DEAI
PENINSULA

Military Aircraft Accidents
on and around Kintyre 1940 -1994

David W.Earl & Peter Dobson

Hanover Publications

© David W. Earl and Peter Dobson. 2018

ISBN: 978-0-9523928-9-7

All rights reserved. No part of this book may be reproduced or transmitted in any form or by any means, electronic or mechanical, including photocopying, recording or by any information storage or retrieval system, without prior permission from the authors/publishers in writing to: Hanover Publications, 25 Hanover Street, Stalybridge, Cheshire. SK15 1LR. England. All photographs contained herein are copyright of their respective owners.

British Library Cataloguing in Publication Data - A catalogue record for this book is available from the British Library.

Front cover: Stranraer Flying Boat K7299. Photo: From a painting by Alan E. Jones

Back cover: Memorial for Neptune WX545 Photo: Author`s Collection

and Avro Shackleton WB833 on Glenmanuilt Hill. Photo: KMRT.

INTRODUCTION

To anyone south of the border, Kintyre is known as the Mull of Kintyre, perhaps due to a certain song of that name by Mr McCartney. In reality the Mull is the headland in the far southwest of this Argyll peninsula and mention that you are writing a book on aircraft that crashed there and most thoughts will be of the Chinook in June 1994, however, many aviation and local historians know only too well that the helicopter was just one of many aircraft that came to grief here and though loss of life in each individual accident was nowhere near that of the Chinook, it was felt by the authors that the others who lost their lives also deserve to be remembered, as do those who by some miracle or sheer luck managed to survive and lived to fly another day.

Research for aircraft in this book began originally around 2002 when the late Kintyre man Duncan McArthur contacted the authors to ask about a couple of the crash sites on the Mull and while Duncan progressed along with other interested parties to produce a small booklet on aircraft accidents on Kintyre, unfortunately, due to the limited resources at that time, several inaccuracies crept in, however, through his early efforts and that of other amateur researchers, the authors were able to progress further and produce this book.

Written in a similar format to the `Lost to the Isles` series, `Deadly Peninsula` tells the stories behind 53 accidents and incidents on and around Kintyre, compiled from both official and unofficial sources, with over 170 biographies on aircrew and passengers and around 350 photographs, many of which have never previously been published.

The aircraft included in this book represent only a small percentage of all those lost around Kintyre, of course many more were lost at sea or during accidents and incidents at the airfield, but because of limitations and fear of becoming too repetitive, it was decided to cover a variety of types with more interesting histories or aircrew.

As interesting as the various aircraft types here may be to aviation historians and archaeologists, many of the airmen and passengers involved, appear to have led fascinating lives and it is certain, were it not for a cruel twist of fate, they would have gone on to achieve much greater things.

David W. Earl

Stalybridge, Cheshire.

2018

CONTENTS

INTRODUCTION.. 3

ACKNOWLEDGEMENTS... 7

KINTYRE MAP.. 8

CRASH LOCATION CHARTS.. 9

Right place ~ Wrong time - Swordfish P9215... 12

Last flight of C for Charlie - Whitley P5041... 21

Seven adrift - Stranraer K7299.. 29

A Fulmar on Kerran Hill - N4038... 46

Deadly decision - Hudson AE640.. 51

Tragedy at Low Smerby - Martlet AL259... 62

The Arinarach ferry plane - Liberator AM915.. 66

Nightmare Navex - Blenheim Z6350... 82

In the drink - Swordfish W5982.. 87

Campbeltown Annie - Anson R3344... 91

Too many fish in the harbour - Swordfish V4441, V4312 & V4489............ 96

Bomber on Torr Mor - Beaufort N1180... 104

No place to land - Anson K6309.. 110

Sole survivor - Albacore N4330... 114

Target tug turmoil - Skua L2907 & Swordfish 119

Sgreadan Hill Wellington HX420... 125

Way off course - Wellington HX779.. 134

Low level hell - Albacore X9165.. 140

Flat calm chaos - Swordfish DK744... 144

Lost at sea - Barracuda P9748	148
Close call - Hudson FK780	151
Into the fog - Beaufighter LZ156	158
Mid-Air mishap - Sea Hurricanes NF867 & NF701	162
A grim discovery - Anson EF820	166
Beinn Bhreac Beaufighter LZ455	172
Man overboard - Barracuda P9737	176
A valiant effort - Swordfish HS448	180
Lost in the clouds - Wellington LB137	187
Death dive off Bellochchantuy - Swordfish HS454	200
Trawler rescue - Anson N4988	204
Another ditching - Swordfish LS426	208
No more happy returns - Seafire MB145	212
A lucky escape - Wildcat JV494	216
No turning back - Barracuda LS582	223
Down off Carradale - Avenger FN878	227
Dead engine dilemma - Whitley BD393	230
Fallen Fulmar X8751	233
Avenger on Deer Hill - FN867	237
Lost contact - Firefly Z1891	242
The Calliburn Avenger FN772	245
No place for a peer - Beech Traveller FT529	251
Cruel forces of nature - Wellington LP351	256
Mystery Seafire `411`	264
Lost beneath the waves - Barracuda ME121	266

The Kilkenzie Seafire SW857......... 269

Twelfth tee trauma - Firefly VT490......... 273

Maritime mishap - Neptune WX545......... 276

Grey lady down Shackleton WB833......... 293

A sting in its tail - Wasp XT789......... 304

Bird strike - F-111 68-008......... 309

Carskey Bay Sea King XV706......... 324

A high price for peace - Chinook ZD576......... 328

APPENDICES

AIRCRAFT IN DATE ORDER......... 339

ROYAL NAVAL AIR STATIONS LAND & SEA......... 341

BIBLIOGRAPHY......... 342

OFFICIAL & OTHER SOURCES......... 344

ABBREVIATIONS......... 345

HP PUBLICATIONS BOOKS......... 347

`Lest We Forget`

Dedicated to all those who lost their lives in flying accidents described in this book.

"To live in the hearts of those we leave behind is not to die".

ACKNOWLEDGEMENTS

Alan Clark, *Aviation Historian/Author, Romiley, Stockport, Cheshire*. **Alan E. Jones**, *Artist/Aviation Historian, Stalybridge*. **Alan Leishman**, *Aviation Historian, Ardrossan, Scotland.* **Allanna Brough**, *Kintyre.* **Angie Ingles**, *Southend, Kintyre.* **Angus Martin**, *Campbeltown, Kintyre*, **Arthur Helsby**, *Ex-RAF MRT Leuchars* **Brian Gee**, *Ex-RAF Machrihanish, Carradale, Kintyre.* **Brian Leeming**, *Nephew of F/O Ronald M. Leeming, 105 (Transport) OTU.* **Dave Ramsey**, *A.R.G.O.S, Heywood, Manchester.* **David Stirling**, *Aviation Historian, Ardrossan, Ayrshire, Scotland.* **David Whalley. BEM. MBE.** *Ex-RAF Kinloss MRT, Burnhead, Moray,* **Duncan McArthur**, *Kintyre.* **Errol Martyn**, *NZ Forces Aviation Historian, Wellington, New Zealand.* **Fran Ralli**, *Daughter of Elizabeth Booth. WRNS* **Gary Nelson**, *Blyth, Northumberland.* **Geoff Bland**, *A.R.G.O.S, Silloth, Cumbria.* **Ian Davies**, *Ferry Command researcher, Altringham, Cheshire.* **Ian Thompson**, *Cousin of Sub/Lt (A) Ian Geoffrey Cuthbert, RNVR, 836 Sqn.* **Jenny Paterson**, *Relative of Sgt Harry Harley Newbury, RAF, 240 Sqn.* **Jim Corbett**, *Aviation Historian/Author, Belingham, Northumberland* **Joan Ward**, *Cousin of Sub/Lt (A) Ian Geoffrey Cuthbert, RNVR, 836 Sqn.* **John Evans**, *Pembroke Dock Sunderland Trust.* **Ken Davis**, *P.O. RN TAGs Assn.* **Ken Sims**, *P.O. RN. TAGs Assn.* **Keith Peloquin**, *Son of Lt/Col Andrew J. Peloquin, USAF 20th TFW.* **Lesley Cooper**, *niece of AC1 Herbert Gordon Brooks, 2 OTU.* **Mark Davey**, *Editor, Campbeltown Courier, Kintyre.* **Mary Muir**, *Campbeltown, Kintyre.* **Margaret McNair**, *Low Smerby Mill, Kintyre.* **Mark Jones**, *Sqn/Ldr Ret, son of W.O. Jack Jones, W/AG 7 (C) O.T.U and 221 Sqn.* **Mark Sheldon**, *Aviation Historian/Author, Pointon, Cheshire.* **Marion Titmuss**, *Niece of Lt Eric Benson Gray, RN, 1832 Sqn.* **Pat Juby**, *Daughter of Air Sig. Sgt Roy Vincent Smith, 36 Squadron.* **Pavel Vancata**, *Aviation Historian, Prague, Czech Republic.* **Phillip Jones**, *Aviation Historian / Author, Llandindrod Wells, Powys.* **Richard Allenby**, *Aviation Historian, Pickering, North Yorkshire.* **Sarah Mitchell**, *Niece of AC1 John Victor Hanaghan RAF, det to 816 FAA Sqn.* **Steven Spink**, *A.R.G.O.S. Maddiston, Falkirk.* **Valerie Garlick**, *Daughter of Sgt Peter William Hewitt, RAF, BEM. 204 Squadron.*

Thanks to all those who contributed information and photographs over the past couple of decades. Every reasonable effort has been made to trace the copyright holders but if there are any errors or omissions, we will be pleased to insert the appropriate acknowledgement in any subsequent printings or editions.

Our thanks also to the various crofters and estate owners who allowed access to their land for site visits and to the friendly staff at Campbeltown Heritage Centre and of course to anyone else inadvertently omitted who aided research along the way. Also a special thanks to artist and friend Alan E. Jones of Stalybridge for his excellent painting of Supermarine Stranraer K7299 for the front cover of this book.

KINTYRE MAPS

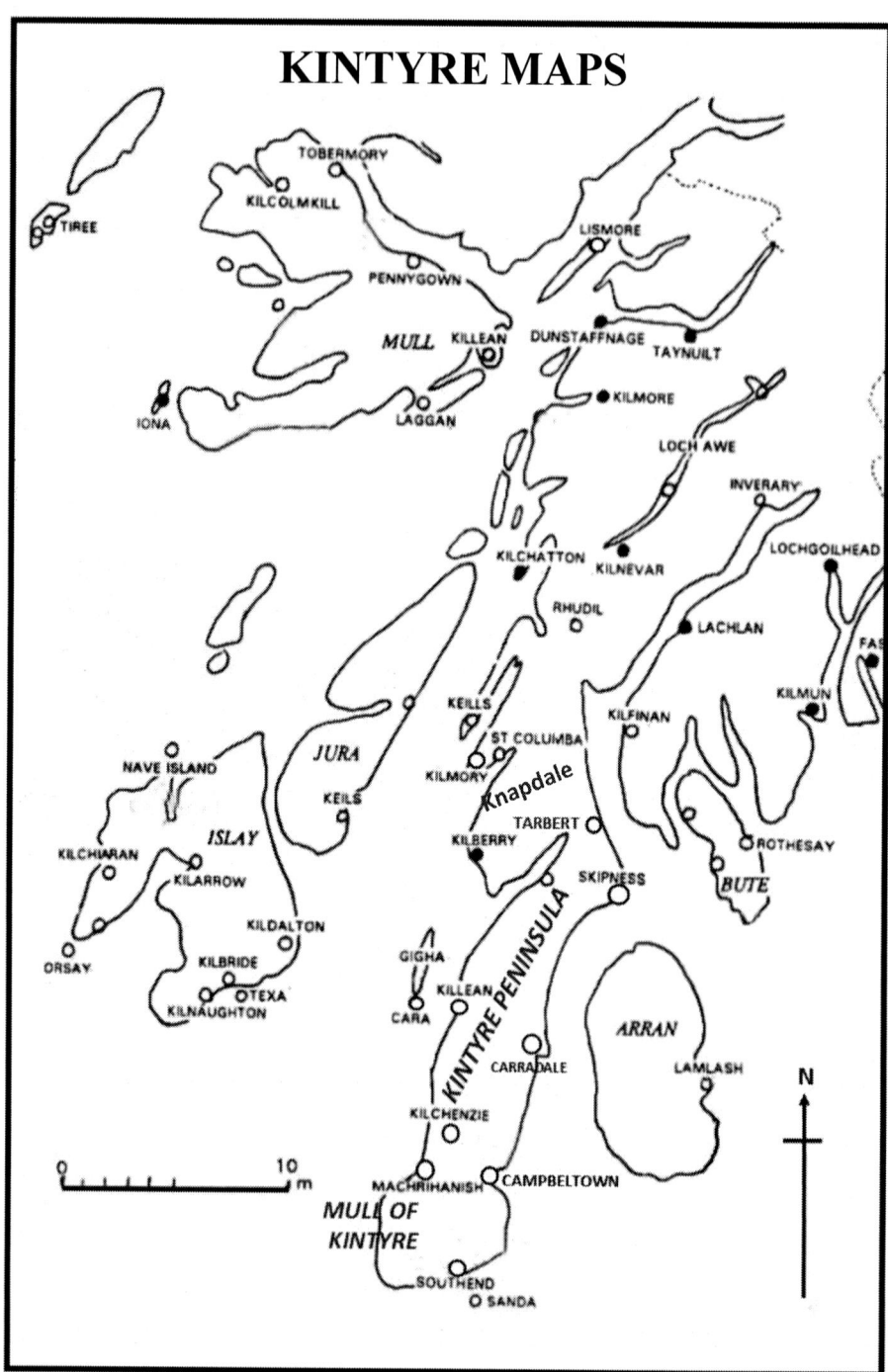

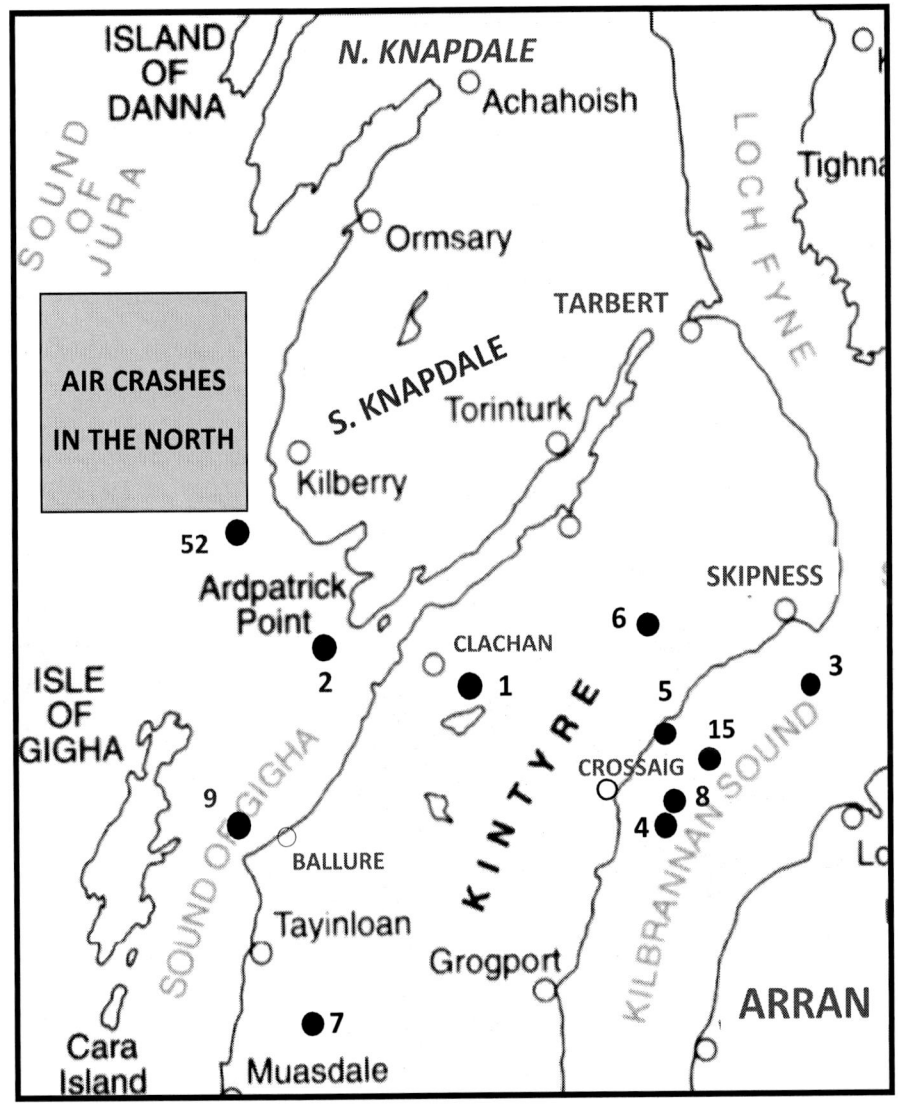

1.	WELLINGTON HX779	6. F-111E 68-008	11. MARTLET AL259
2.	ALBACORE X9165	7. BLENHEIM Z6350	12. LIBERATOR AM915
3.	SWORDFISH DK744	8. ALBACORE N9330	13. SWORDFISH P4215
4.	BARRACUDA P9748	9. BARRACUDA ME121	14. ANSON R3344
5.	SWORDFISH HS448	10. HUDSON AE640	15. ALBACORE N4330

16. SKUA L2907 / S`FISH
17. WELLINGTON HX420
18. HUDSON FK780
19. BEAUFIGHTER LZ156
20. HURRICANE NF867
21. ANSON EF820
22. BEAUFIGHTER LZ455
23. BARRACUDA P9737

24. WELLINGTON LB137
25. SWORDFISH HS454
26. SWORDFISH LS426 *
27. SEAFIRE MB145
28. AVENGER FN878
29. FULMAR X8751
30. AVENGER FN867
31. FIREFLY Z1891 *

32. AVENGER FN772
33. TRAVELLER FT529
34. SEAFIRE 411
35. SEAFIRE SW857
36. FIREFLY VT490
37. NEPTUNE WX545
38. SHACK` WB833
39. WASP XT789

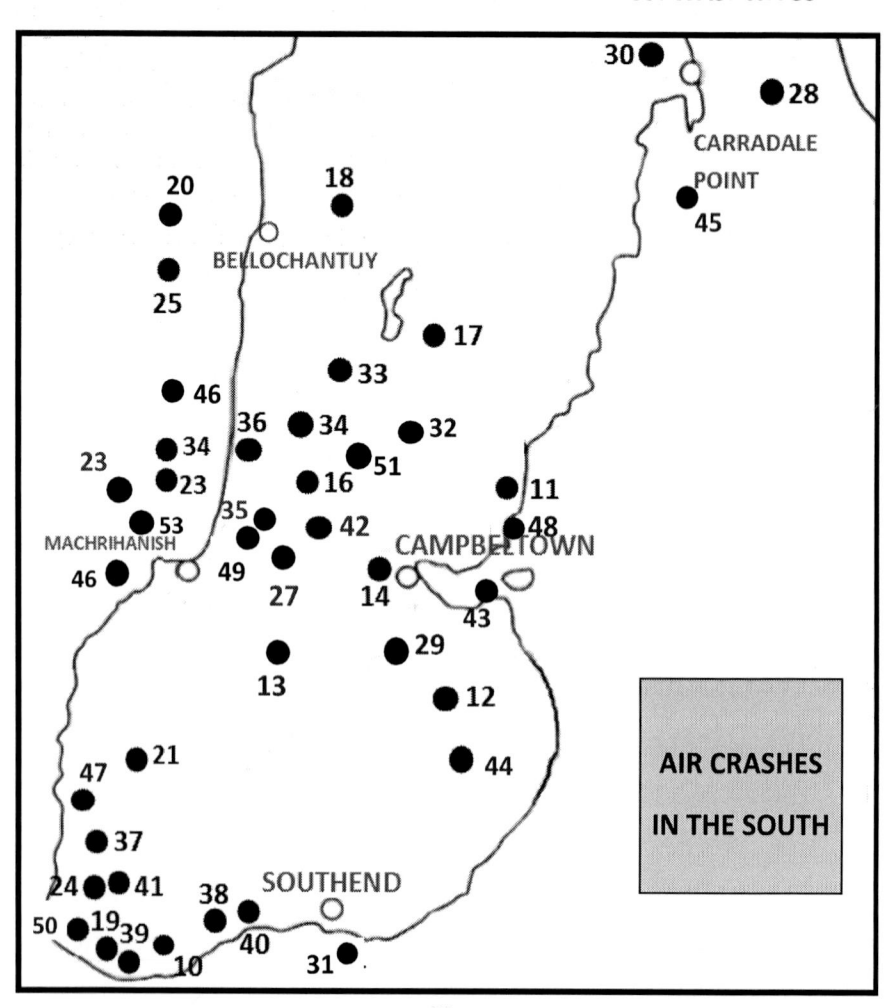

AIR CRASHES IN THE SOUTH

40. SEA KING XV706
41. CHINOOK ZD576
42. WHITLEY BD393
43. SWORDFISH V4441, V4312 & V4489
44. FULMAR N4038
45. ANSON N4988
46. SWORDFISH W5982

47. WHITLEY P5041
48. STRANRAER K7299
49. WILDCAT JV494
50. BEAUFORT N1180
51. BARRACUDA LS582
52. WELLINGTON LP351
53. ANSON K6309

Note: Many of the locations of accidents both on land and in the sea are estimated based on information found in official records or described by eye-witnesses, so should not be wholly relied on as being completely accurate, but used as a general guide as to where these aircraft crashed. Several of these crash sites you will notice have been visited by either the authors, or associates over the years, so details of locations within these accounts will be fairly accurate. Within the accounts that follow on these aircraft, all Royal Naval Air Stations ship names are given in brackets and RN sailing vessels are preceded with HMS, both are in italics.

* It has not been possible to establish where precisely these aircraft crashed, they are only described in official records as being off the Mull of Kintyre.

RIGHT PLACE ~ WRONG TIME - SWORDFISH P4215

Requisitioned by the Royal Navy on 12th February 1940, the civilian aerodrome used by Scottish Airways at Campbeltown, so named after the main town to the east, was described by one pilot as being:

"Really quite primitive. Ground-to-air signals were still in the stone age and there was only one small hangar, supplemented by a Bessonneau (Timber hangar with canvas cover as used in WW1) with a tendency to fly off on its own.

The control tower consisted of Mr. McGeachy, the Scottish Airways agent, a stove, ample supplies of tea and a telephone. During night flying one of the observers was laid on with an Aldis lamp.... It was an unmistakeable Admiralty selection. Between two sharp ranges of hills and terrain up and down in all directions like an ocean wave in six cross-winds"

This old airfield was sited just to the south of Bleachfield and north of the B843 road, roughly 2 miles west

A typical Bessonneau hangar similar to the one used at Campbeltown

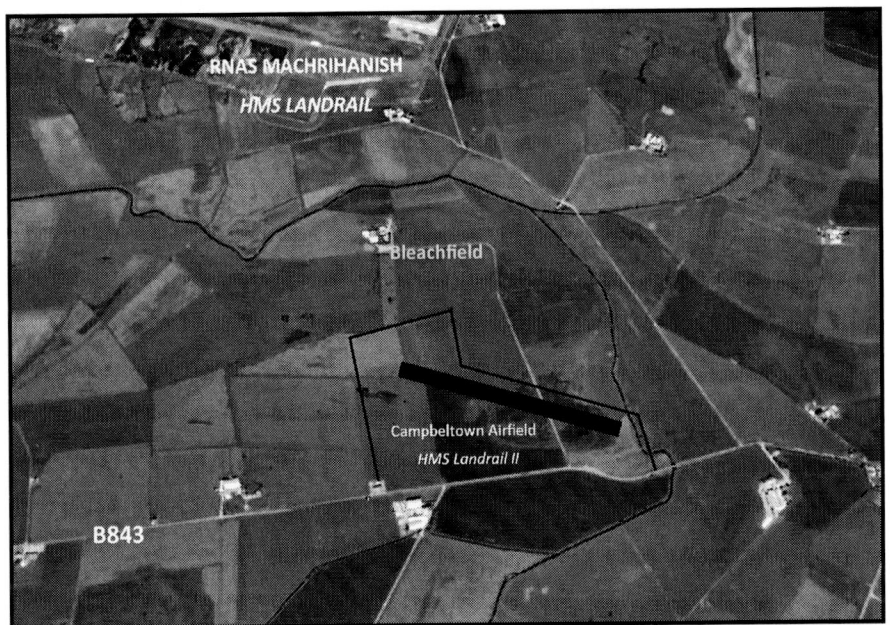

Aerial shows where the old airfield and grass runway was at Strath, Campbeltown

Photo: Author's Collection

of Campbeltown town centre. This airfield was also known locally as Strath or Dalivaddy, before the Royal Navy commissioned it as (*Landrail*) in April 1941, but the name was changed to (*Landrail II*) when RNAS Machrihanish, a new airfield to the north was completed on 15th June that year.

Temporarily shore based at Abbotsinch from 4th Jan 1940, then at Campbeltown airfield from 19th February, whilst the ship HMS *Furious* (D47) was under refit at Devonport, were 816 and 818 Squadron's Fairy Swordfish Mk Is.

At 06:10 on Wednesday 3rd April 1940, Swordfish P9215 of 816 Sqn had taxied to the end of the grass airstrip and was awaiting the take off signal for a routine dawn reconnaissance flight off the west coast of Scotland.

The pilot briefed for the flight that day was Sub/Lt (A) John D. Stern, RN, accompanied by two crew: Observer Lt Bruce E.H. Stranack, RN and TAG N/A 1 James W. White, RN.

On a cold damp morning with light winds forecast, the Swordfish was finally given the green light and at 06:25 proceeded to take off, but just as it got airborne, a side wind caused the aircraft to swing to starboard, the pilot Lt Stern unable to hold her steady, soon lost control and the Swordfish collided with aircraft on the ground.

It immediately burst into flames and exploded killing all three crew along with an aircraft maintenance man AC1 John Victor Hanaghan, RAF, who had been working alongside seven other Swordfish picketed around the field.

Above: Looking NW to where the old airfield used to be off the B843.
Photo: Author's Collection.

Below: Ratings swinging the wings into place on a Fairey Swordfish
Photo: Dickie Stark Ex-RN FAA 771 Sqn.

Pilot Sub-Lieutenant John Douglas Stern, (A) RN, born in Bristol in 1912, was the eldest son of Reverend John and Constance Idonia Violet Stern (née Douglas-Hamilton) of Crackington Haven, Bude, Cornwall. John had one brother and four sisters.

John's father was ordained in 1902 and in 1908 married Constance Idonia Violet Douglas-Hamilton in Hammersmith, but the couple later moved to Clifton, Bristol where they raised a family.

The children were all educated in Bristol until 1921 when they moved to Fowey, Cornwall, where John's father took up the post of vicar at the local church. However, during two harsh winters in the town, he suffered ill health and was forced to go into a nursing home in Plymouth. Sadly, following an operation for pleurisy, he passed away on 4th May 1923.

John joined the RAF in 1935 and following basic and theoretical training he was granted a commission to Acting Pilot Officer on probation on 23rd March 1936 and posted to 9 FTS at Thornaby, Yorkshire, on 4th April for training on Hawker Harts.

Whilst at Thornaby, on 20th June 1936, John had a lucky escape in K5805 when the aircraft was involved in a collision on the ground with K5813 fortunately without serious injury, but it resulted in John's aircraft being written off. K5813 was later repaired.

John was posted to 58 Squadron at Driffield, Yorkshire, on 10th October 1936, but spent just a few months here before joining 114 Squadron on 1st December at Wyton, Cambridgeshire. Once again he flew the Hawker Hart and at the end of January was confirmed in the rank of Pilot Officer.

Hawker Hart from a Flying Training School similar to those used at Thornaby

In July 1937 John passed his navigation course and was awarded a Second Class Navigation Licence. A year later he relinquished his commission on appointment to the Air Branch of the Royal Navy to become an Acting Sub-Lieutenant on 22nd August 1938.

On 27th January 1939 he was promoted to Acting Lieutenant and attached to the Fleet Air Arm at Lee-on-Solent, prior to joining 815 Squadron aboard HMS *Furious* in October that year.

At the request of his wife, after the accident on Kintyre John was returned home for burial in Fowey Cemetery, Cornwall and has a private headstone purchased by relatives in Section H. Grave 51.

It is interesting to note that John's Great, Great Grandfather on his Mother's side was Admiral Charles Powell Hamilton RN, who in turn was a descendant of Lt.Gen James Hamilton the 4th Duke of Hamilton.

Observer Lieutenant Bruce Edwin Harington Stranack. RN, born 25th August 1910, was the son of Colonel Cyril Edwin Stranack. DSO. OBE. RA (Ret) and Violet Stranack. Also husband of Rebecca Daffodil Ann Stranack, c/o married quarters Machrihanish House, but formally of Alverstoke, Hampshire.

Bruce's father Cyril was ex-British Army and a long serving officer in the Royal Horse & Field Artillery. Having been commissioned a Second Lieutenant on 21st Dec 1901 for a time he had served in India.

By the time the First World War broke out in 1914, he had attained the rank of Major and later Lt/Col in the Royal Artillery and been credited with the DSO.

Having retired in 1935, in 1943 he returned to active duty as a Temporary Colonel. He passed away on 29th April 1953.

Bruce, having attended Cheltenham College from 1921-1924, was a keen sportsman and played cricket for the College in the 1900 XI team and later got his colours for cricket, racquetball and hockey for Woolwich and the Royal Artillery.

Bruce enrolled in the Royal Navy at Devonport, Plymouth on 15th May 1924 then served for three years as a cadet and Midshipman in the Royal Sovereign in the Mediterranean and following promotion to the rank of Sub-Lieutenant in November 1931, he served aboard the destroyers HMS *Torrid* and *Anthony* and became a Lieutenant in November 1934.

On 4th May 1936 Bruce, along with seven fellow officers, was selected to undergo a Naval Air Observers course at Portsmouth. The course lasted for nine months and included instruction in signals, tactics and gunnery at various other Naval establishments.

After this he would be sent to the School of Naval Co-Operation and working with the RAF he was given instruction in air tactics, navigation, photography, airmanship and bombing etc at Lee-on-Solent.

During the Abyssinian Crisis Bruce had served as an Air Observer aboard the flotilla leader HMS *Montrose* and later the battle cruiser *Repulse* and the carrier *Courageous*, before ending up with *Furious*.

For reasons unclear his fellow shipmates referred to him at 'Tony' and in a copy of 'The Times' published soon after his death and later reprinted in the 'Gloucestershire Echo' great tributes were paid as follows:

"The death of Tony Stranack at the age of 29 comes as a sad blow to his many friends among officers and men in the Navy. It leaves a gap for those lucky enough to have served with him that no one can fill in quite the same way. He was the best of messmates, with a sense of humour and a lightness of touch that endeared him to everyone".

Others described him as :

"A tireless worker who never became harassed or impatient.... However much he had to get though and however many things he might have to worry about, he never showed it by the slightest hint. Only those who were privileged to know him best, realised how much he had accomplished and how deeply he felt things.

The greater part of his spare time was employed in using his gifts of writing and acting, along with his spontaneous humour for the entertainment of the men with whom he served. In these ways he was entirely selfless and when he left the ship, no one was missed more".

"He typified one's idea of a Christian gentleman and his witty and sensitive mind and fine character will live on as his memorial to be an inspiration to all

his friends. He lost his life in the course of his duty, which he loved and which for him, always came first".

Alas, due to the nature of this accident, Bruce's body was never found and he is commemorated on Bay 1. Panel 2 of the Lee-on-Solent Memorial in Hampshire.

NA1 James Wilfred White's grave

Photo: Author's Collection

Telegraphist Air Gunner Naval Airman 1st Class, James Wilfred White, RN, born 8th April 1917, was the son of Thomas James and Mabel Alice Mary White (née Hellyer) of Bognor Regis, Sussex.

Often referred to as Wilfred or Wilf by family and friends, his parents had been married in Westhampnett, Sussex, in April 1912 and aside from Wilfred they had two younger sons James W and Phillip A. White.

The family lived in Hawthorn Road and were great Catholics. Wilfred and his brothers attended local Roman Catholic Schools. He was a keen amateur boxer and a member of Bognor Regis Boxing Club, winning several prizes in the sport, which, when in the Navy earned him the nickname 'Knocker'.

Wilfred's brother Philip, was also in the Royal Navy and was an Ordinary Seaman aboard HMS *Royal Oak* when she was torpedoed in Scapa Flow, Orkney by Gunther Prien in the German U-boat U-47 on the night of 14th October 1939. Fortunately he was one of the survivors of that tragedy in which 834 men lost their lives. Wilfred was accorded a full military funeral at Campbeltown (Kilkerran) Cemetery, Kintyre. Division 4. Grave 579A .

Groundcrew Aircraftman 1st Class John Victor Hanaghan. RAF, born 4th March 1920, was the son of Major Albert Victor and May Clare Hanaghan (née Kilner) of Lewes, East Sussex. John had one younger sister Maureen. His father Albert, as a Sergeant and later Warrant Officer in the British Army Service Corps served in the First World War as a Mechanist and staying on in the Army throughout WW2 he retired from the service as a Lt/Col in 1946.

John was born in the Dorset Arms, Lewes, where his grandmother was the landlady. He was educated locally and is noted to have attended Lewes Priory School, the county grammar school for boys from 1932-1935. He was a choirboy at one of the schools and also a member of the Cliffe Bonfire Society based in Lewes, which formed in 1853 and celebrates the discovery of the Gunpowder Plot of 1605 every 5th November, with organised meetings being held at the Dorset Arms.

John also spent some time with the family in India where his father served in the Royal Indian Army. A ship's passenger lists stated that he sailed from Bombay aboard the P&O Steam Navigation company Liner, the SS *Stratheden,* a Barrow built 23,722-ton ship, arriving in London on 16th May 1938.

It would appear that not long after his arrival back in England, he joined the RAF and trained as a fitter/rigger. For a time in 1938 John had been stationed at RAF Cardington, Bedfordshire, which had formally been an airship station, but was then a Care & Maintenance shop and balloon station.

AC2 John Victor Hanaghan. RAF Taken shortly after enlistment

Photo: Sarah Mitchell

AC1 John Victor Hanaghan. RAF
Photo: Sarah Mitchell

John's niece recalled a nice little story about when her Mother moved to the area in 2014 to be closer to her. She had been to afternoon tea in the local residents community centre when an old lady kept saying that her face looked very familiar. She said that she couldn't possibly know her since she had only just moved to the area, but the old lady then asked if she had a brother, to which she remembered that her uncle John had served in the area and said she would bring along a photo to show her.

Sometime later she took the photo into the centre and showed it to the old lady, who recalled instantly that when she was around 12, her brother, who had also been stationed at Cardington, was one of John's friends and he had been to their house in Bedford a few times.

AC1 John V. Hanaghan's headstone

Photo: Author's Collection

Having completed his training and with the Navy having a shortage of fitters, John was posted to 816 FAA Squadron. Apparently when control of the Fleet Air Arm was passed to the Admiralty in 1938, the Air Ministry allowed those men of the RAF who were serving with naval squadrons to remain if they so wished.

It would appear that John was happy to work alongside the Swordfish squadrons or he could easily have moved on. It was no doubt quite a thrilling experience for the young 19 year old to watch all the air activity around the airfield, when he wasn't busy preparing them for flight of course.

John, was a tragic victim of circumstance and appears to just have been in the right place, attending to his aircraft, but sadly at the wrong time.

Following the accident, which even more tragic had occurred just a day before his 20th birthday, John was accorded a full military funeral at Campbeltown (Kilkerran) Cemetery and was interred in Division 4. Grave 580. His epitaph reads:

`A tragic loss to those who loved him`

John's name was missing from the Lewes War Memorial, so shortly before her passing his sister Maureen campaigned to have his name added to the memorial. He is also commemorated on the Lewes Prior School Roll of Honour.

LAST FLIGHT OF C FOR CHARLIE - WHITLEY P5041

Originally formed at Aldergrove, County Antrim, Northern Ireland on 15th May 1925, with a complement of Vickers Vimy twin engine heavy biplane bombers, was 502 (Ulster) Auxiliary Air Force Squadron, under command of S/Ldr Robert D. Oxland. CB.CBE.

Throughout the late 1920s and 1930s the squadron would operate various aircraft types: Handley Page Hyderabad, Vickers Virginia, Westland Wallace, Hawker Hind, Avro Anson and the Blackburn Botha, before finally receiving the Armstrong Whitworth Whitley Mk.V twin engine bomber in October 1940.

Commanded at that time by W/Cdr. L.R. Briggs and succeeded in December by W/Cdr. T.C. Cooper, the squadron was actively involved in Convoy Escort duties, combing the North Atlantic for dreaded U-boats.

At 12:22 on Thursday 23rd January 1941, Whitley P5041 YG-C skippered by F/Lt Phillip Leslie Billing RAF, along with four crew consisting: F/O Arthur P. B. Holmes, AuxAF, Sgt Herbert Pilling RAFVR Sgt David John Peter Bradley, RAF and Sgt Alec Raymond Hooker, RAF, took off from Aldergrove to provide an escort for convoy HG.50 which had departed from Gibraltar on 8th January with 10 ships bound for Liverpool. The convoy had been spotted at 10:05 by allied escorts in position 54.56N—13.54W and from then on aircraft were present at intervals every day during daylight hours for the rest of the voyage.

Having completed their part of the cover, the crew of C-Charlie turned for home and made their way eastwards. Weather conditions were not good, with freezing temperatures, heavy snow, rain and hail showers and poor visibility. In fact the ORB states that this was the first day of operational flying for 3 days due to adverse conditions, the national press described much of the country was lying under a blanket of snow.

Still in the thick of all this weather and no doubt struggling to keep their aircraft in the air, it is believed the crew drifted slightly off course in cloud and having flown by Northern Ireland were too far east and heading for the Mull of Kintyre, where in darkness the Whitley crashed into the rising ground above the old

21

A 502 Squadron Whitley

abandoned 17th century settlement of Balmavicar on the west coast, north of the Kintyre lighthouse. The aircraft exploded on impact and was totally wrecked. F/Lt Billing and crew all died instantly.

The time of the crash according to the accident card was 19:45, so the Whitley had been airborne for 7hr 23m. The weather greatly deteriorated as the Whitley neared Northern Ireland and

The area of the crash today where only small pieces remain, though a few larger parts lay amongst the Neptune wreckage. Photo: Author's Collection

The shattered rusty remains of one of the main undercarriage units.

Photo: Author's Collection

the cloud base had dropped below a thousand feet. No doubt the freezing temperatures and ice had also been causing problems. The investigation put the cause of the accident down to a 'Navigation Error' though the undoubtedly weather played a major part.

AOC stated that 'Deteriorating weather after dark' was definitely a contributory cause and mentions an error in the W/O frequency and perhaps a missed recall signal? The aircraft apparently flew by the lighthouses at Innistrahull and Islay, but either didn't see them or failed to recognise them? C of I: 'recommended a review of the navigation and wireless procedure'.

The following day F/O L.J. Ward and crew in Whitley T4168 `YG-H` from 502 Squadron, were returning from a search for tugs seeking bombed ships when their aircraft ran out of fuel and crashed off Quigley Point, Lough Foyle, Eire. The 2nd pilot P/O Johnson, Obs Sgt J.E. Hogg and A/G Sgt L. Greenwood were all killed, with the latter two being listed as missing.

Johnson was accorded a military funeral at Rickmansworth Cemetery, Hertfordshire but because Eire was a neutral country in the Second World War, the two crew who survived, Skipper F/O Ward and W/Op Sgt C.V. Jefferson were both interned by Irish authorities.

Captain and Pilot Flight Lieutenant Philip Leslie 'Peter' Billing, RAF, born 1916, was the son of Percy and Lilian Grace Billing (née Butler) of Worth, Kent and husband to Jane Olive 'Jenny' Billing (née Elliott) of Ballintoy, Co.Antrim, Northern Ireland.

Referred to as Peter, for reasons unclear, he was commissioned Acting Pilot Officer on probation on 21st December 1936, then following assessment he was sent to a Flying Training School as a U/T pilot where he finally gained his wings nine months later.

Peter flew various aircraft during training and also completed a course in navigation. He was promoted to full Pilot Officer on 23rd November 1937, prior to further training on twin engine aircraft and later flew Anson's with 269 Squadron at Montrose.

A promotion to Flying Officer came on 12th April 1939, by which time he was serving with 502 (Ulster) squadron flying the Avro Anson on reconnaissance anti-sub patrols and for his fine work here he was Mentioned in Dispatches on 20th February 1940.

F/Lt Peter Billing and his bride Jenny at St.John's Church in December 1940

Photo: Author's Collection

A further promotion to Flight Lieutenant came on 3rd September 1940 and Peter became one of the squadron's more senior officers. He continued to fly anti-sub patrols and is noted on several occasions to have flown with Sgt Bradley (then an aircraftman) as his wireless operator and sometimes F/O Holmes flew as his navigator. Apart from encountering murky weather most of his flights were fairly routine.

One example being on 1st July 1940 when Peter, F/O Holmes, Sgt Wilson as A/G and AC Fisher on W/T took off in rain and drizzle in Anson N5215 'S' at 03:55 for A/S dawn patrol. There were no enemy encounters but the crew spotted 2 British tankers *Winawac* and *Hong Kong* at 06:31 in position 55.32N – 06.25W on a course of 120 degrees traveling approx. 12 knots, plus an Admiralty trawler at 55:25N—06:45W and they returned to base at 07:40.

Late August, Peter and other selected pilots and aircrew were sent to 19 OTU at RAF Kinloss near Forres, Grampian, for a conversion course on the Whitley. They were allocated five Whitley Vs kitted out with ASV radar. The crews flew these operationally and were given the name '502 Sqn Special Flight'.

Peter and the other crew members returned to Aldergrove at the end of October and from here flew their first operational sortie in a Whitley on 3rd November, by which time other aircraft had arrived and the whole squadron would be flying the Whitley before the end of the year.

On 11th December 1940 Peter married his fiancée Miss Jane Olive (Jenny) Elliott, at St. John's Church, Crumlin, Northern Ireland. Both Peter and Jenny's parents were at the wedding, with a squadron pal F/Lt S.J. Harrison acting as his best man. Jenny's parents Jean and Christopher Elliott were farmers from Ballintoy, Co. Antrim before the war and Christopher himself was a Squadron Leader in the RAF.

At the time of the accident F/Lt Peter Billing, a very experienced Coastal Command pilot, had logged a total of 1,005 solo flying hours, 80 of which were on the Whitley.

Peter was interred with full military honours in Glenavy (St.Aidan) Church of Ireland Churchyard, County Antrim, Northern Ireland. Plot B. Grave 6A.

Navigator Flying Officer Arthur Peter Buckley Holmes, RAF (AAF), B.A, born at Deganwy, Caernarvonshire on 26th November 1908, was the son of Buckley and Ethel Maud Holmes (née Wensley) and husband of Dorothy Margaret Probert Holmes (née Newman), of Belfast.

Known to all as Peter, as a commoner he attended Malvern School and matriculated in 1927 to enter Queens College Oxford where he studied law and achieved a First Class Honours degree in 1930. Like all colleges sport was encouraged and Peter was on the college rowing team.

After leaving Oxford he studied at home for the Civil Service, which he entered in Northern Ireland in 1931. Here he took up the post of Secretary to the Minister of Finance in Ulster.

On 5th May 1935 Peter became an Acting Pilot Officer with 502 (Ulster) Special Reserve Squadron at Aldergrove, at which time the squadron had a complement of Vickers Virginia twin engine heavy biplane bombers.

Peter was awarded his Observers brevet with 502 (B) Squadron on 23rd May 1937 and on 1st July the SR Squadron converted to an Auxiliary Air Force unit and were now equipped with Hawker Hinds.

Granted a commission to P/O on 17th January 1939, the squadron had now received Ansons and after war broke out Peter flew on several occasions as navigator for F/Lt Billing. He was promoted to F/O on 3rd September 1940.

Following the Whitley accident in which he is listed as 2nd Pilot in ORB, Peter was interred in Drumbeg (St. Patrick) Church of Ireland Churchyard, Co. Antrim, with a private headstone in Section F. Grave 12 attended by family and friends from his squadron.

Observer Sergeant Herbert Pilling, RAFVR, born 1917 in Doncaster, was the only son of Arthur and Louisa Pilling (née Nicholson). He had one younger sister Constance.

The family lived in the large market town of Doncaster, South Yorkshire, where his parents had married in 1915. Bert attended local schools here.

Last resting place of F/O Holmes in Drumbeg (St.Patrick) Churchyard

Photo: Author's Collection

He joined the RAF as a Volunteer Reserve prior to the Second World War and applied for aircrew. After basic training he was selected to become an observer (navigator) and was sent to Air Navigation School.

There is no mention in the ORB of him prior to the accident, where his crew position is given as Navigator, so it is thought he had only just arrived on the squadron after graduating from the ANS.

Bert was returned home for interment in a family plot, but has a Commonwealth War Graves headstone in Conisbrough Cemetery. Sec C. Gr.94.

Sgt Herbert Pilling's grave, Doncaster

Photo: Author's Collection

Wireless Operator Sergeant David John Peter Bradley, RAF, born in Willesden, Middlesex in 1921, was the son of Peter Rooney Bradley and Lily Elizabeth Bradley (née Martin) of Eastcote, Pinner, Middlesex and husband of Phyllis Bradley (née Howlett).

David joined the RAF when war broke out in September 1939, and following basic training in Blackpool he was sent to an Air Gunnery School followed by Wireless School, where he graduated as a W/AG in the spring of 1940 at the age of just 18.

David was posted to 502 Squadron in April and served throughout the year as a W/Op on both Anson and Whitley aircraft. Being a surplus to requirements Wireless Operator, he flew with any crew that needed him and is mentioned in the ORB on numerous occasions.

On 20th April David was flying as W/Op for P/O Gilmour and crew consisting: P/O Walker and LAC Granston. They had taken off from Aldergrove at 12:07 in Anson N5048 'A' in order to provide escort for the aircraft carrier *Ark Royal* which had sailed from Plymouth with destroyers *Saladin*, *Bulldog* and *Westcott* on the 19th.

The plan was for the ship to be met by two other destroyers *Juno* and *Hasty* and along with *Saladin* and the aerial patrol the carrier would have safe passage up the Clyde to Greenock.

The Anson flew to the designated rendezvous point at 55.30N-06.30W in rain and low cloud, but there was no sign of the carrier or the ships, so with fuel getting low the Anson returned to base at 16:40. It was noted that an hour later than expected due to headwinds, the carrier turned up at 55.32N—06.01W and was eventually escorted by F/Lt Billing and crew in Anson N9918 'B'.

A bit of excitement for David came on 2nd September when flying an Anti-Sub patrol with P/O Pettit and crew in Anson 'C', they spotted a periscope of a submerged submarine at 13:05 in position 55.18N—07.07W and released two A/S bombs, however, no hits were observed and the periscope was immediately withdrawn. At 16:00 the crew sighted two RN destroyers and informed them of the sighting and dropped smoke floats to guide them to the area. Alas, the U-boat managed to escape detection.

During September David went on leave and married his fiancée Phyllis L. Howlett of King's Lynn, Norfolk. The couple were wed in Uxbridge, Middlesex. Having returned to his squadron he went on to flying the Whitley and according to the ORB is noted as having the rank of Aircraftman throughout his time with 502, so either he was posthumously promoted to Sergeant, or the duty clerks made an error?

After the accident David was returned home for burial and was accorded a full military funeral in Willesden New Cemetery, Middlesex, Sec E. Grave 614.

Sgt David Bradley in Willesden Cem.

Observer Sergeant Alec Raymond Hooker, RAF, born in Preston, Faversham, Kent in 1920, was the son of Leonard P and Helen M. Hooker (née Wardle) and brother of Roy, Brian, Edna and Joyce of Kent.

Alec left school wanting to join the RAF but being too young he became a junior clerk at the Post Office. He was mentioned in the `Assigned to Clerical` list in the London Gazette on 10th Sept 1937. At the age of 18 he tried again for the RAF and was accepted, and following basic training was sent to a Air Navigation School.

Following a service by Rev. F. D. Foster, Alec was interred with military hons in Faversham Cemetery, Sec E. Grave 25.

Sgt Alec Hooker in Faversham Cem.

SEVEN ADRIFT - STRANRAER K7299

Based at Stranraer, but also operating from a secondary advanced base at RAF Castle Archdale, Lough Erne, N. Ireland, 240 Sqn with their large twin engine biplane flying boats, regularly patrolled the North Atlantic and North Channel between Ireland and Scotland, protecting incoming and outgoing convoys against the dreaded U-boats.

On 25th February 1941, F/Lt Furlong, P/O Sumner and crew took off from Lough Erne, County Fermanagh at 11:25 hours to patrol coastal waters north of Rathlin Island, then rendezvous with convoy OB 290 which was heading west with 38 Merchant Vessels and 7 RN Escort ships.

F/Lt Furlong in Stranraer K7299 located the convoy at 13:31 on a heading of 270 degrees with an estimated speed of 6 knots, by which time a Blenheim was also in the area. Enemy activity was rife and at 15:28 while patrolling the area north of the convoy, Furlong sighted a Norwegian lifeboat with eight or nine people on board and immediately returned to the convoy to give a bearing and distance for the lifeboat.

It was discovered the lifeboat contained seven survivors from the Norwegian Merchant Vessel *Benjamin Franklin* (Master Alf Andersen) which had been inbound to Liverpool from Halifax Nova Scotia on the 19th February with convoy HX107, when due to engine trouble in rough seas it fell behind from the rest of the convoy, and was struck on the port side by a torpedo from U-103 (KovKapt. Victor Schütze—Knights Cross / Oak Leaves).

The ship had been hit in the engine room and began to list with the crew of 36 having just abandoned ship when a second G7e torpedo was fired and hit the starboard side under hatch No.4, where a cargo of 1700 barrels of acetone were stored, there was a huge explosion and the ship disintegrated and sank.

The seven survivors picked up from the lifeboat by HMS *Pimpernel* K71 were all that was left of the 36 strong crew, some of their shipmates had perished in the high seas from exposure, while others that were picked up by an Egyptian steamship *Memphis*, died later when she foundered off NW Ireland.

Supermarine Stranraer of 240 Squadron at Lough Erne

Having set a course for Rathlin and arrived back at Lough Erne at 19:25, the crew of K7299 were debriefed, ate a well earned meal, and retired to reflect on the days events.

The following day the crew had been out on patrol again, but this time, they themselves were the ones in distress.

Just before midnight on Wednesday 26th February 1941, service personnel on guard at the harbour observed a large flying boat out to sea, seemingly drifting and out of control as it was pounded by the waves in Campbeltown Loch.

At 23:45 the aircraft had grounded on the foreshore, allowing enough time for the crew to scramble clear, climb aboard the dinghy and paddle towards the shore.

Earlier that evening the aircraft Supermarine Stranraer K2799 coded BN-M of 240 Squadron, Captained by F/Lt Vincent Howard Furlong, Co-pilot Sgt Pete Hewitt and five crew, had encountered strong headwinds from a passing cold front, which in turn had caused the aircraft's wings and ailerons to ice up.

The flying boat had become difficult to control and the battle with the harsh elements had taken its toll on their rapidly diminishing fuel reserves. As conditions deteriorated with recorded gusts of 79 to 80 mph, F/Lt Furlong knew they were in trouble.

Navigator 'Dimi' Havlicek recalled the events to his Nav friend John Iverach:

"What's our fuel reading?" said Dimi, Furlong checking his gauges replied:

"About 30 gallons. Half an hour maybe, no more". "Well" yelled Dimi, *"unless the wind swings around again or lets up, we'll never make it. We're only twenty miles from Milleur Point,* (North of Stranraer) *but the wind is up to seventy knots head on, ground speed's only fifteen. Can we divert?"* asked Furlong. Dimi shook his head. *"Not a chance. No place is closer than home. Anyway, everywhere is socked in tight".*

The two pilots undertook the difficult decision to land the heavy biplane on the open sea, normally not recommended in such conditions, but with the two Bristol Pegasus X engines still providing some power, they had little choice.

"We'll go as far as we can in case there's a wind change" said Furlong *"Tell the crew to start getting ready, then get as accurate a position you can . We'll dump the depth charges now!"*

On the order from the skipper, Co-pilot Sgt Hewitt jettisoned the depth charges, as Furlong re-trimmed the aircraft to compensate the weight loss.

"OK everybody" said Furlong, *"Mae Wests on. Ready for ditching in a few minutes. You all know your stations and the drill. Elwell, Wilson, Hesk - don't forget the rations, water and signals, and make sure the oars, life-lines and bellows are in the dinghies. Dimi, remember the Very pistol and cartridges and give your latest position to Newbury* (The Wireless Operator) *- Newbury, start sending your S.O.S. and position in plain language".*

At this point, now around 500 feet off the water, Sgt Hewitt began stuffing a canvas sack with all the sensitive material: Syko coding machine, code books and any official documents. Its destination, the ocean floor, where it couldn't fall into enemy hands.

With the crew now at their ditching stations, everything seemed ready when suddenly one of the crew called up the Skipper: *"Elwell here sir, I - I seem to have forgotten my Mae West, and I can't swim!"*

There was a long silence, broken only by Dimi *"Here"* he said, *"take mine. It never did fit and it chafes my neck. Anyway, everybody knows I can swim rings around all of you guys".*

"What's our position now?" said Furlong. *"Just five miles from Corswall Light, tracking one thirty"* came the reply. *"Alright Newbury, send that off with our ditching message. Pete, I'll head her dead into the wind and when I yell, you drop three flame floats five seconds apart. Then fire a couple of parachute flares. We'll do a tight three sixty and try to get down in one piece. Everybody get strapped in tight. This could be the roughest landing you'll ever have. OK Pete, NOW!".*

The flame floats were released and the whole area lit up like a football stadium. Then, at approximately 20:15 hours, F/Lt Furlong with exceptional skill, successfully ditched the heavy flying boat, though due to the rough sea a wing float had been torn off, and the starboard wing tip was damaged, but the aircraft's hull, much to the relief of everyone on board, was still in one piece.

Though a few of the hull seams had ruptured and water began to pour in, these could be patched up, but it was soon realized that with the port wing float broken, the light wing would start to rise and cause the aircraft to list, fill up with water and eventually sink.

The engines were still ticking over and this would keep her headed into the wind, but once the fuel was gone Furlong knew she would start drifting far out into the open sea.

"Quick Elwell, throw the drogues from the nose!" yelled Furlong. These drogues were normally used as a last resort to slow the aircraft down when alighting on the water into a light wind, but it was hoped that by releasing them from the nose, hey would help to stop it from drifting too far once the fuel expired and the engines stopped.

Though the dinghies were prepared, Furlong knew they crew wouldn't last long on the ice cold sea, so hoped they could keep the aircraft afloat until rescue services arrived.

Sergeant's Newbury and Hesk managed to start the auxiliary power unit, and soon got to work on the bilge pump, meanwhile Elwell and Hewitt plugged the cracks in the hull, but the damaged float was still pulling them over and threatening to sink them.

While others worked on bailing the water and repairing leaks, Dimi, had been gathering lengths of rope, tying them together, and after lashing one end around his waist, without a word he climbed up past Furlong, onto the empty co-pilots seat and went out of the escape hatch.

Clambering along the port wing on his hands and knees in pitching seas, he then tied himself to wing struts and with his weight distributed the Stranraer's wing began to drop and after a short while was almost on an even keel, when moments later the engines died.

Furlong kept the rudders straight and every so often would give the thumbs up to Dimi as a sign of encouragement, at first Dimi acknowledged this by waving

Supermarine Stranraer K7295 BN-L of 240 Squadron

Stranraer K7299 BN-M the day after it was washed up on the beach
Photo: Vince Furlong Via John Evans and Pavel Vancata

back, but the cold sea, his wet gear and fierce winds were taking their toll, and after a while his body just lay motionless. The crew didn't know if he was alive or dead, but knew that he was all that was keeping them from capsizing, a truly selfless heroic act by the young Czech in every sense of the word.

The crew kept bailing all night, then, just as dawn broke, those in the back were thrown to the floor, the aircraft pitched high in the air, then came crashing down on its starboard side.

"This is it!" someone shouted, as they prepared to make a hasty exit. Furlong then wiped the window to see a long coarse gravel beach with dark hills silhouetted against the sky in the distance, he realized then they had grounded.

"Christ" said Furlong, *it's got to be the Mull of Kintyre".*

Kintyre it was, they had drifted over forty miles in the gales, but had finally reached dry land in the form of a beach near Campbeltown. Further north and they would have hit rocks, further south and the aircraft could have ended up off Ireland, if it hadn't broken up first. They had indeed been very lucky.

Once out they untied Dimi from the wing and laid him on the beach, he was unconscious and in a bad way, but the crew managed to revive him while Furlong and Newbury set off for help.

A motor launch arrived in Campbeltown later in the day and the crew were all taken back to Stranraer. Dimi was taken to hospital, though eventually he

33

made a full recovery. Furlong recommended that he be awarded a decoration for his gallant efforts in saving the crew, but it would appear his request fell on deaf ears with the C.O. and his only reward was the gratitude of his crew. In a cruel twist of fate, of those seven men on the Stranraer, only Furlong and Hewitt survived the war, the rest all perished in accidents before the end of 1941.

An inquiry into the loss of the Stranraer concluded that the crew having obtained inaccurate D/F fixes, had a stronger than forecast headwind, this resulted in them running low on fuel and being unable to reach Loch Ryan at Stranraer.

Designed by Reginald J. Mitchell, the Stranraer was generally crewed by up to seven personnel and armed with 2 x 7.7mm Lewis machine guns. She had a wingspan of 85 feet with a length of 54 feet, 9 inches. Maximum speed was 165 mph and with a range of 1,000 miles was able to operate at ceilings of 18,500 feet.

Of the few that were built, RAF crews found the aircraft to be very sluggish and many unappealing nicknames for the type soon emerged. Regardless, the new aircraft served in the all-important anti-sub coastal patrol role, though none ever saw real combat action in World War Two.

K7299 was one of only seventeen to be purchased for the RAF and manufactured by Supermarine Aviation Works (Vickers) Ltd, Southampton under contract no. 419705/35. The aircraft was delivered to 228 Squadron at Pembroke Dock on 10th October 1938 and later served at Calshot and Oban, before eventually arriving at Stranraer and Lough Erne in July 1940 to serve with 240 Squadron as BN-M.

F/Lt Vincent H. Furlong. RAF

Photo: John Evans—
Pembroke Dock Sunderland Trust

It was Struck Off Charge having logged a total of 817 flying hours. The type was withdrawn from frontline service as early as March 1941 as PBY Consolidated Catalinas began to arrive.

Pilot Flight Lieutenant Vincent Harold Furlong, RAF, born in Chiswick on 20th February 1917, was the son of Walter John and Florence Sarah Furlong (née Healy) of Brentford, Middlesex. Vincent had one younger brother Bernard.

Having passed through Cranwell as a flight cadet, Vince, as he was referred, was granted a commission on 1st August 1936 with a permanent commission in the RAF and an Acting Pilot Officer on probation from 24th August. He was then sent to 8 FTS at Montrose on 5th September followed by an OTU prior to joining a squadron.

A posting to 217 Squadron at Boscombe Down, Salisbury, came next on 24th April 1937. Here Vince flew the twin-engine Avro Anson on general reconnaissance sorties, mainly on the lookout for ships or aircraft in distress.

Soon after war broke out the squadron moved in to St. Eval in Cornwall, where aside from the Anson, the new Beaufort 1s arrived in May 1940, but teething troubles led to the Anson still being used until December for patrols over the English Channel and Western Approaches.

Promotion to Flying Officer came on 29th January 1939, though Vince continued to serve with 217 Squadron until 3rd September 1940, when it would appear, as a rest from operations, he was posted to No2 (C) OTU at RAF Catfoss, Yorkshire, presumably as an Instructor.

Vince had been returning to Catfoss from a routine exercise on 8th January 1941 in Blenheim L6775, when a heavy landing caused the undercarriage to collapse, luckily there were no injuries to himself or his crew and the aircraft was soon repaired and put back into service.

Ironically, Vince was posted to a flying boat squadron just six days later, and would soon be flying the Supermarine Stranraer flying boat, which of course had no need of an undercarriage.

American Lt. Eddy Wagner, USN and F/Lt Vince Furlong. RAF
Photo: Vince Furlong via John Evans and Pavel Vancata.

Having been posted to 240 Squadron at Loch Ryan, Stranraer, Vince flew Stranraers until March when the squadron saw delivery of Consolidated Catalinas.

Promoted to Flight Lieutenant on 21st June 1941 and still with the Squadron, he was now flying the Catalina from Lough Erne and continuing convoy protection with anti-sub patrols.

In June the following year he was promoted to Squadron Leader and on 1st August joined 95 Squadron in West Africa. A further promotion to Wing Commander came on 1st September when he became the squadron C.O. serving at Bathurst in Gambia.

The squadron here operated the Short Sunderland with 10 man crews, though for Vince his rank and status meant his flying days were numbered, though he did manage a trip with F/O Welton and crew on 20th February 1943, when they flew on convoy escort in DV963.

Wing Commander Percy Robert Hatfield. DFC. AFC. RAF assumed command of 95 Squadron on 24th March when Vince became the O.C. of RAF Bathurst.

F/Lt Vince H. Furlong. RAF
Photo: Author's Collection

Vince remained in the RAF for a short while after the war ended, but in more of an admin role, though his Wing Commander rank was reduced to that of Squadron Leader. He married his fiancée Kathleen in 1947 and left the RAF in 1949.

His movements in civilian life are somewhat sketchy, but his occupation when visiting his brother in Canada in February 1952 was noted to have been a foundry technician, and again this was his occupation on a border pass from Rio De Janeiro, Brazil to Niagara Falls, N.Y. in 1963. Vince passed away in Ludlow, Shropshire in 1998.

A Short Sunderland makes a landing at Bathurst, Gambia

Sgt Peter W. Hewitt RAFVR as an AC1

Photo: Valerie Garlick

following a series of flying lessons by Instructor J. H. Lacey, who later became known as the famous WW2 fighter ace `Ginger` Lacey DFM & Bar, he obtained his pilots certificate in a Gipsy Moth 95 on 18th March 1939. Pete was also in the Civil Air Guard during the build up to war.

When war broke out on 3rd Sept, Pete joined the RAF and after basic training was posted to 7 EFTS at RAF Desford, Leicestershire as an LAC U/T pilot flying Tiger Moths, then No1 School of General Reconnaissance at Squires Gate, Blackpool, flying Anson 1s.

Co-Pilot Sergeant Peter William Hewitt, RAF, born 28th February 1914, was the eldest son of George Arthur and Sarah Hewitt (née Hutchinson) of Bradford, West Yorkshire. He had one younger brother Martin.

Pete`s father was a timber merchant with a firm in Hull, which provided the income for a good standard of education for the children. After High School Peter attended Scarborough College.

In the late 1930s Pete, always a sports enthusiast, was a member of the West Riding Sailing Club, Secretary of the Bradford Amateur Rowing Club, a member of the Yorkshire Sports Car Club and also the Yorkshire Aeroplane Club at Yeadon (Leeds/Bradford airport) where

Sgt Peter W. Hewitt. RAFVR

Photo: John Evans - Pembroke Dock Sunderland Trust

37

No 25 Course 1940 - No.1 School of General Reconnaissance, Squires Gate

Sgt Peter Hewitt is pictured middle row far right.   Photo: Valerie Garlick

He eventually ended up on Flying Boats with Coastal Command, so needing practice landing on water he was sent to a FBTS at Stranraer to train with members of 240 Squadron for a few weeks, which is how he came to be on the Stranraer that beached on Kintyre.

In March 1941 he was posted to the FB OTU at Invergordon before going on to fly as Co-Pilot on Sunderlands with 204 Squadron. It was while serving with this unit at Bathurst, Gambia, that he almost lost his life in Sunderland T9041.

The aircraft coded 'V' was on convoy escort duty on 28th June 1942 and Pete, now a F/Sgt was with F/Lt Ennis and crew when all four engines failed, the flying boat ditched off West Africa in a heavy swell at 13:30 and started to sink. Of the ten on board, all except F/Sgt Henry John Humphrey, who was lost with the aircraft, managed to scramble clear before it sank.

The events which followed earned Pete a B.E.M and the citation appearing in the London Gazette was covered in the national press at the end of the year. Here is what it said: *"Flight Sergeant Hewitt was the 2nd pilot of a flying boat which crashed whilst alighting in a heavy swell, and sank. The crew were in shark-infested waters, 180 miles from land, with one rubber dinghy and four life belts. The captain of the aircraft was injured, and the dinghy would support only two people……..finding that one of*

38

Short Sunderland T9041 at Bathurst, Gambia

the crew was drowning, he managed to get him on to the damaged dinghy and spent the whole of one night swimming alongside, holding the man's head out of the water, until sadly he died. Even then Flight Sergeant Hewitt made strenuous efforts to effect resuscitations, to his own detriment and exhaustion.

Later, when dinghies with food and water were dropped by an aircraft, Flight Sergeant Hewitt was the first to swim out to collect those within range. The crew were on the water for 70 hours before they were rescued, and it was largely due to the magnificent example of self-sacrifice and endurance of Flight Sergeant Hewitt and his cheerfulness in spite of the apparently hopeless situation, that only one of the crew was lost. When rescued he was in a far worse physical condition than any of his companions". (LG. 29.12.42).

The crew of the Sunderland had been spotted by F/Lt Henry and crew in Hudson FH236 'E' of 200 Squadron. This aircraft, after dropping dinghies and supplies, then directed the RN destroyer HMS *Velox* to the scene and the Sunderland crew were taken aboard. Sadly, during the last night F/Sgt John Thomson the man Pete had tried to save, had passed away.

Following a period of survivors leave, Pete continued to serve with 204 Squadron and was promoted to Pilot Officer on 29th July 1942. His B.E.M was presented at Buckingham Palace on 29th December that year and a further promotion to F/O came on 28th January.

On 30th October 1943 whilst serving at RAF Alness, Ross-shire, he was given leave to marry his fiancée Miss Margaret Brodie at St.Michael and All Saints Church, Hendon. Pete achieved the rank of F/Lt and left the RAF after WW2 retaining this rank as a reservist.

On leaving the RAF he went home to Yorkshire with his wife and four daughters, Valerie, Alison, Patricia and Sylvia and worked with his father in timber business, but when his father passed away, he decided to run a newsagent and booksellers shop in Beverley, before finally retiring in 1989.

Navigator Pilot Officer Vladimir Viktor Havlicek, RCAF, born in Praha, Czechoslovakia on 23rd October 1909, was the son of Vladimir J. and Zdenka Havlicek (née Zatkoka) of Praha (Prague), Czechoslovakia.

Dimi, as he was referred, went to Public School in Vienna until 1915, then to High Schools in Prague and Zurich, Switzerland until 1929 when he won scholarships for Frankfurt University and the University of Prague, graduating as a Doctor of Political Science in 1932. Dimi also spoke five languages, Czech, German, French, English and Polish.

In 1932 he became a 2nd/Lt in the 1st Cavalry Regiment of the Czech Militia and in 1935 was promoted to 1st/Lt. This unit was basically a small army of non-professional soldiers, citizens and/or subjects of the state, who can be called upon for military service during a time of need and Dimi had served part time, while being employed as an export manager for the Bata Shoe Company.

Dimi was an excellent sportsman and was awarded the Knights Order of the Romania Crown 2nd Class, for winning the International Military Ski Patrol events in the Czech Olympic Games. He also took part in tennis, swimming and football events and travelled the world.

Due to the uprising of Nazi Germany and the threat of invasion, many Czechs fled the country while they still had some control over the borders. Dimi, no doubt influenced by his father, was one of those who left while he still had the chance, he

Vladimir Viktor Havlicek

had been informed by his boss Tomas Bata, that the firm would be looking to build a new factory in Canada and that he would have a job there once this happens.

Dimi Arrived in Cherbourg, France on 14th April 1938 and on the 20th sailed aboard the Queen Mary for New York, he then travelled by rail to Canada and for a while lived in Toronto as a representative of a Czech Commercial House.

He was once again employed with his old firm, the Bata Shoe Company on newly built premises at Batawa, Southeast Ontario. The company provided low cost housing for its employees and Dimi began to settle into a new life, he became a tennis star playing singles and doubles with the Toronto Lawn Tennis Club, winning many matches.

For a short time life was good, but the threat of war in Europe became a startling reality when he heard his country had fallen to Nazi Occupation in March 1939, followed six months later by Poland.

On 7th December 1939 Dimi and a Czech friend Jan Gellner from Trieste both applied for the Canadian Air Force, and on being accepted and undergoing a medical exam and recruitment test, they were finally accepted on 11th May 1940 and arrived at No1 MD a basic training camp in Toronto as AC2s.

Leading Aircraftmen J.P.MacKay and Dimi Havlicek just back from a training flight in a Harvard in Canada 1940

Photo: Toronto Star

Next came three weeks at 1 I.T.S where they would finally be assessed as to whether they were suitable for air or ground duties. It was here that Dimi and the boys got their first taste of flying in an Avro Anson.

Both Dimi and Jan were selected for aircrew and were informed that they would later train as Navigators. Arriving at No.1 AOS at Malton, Ontario on 21st June, Dimi and the others were instantly promoted to LAC and became U/T Observers (the early term used for navigators).

A few months later Dimi went for gunnery training at No1 B&GS, Jarvis, Ontario. Arriving on 15th September, he would complete the course by the end of October, having earned 'Above Average' marks, then on the 28th he was awarded his Observers brevet and promotion to Sergeant.

More classroom work, periods of leave and an advanced navigation course at Rivers, Manitoba followed, prior to Dimi arriving with others at Halifax, Nova Scotia, for embarkation to the UK on 15th December 1940 aboard an old Dutch liner the SS *Pennland*, and arrival in the Clyde on Christmas Day morning. Based on his excellent grade at ANS, Dimi had applied for a commission and was now a Pilot Officer.

After travelling south by train he and others checked in at RAF Uxbridge on the 26th, and the following day were all given passes to explore London and the likes before being posted to 240 Squadron at Loch Ryan, Stranraer.

41

Pilot Officer Vladimir Viktor `Dimi` Havlicek RCAF
Photo: Vince Furlong Via John Evans and Pavel Vancata

He stayed with 240 Squadron, first flying Stranraers, then Catalinas from March 1941 before losing his life in a tragic accident at the end of the year.

On the day in question, 23rd December Dimi, now a F/O was the Navigator for P/O K.A.W. Patterson and crew on Catalina W8418 when it was badly damaged at Pembroke Dock.

The aircraft had taken off at 02:40 and was returning to base after a long patrol, soon after reaching base the flying boat landed heavy, a float dug in and as the aircraft began sinking, Dimi heard shouts from men trapped inside, so went back to help one of the W/Ops but soon after pushing him up through the hatch, the aircraft sank taking Dimi and three of the ten man crew with it.

Dimi Havlicek's body was never found and he is commemorated on the Runnymede Memorial, Surrey, Panel 59, and as per Canadian rules posthumously promoted to Flight Lieutenant.

Wireless Operator & Air Gunner Sergeant Harry Harley Newbury, RAF, born on 7th October 1921 in Trinidad, was the son of Leoniel and Louisa Newbury (née McIntosh) of Warsash, Hampshire. He had two brothers Alec and Raymond and two sisters Violet and Grace.

As mentioned earlier Harry was born in Trinidad where his father, known to family and friends as Len, was the manager of a hotel. In 1924 the family left from the port at Curaçao, Trinidad, aboard the SS *Venezuela*, a steamship of the Royal Netherlands West India Mail Company, and arrived in Plymouth on 11th February.

Sgt Harry H. Newbury. RAF

Photo: Gill Overton via Jenny Paterson

The family lived in Kent for a while, before moving back to his father's birthplace of The Nook, in the coastal village of Hook-with-Warsash in South Hampshire at the mouth of the River Hamble.

A former pupil of Locks Heath Junior School in Warsach, Park Gate, Southampton, Harry appears to have been well liked by all the staff and former classmates there.

When war broke out two Newbury brothers joined the RAF and after basic training Harry was selected for a three month Wireless course at Blackpool, where he would learn Morse Code etc later qualifying as a W/Op he received his `Sparkes` badge, promotion from AC1 to LAC and an increase in pay to 28 Shillings (£1.40) per fortnight. He was then sent to an Air Gunners School for a gunnery course prior to joining a squadron. At the end of the course Harry would be awarded his gunners brevet and a promotion to Sergeant would swiftly follow.

It is not certain whether he was one of the crew, or a passenger on this occasion, but on Friday 2nd February 1940, a Saro London flying boat belonging to 240 Squadron, at that time based in Sullom Voe, Shetland, had left its base for a transit flight to RAF Calshot for a major inspection, but had failed to reach its destination.

The pilot that day was P/O H.A.B. Porteous with P/O N.A.L. Smith as co-pilot with five crew and four passengers. The aircraft was K6927 and the route would be down the west coast of Scotland and Wales via the Isle of Man and should have taken them no more than a day, but the weather was poor and with visibility getting worse the crew landed at Oban and were closed in over the weekend.

With a slight let up they took off on Monday 5th but again conditions got worse and while flying in low towards the harbour at Holyhead, Anglesey, they tore the trailing aerial off on a ships mast, dropped, hit the sea hard and the aircraft was wrecked. Fortunately the crew and passengers all got out and were picked up by a rescue boat, then taken ashore to a nearby Mariners Mission where they received dry clothes and hot drinks.

The remains London K6927 at Holyhead

Photo: Danny Lockyer BEM- 240 Sqn. W/AG

Remaining with 240 Squadron, Harry would operate in London and Singapore flying boats from Invergordon and Pembroke Dock, before moving to Loch Ryan, on Stranraers in July 1940 until the end of March 1941.

The incident at Kintyre would have been one of the last times Harry flew in the Stranraer, as the squadron began converting to Catalinas. John Iverach recalled in his memoirs that on 20th March he had been at Lough Erne when two of the new Catalinas arrived, one had Harry on board and John had gone to pick him and the crew up in a truck, then having shown them their quarters, they all had a drink and a laugh together in the bar before retiring.

The following evening came the sad news that AM265 BN-A crashed into a hill at Glenade, Co.Leitrim with P/O Harold L.Seaward and seven other crew including Harry Newbury, and all had perished. He was interred with full military honours in Irvinestown (Sacred Heart) Roman Catholic Cemetery. Co. Fermanagh. Grave No.1.

Wireless Electrical Engineer and Air Gunner, Sergeant John Sterling Hesk, RAF, born 1920 on the Isle of Wight, was the youngest son of Robert Chantry Dawson and Ruby Hesk (née Sterling), of Shanklin, Isle of Wight. He had one older brother Harold Valentine Hesk

John's father was a carpenter and an electrician and the family lived on Landguard Road, Shanklin. John had been a pupil at Sandown Secondary School before going on to Cranmore Training School, Yarmouth, Isle of Wight. His older brother Harold was in the Merchant Navy.

Having survived the ordeal in the Stranraer, John was to lose his life just weeks later, when on 7th May he was returning to Lough Erne at 04:30 with Pilot F/O P.C.Thomas and 8 other crew when on landing without a flarepath, the aircraft Catalina AH536 crashed and sank in deep water. Only one of the crew was found, the rest including John, are commemorated on Runnymede, Panel 45 and on a memorial on the shore of Loch Erne.

A memorial for the crew of AH536

Photo: Kenneth Allen. Under CC Licence.

Wireless Operator & Air Gunner Sergeant Joseph Leslie Elwell, RAFVR, born 27th September 1918 in Dudley, was the son of Joseph and Laura May Elwell (née Skeldon) of Coseley, near Bilston, Staffordshire. He had one older sister Winifred Laura.

Joe's parents, both natives of Dudley, Worcestershire, were married in the town on 29th December 1912 and the happy couple lived on Millbrook Street where their daughter Winifred was born the following year.

With the First World War in Europe raging, Joseph's father was called up and joined the Kings Own Scottish Borders in June 1915 and had reached the rank of Sergeant by the end of the war. He returned home in 1917 and their only son Joseph Leslie was born the following year. Joe lost his life in Catalina AH536 on 7th May 1941. He is commemorated on Panel 43 of Runnymede.

Wireless Operator & Air Gunner Sergeant Henry Ernest Wilson, RAFVR, born 4th May 1917, was the son of Henry Charles and Agnes Mary Wilson of Haley Green, Warfield, Bracknell, Berkshire. He had one older sister Eileen.

Henry attended schools in Warfield and prior to joining the RAF in 1939. he was working as a plumber and living at Council Oakes, Easthampstead, Berkshire.

Henry was also a crew member on board Catalina AH536 with his pals John Hesk and Joe Elwell. He is commemorated on Panel 55 of the Runnymede Memorial.

A FULMAR ON KERRAN HILL - N4038

On Christmas day 1940, a little after 14:00, six Grumman Martlets of 804 Squadron Royal Navy Fleet Air Arm based at Skeabrae, took to the skies over Orkney in hot pursuit of a Junkers Ju.88, alleged to have been flying a photo-reconnaissance mission off the Northern Scottish islands.

The aircraft coded 4N+AL was soon intercepted by two of the Martlets, Lt Rodney Carver flying as leader in BJ562 `A` and Sub/Lt (A) Thomas Parke in BJ561 `S7L`. Moments later several hits were made on the raider causing damage to the starboard radiator and port engine oil pipe, other hits riddled the tail-plane and dorsal fin, leaving no option for its pilot Leutnant Karl Schipp but to make a crash landing in the nearest field. With its air gunner badly wounded and the undercarriage still retracted, the pilot made a very skillful crash landing in a field near Flotterston, Sandwick, close to Loch Skail, on the west coast of the Orkney Mainland (Pomona). The Luftwaffe crew were soon met by farmers armed with shotguns and swiftly led away from the crashed aircraft, before they had a chance to set fire to it.

This Ju.88 from the unit 3(F)/22 at Stavanger, Norway, became the first enemy aircraft to be shot down by American aircraft flown by British pilots in WW2, the victors returning to Skeabrae to a heroes welcome and great cheers from fellow pilots.

Ju.88 4N+AL at Flotterston. Photo: Orkney Library Archive Gregor Lamb Collection

HMS Pegasus

By March 1941 804 Squadron had already received the first of its Fairey Fulmar Mk1s and IIs, providing allied convoys some protection. These aircraft operated from catapult armed merchant ships (CAMs), a forerunner to the RAF merchant ship fighter unit employing Hawker Hurricanes in a similar role.

It was whilst engaged in one of these operations from HMS *Pegasus*, a converted collier, that Lt Parke would lose his life on 7th July 1941.

He was now a Lieutenant and along with his TAG L/A Edwin F. Miller, the pair were launched from *Pegasus* in Fulmar N4038 at 07:58 in order to

Fairey Fulmar

locate and intercept a German Fw.200 Condor, known to have been shadowing convoys SL78 and OG57 prior to them arriving in Sierra Leone and Gibraltar.

However, due to poor visibility caused by low cloud and rain, contact with the convoy proved impossible, Parke and Miller therefore plotted a course to Aldergrove, Northern Ireland, but due to the prevailing weather conditions and lack of height, their aircraft flew into high ground at Kerran Hill, south of Campbeltown at 11:00. Sadly there were no survivors.

On discovery of the wreckage on the hill above Glen Hervie some hours later, the bodies of the two young airmen were recovered and taken back to Campbeltown, where following a service, Parke and Miller were laid to rest in Campbeltown, (Kilkerran) Cemetery with full military honours in Division 4. Graves 583 and 584 respectively.

Pilot. Lieutenant (A) Thomas Robert Verner Parke, RN, was born in 1920. He was the son of William 'Willie' Alexander and Isabel Emily 'Ella' Parke (née White) of Crossmoyle Clones, Co.Monaghan, Ireland. He had one older brother William Cecil and a sister Jean Marie.

For young Thomas tragedy struck at an early age. First his father passed away in 1928, then his mother died in 1934. so At the age of 14 he went to live with his aunt and uncle at Morwenna, Great Orme Road, Llandudno, North Wales.

Lt (A) Thomas Robert Verner Parke RN as a young Sub-Lieutenant.

His uncle was James Cecil Parke, a former army Major who had fought at Gallipoli in WW1 with the Leinster Regiment and was twice wounded.

Major Parke had also excelled in sports and once captained the Ireland Rugby Team, won an Olympic silver medal in Tennis mixed doubles and among other achievements helped Britain win the Davis Cup in 1912 by beating Australasia. At the outbreak of World War One he ranked sixth in the world.

In civilian life his uncle was a solicitor in offices at Trinity Square, Llandudno and his position here provided income for a good education for his young nephew Thomas throughout his teen years.

Thomas joined the Air Branch of the Royal Navy as a Midshipman (A) on 1st May 1939 and conducted his elementary flying training at Elmdon, (now Birmingham Airport) with 14 EFTS, then on 6th November he joined 6 Course with No1 Flying Training School at Leuchars, Fife.

At RNAS Yeovilton (*Heron*) on 21st April 1940, Thomas was awarded his pilots wings and promoted to Acting Sub-Lieutenant. Following a spot of leave and some operational training, he eventually joined 804 Squadron on 4th July flying Gloster Sea Gladiators from Hatston, Orkney on coastal defence of the Home Fleet in Scapa Flow.

Grumman Martlet of 804 Squadron from Skeabrae, Orkney

Gloster Gladiator

On 28th October 1940 the squadron, at this time under command of Lt/Cdr. J.C. Cockburn, moved to Skeabrae and was re-equipped with 12 Grumman Martlet 1s.

As we know it was whilst flying a Martlet that Thomas shot down the Ju.88 over Orkney, so quite possibly inspired by his younger brothers actions, and later coming to terms with his loss, William, who was a Corporal Fitter in the RAF, applied for aircrew and went on to train as a pilot, both in the UK and in Canada.

William eventually won his wings, and conducted his operational training on Oxfords and Wellingtons, before being posted to 15 Squadron flying Stirlings and Lancasters on bombing raids over occupied Europe, which earned him a DFC in December 1944.

After the war he left the RAF with the rank of Flight Lieutenant and became a civilian pilot for BOAC. He passed away in October 2010.

Be it their competitiveness in sport, or their devotion to duty in the armed forces, the Parke family are certainly an inspiration to us all.

Telegraphist Air Gunner 3rd Class Leading Airman Edwin Francis Miller, RN, born 27th January 1922, was the only son of Oswald George and Charlotte Ellen Miller (née Blazeby) of Stutton, Suffolk.

Edwin's parents had been married in Edmonton, Middlesex in 1920, his father had served in Royal Navy in the First World War and reached the rank of Petty Officer. In 1939 the family moved to the village of Stutton, Suffolk.

Edwin joined the RN FAA in 1940 and trained at Worthy Down and Gosport as a TAG. He was interred in Kilkerran Div 4.Grave 584 and commemorated on the Stutton Village War Memorial and the Roll of Honour in Stutton Church.

L/A Edwin F. Miller in Kilkerran

Photo: Author's Collection

Lt (A) Thomas R,V. Parke. RN

Photos: Author's Collection

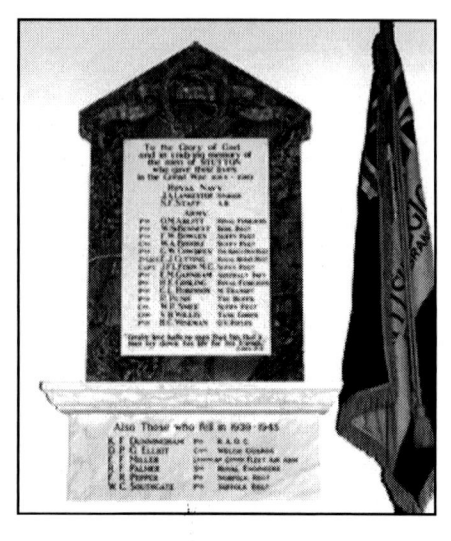

Roll of Honour in Stutton, Church

DEADLY DECISION - HUDSON AE640

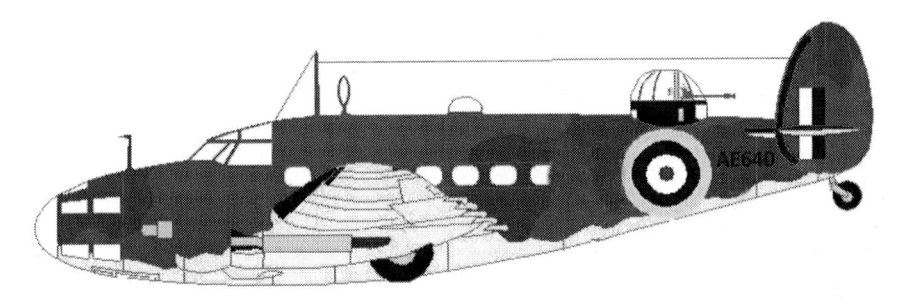

Designed by Clarence Leonard 'Kelly' Johnson, the Hudson was constructed at the Lockheed Aircraft Corporation works at Burbank, California and supplied to the Royal Air Force under the Lend Lease Scheme as 41- 42993 (USAAF) a Mk V of which 309 were produced. It was powered by two 1,200 hp Pratt & Whitney Twin Wasp 14-cylinder two-row radial engines and allocated to the Overseas Aircraft Despatch Flight, for delivery to the UK and given the serial AE640.

Initially delivered to Dorval, Canada, the Hudson commenced the long and hazardous journey to RAF St Eval, Cornwall via Prestwick, Ayrshire, navigating via the North Atlantic ferry route with a crew of three: Pilot F/Lt Keith Fergus Arnold. DFC. RAF Observer Sgt Percy Keast RAFVR and a civilian Wireless Operator Wilfred Bratherton,

Both Keith Arnold and Percy Keast were noted as being on the strength of 31 Air Navigation School at Port Albert, on the shores of Lake Huron, Ontario, Canada.

Due to deteriorating weather conditions on route, the Hudson was cleared to land at RAF Limavady in Northern Ireland, before continuing the journey to Prestwick where the crew would be accommodated.

Hudson AE610 from the same production batch

51

On Friday 25th July 1941, despite a forecast provided by the Meteorological Officer at Limavady of poor weather, consisting of rain, drizzle and a low cloud ceiling, F/Lt Arnold took off in AE640 on an easterly heading towards Prestwick.

Available records do not state whether the crew had eventually reached Prestwick and were waiting for a gap in the cloud, or if they turned out to sea to descend below cloud with intentions of returning to Limavady.

The burnt out wreckage of the Hudson was eventually located on rising ground at an approximate height of 200 feet, just below Feorlan cottage on the south eastern side of the Kintyre peninsula. This position indicates the aircraft was on a westerly or north westerly heading when it crashed with the loss of all three crew members.

Mr & Mrs Bob Cleland, owners of Feorlan in 1994, with the crash site behind them

Photo: *Geoff Bland*

The crash site at Feorlan in 2017   Photo: Gary Nelson

Members of the Dumfries & Galloway Aviation Museum surveying the site in 2007

Photo: Steven Spink

Parachute hook found at the crash site after the war

Photo: Steven Spink

At an investigation it was stated that the accident occurred at 11:30 hours and that: *"The flight had commenced against the advice of officers at Limavady, in rain, drizzle and low cloud over Scotland"*. The reason for this action will never be known, though possibly it was envisaged that the weather would improve as the flight progressed, or perhaps there was some haste for the pilot to get back to St. Eval to see his wife and newborn son before returning to ops?

A very experienced pilot, F/Lt Arnold had been in the RAF since 1936 and only weeks earlier he had been awarded the DFC for his trips over Nazi occupied Europe flying dangerous photo-reconnaissance missions in Spitfires, and it is interesting to read his hand-written notes in the PRU Operations Record Book on his return from these flights.

For instance, on 13th February 1941, he took off from St.Eval in Spitfire X4333 at 09:50 for a mission to Nantes, St.Nazaire, Vannes and Lorient, daubed as mission No 297. Returning from the flight he recorded:

"S/C (South-Coast) Dodmans - Nantes, Ht.23,000ft. Photographed Nantes—Chateau—Bougon, then went on to St.Nazaire which was cloud covered and at this point `Puffing Billy` was froze up and oxygen failed, so came down to 18,000ft proceeded on to Vannes.

Photographed Vannes, Meugon and another aerodrome near Plumergat. Did a visual of Quiberon Bay, then went on to Lorient where heavy AA fire was encountered, so came down to 16,000ft to avoid the accurate fire.... a hit was later discovered in the fuselage" He arrived back at base at base at 12:20 after a duration of 2.5 hrs.

As the O.C. of ``A` Flight he was always busy and in another entry in the ORB 5 days later he almost got caught

X4786 was one of the PRU Spitfires flown by F/Lt Keith Arnold on 21st May 1941
Photo: The Aviation Photo Company

F/Lt Keith Arnold with his PRU Spitfire in 1941
Photo: Dick & Mary Zandee Via Alan Clark

out on mission No 306 to Brest, when he was attacked by enemy fighters. Having again taken off from St.Eval at 09:30 he crossed the channel in variable cloud down to 1,000 feet, conducting a photo run in from Goulet to Brest he notes:

"flew directly across the docks at 700-800 ft with vertical camera as the oblique camera was on the right hand side. Heavy `Flak` on all sides over Brest and several Me.109s were encountered over Guipauas where 5/10 St.Cu (Strato-Cumulous cloud) *gave small cover. After a dogfight with the 109s, the coast and better cloud cover was reached. Came home at 200ft.. Crossed coast via Lands End".* Duration 1hr 45min.

Pilot Flight Lieutenant Keith Fergus Arnold. DFC. RAF born 1st April 1911 in Kindersley, Saskatchewan, Canada, was the son of Colonel Harry Watson Arnold and Eva Mary Arnold (née Martin) of Saskatchewan. He had one brother Victor Charles, and three sisters, Doris Eva, Frieda Mary and Joan Elaine. He was also husband of Mary and they had one son Wayne McLeod Arnold.

His parents were originally from Essex and his father Harry, had been a Captain in the First World War, and left the army as a Colonel. He married Eva Mary Martin in Tendring in 1907 and later the family settled in Canada.

Keith had spent his early years on his father's ranch where he became a proficient horseman and trick roper and at the age of 16 he was racing horses as a member of the Western Canada Association of Exhibitions in the class A circuit.

Keith was educated at Saskatoon and attended the University of Saskatchewan where he studied accountancy. While at University he developed an interest in aeroplanes and enrolled as a pupil at Moose Jaw Flying Club where he was one of the first to buy shares. He later finished his flying course at the Saskatoon Aero Club where he obtained his private pilots licence.

As part of his national service he became a trumpeter in the 15th Canadian Light Horse, but his heart was set on flying and he later sailed for England aboard a cattle ship to join the Royal Air Force. He was sent to an Elementary Reserve Flying Training School where he eventually gained his pilots wings.

Having been granted a short service commission, he became an Acting Pilot Officer on 24th August 1936 and was sent to RAF Uxbridge to be assessed before being posted to 10 SFTS at Tern Hill, Salop on 9th September, where he flew Hart, Audax and Tutor trainers in preparation for joining a squadron.

Keith's first posting was to 217 Squadron at Boscombe Down on 22nd April 1937, the squadron had just been reformed in March as a General Reconnaissance unit flying the twin engine Avro Anson. Promotion to full P/O came the following month, along with several moves to Tangmere, Bicester, and Warmwell.

A keen golfer, when the opportunity presented itself, Keith played for St.Augustine's Golf Club, Ramsgate and was mentioned in national press on 24th November as having beat RAF Manston 7 matches to 5 at Ebbsfleet.

F/Lt Keith Fergus Arnold DFC. RAF

Photo: Dick & Mary Zandee Via Alan Clark

The article went on to say that P/O Arnold, with a handicap of 13, beat H. R. Port (Handicap of 9) and also won the monthly bogey.

In 1938 Keith, already a former boxer at University, won the RAF Welterweight Boxing Championship, and ended the year on a high with a promotion to F/O on 29th December. A further promotion to Acting F/Lt came in June 1939, and that summer he married his fiancée Mary Hudson in Dorchester and the couple were blessed with a son the following year.

Still with 217 Squadron, at the start of the Second World War, Keith flew patrols over the Western Approaches to the Channel, later moving from Warmwell to the incomplete base at St. Eval on the north-west coast of Cornwall on 2nd October 1939.

There appears to be a bit of a gap in Keith's service record in 1940, though at the end of the year he was O.C. of 'A' flight in 1 PRU at Benson flying Spitfires and from December through to the end of May 1941, he flew numerous photographic sorties over Europe from St.Eval, Heston and Mount Field, the last being to St.Nazaire on 27th May in R6900.

Earlier that month, Keith had been dealt a devastating blow when he received the news that his younger brother P/O Victor Charles Arnold RCAF had been killed in a flying accident in Scotland.

He was undergoing pilot training at 58 OTU Balado Bridge, Grangemouth north east of Falkirk, Stirlingshire, in a Miles Master Mk I T8780, when during the exercise on 5th May 1941,

P/O Victor Charles Arnold. RCAF

Photo: Dick & Mary Zandee
Via Alan Clark

the aircraft was observed to dive into the ground killing Victor and critically injuring Sgt Jack Dunmore, who was rushed to the Larbert Military Hospital but sadly passed away on Saturday 17th May at 07:15 hours.

Sgt Dunmore, an experienced pilot from Egham, Surrey joined the RAF on 15th April 1938 and had served with 266 (Rhodesia) Squadron flying Spitfires from RAF Wittering before a posting on 1st October 1940 to 222 Squadron at Hornchurch, again on Spitfires. On the afternoon of 15th October Sgt Dunmore shared in the destruction of a Bf.109 but had to force land his Spitfire L1089 at RAF Hawkinge due to battle damage.

Victor Arnold was interred in Grangemouth (Grandsable) Cemetery Sec.1. Grave 13. Jack T. Dunmore is in Chislehurst (The Annunciation) Churchyard, Kent. Both were accorded a full military funeral.

On 13th June Keith went on leave to Canada and sailed from Liverpool to Montreal aboard the British Passenger/Cargo Steamship MV *Nicoya*. While on leave he visited his parents to offer comfort in the loss of their youngest son. He also addressed the Kiwanis Club, impressing them with tales of Canadian flyers.

As we know Keith lost his life returning from Canada in July and a service was held at 15:00 on Saturday 2nd August at St. Eval Church, Cornwall, before interment with a full guard of honour with officers and men from his unit in the company of family and friends.

His wife Mary never really got over the tragedy and passed away in 1946. Their orphaned son Wayne went to live with his grandparents in Vancouver, Canada and sailed for Halifax via New York with Lecturer Elizabeth Meredith aboard the Cunard White Star liner *Drotting Holm* on 30th April 1946.

Sadly, the story didn't end here, for tragedy struck the Arnold family again when Wayne was killed in an attempted robbery by a taxi driver at a hotel in Tijuana, Mexico on 25th April 1962.

Observer Sergeant Percy Keast, RAFVR, born November 1916 in St. Austell, Cornwall, was the only son of Percy and Florence Hilda Keast (née Tabb) of Tywardreath, Cornwall. He had one older sister Dorothy.

F/Lt Keith Arnold's grave

Photo: Alan Clark

Percy's parents were married in 1910 and his father, a China clay works foreman, had served with the Machine Gun Corps in the First World War as a driver from December 1915 until demob in Jan 1920.

Tywardreath where Percy grew up is a small hilltop village located on the south coast of Cornwall around 3 miles north west of Fowey.

Percy was educated at St.Austell County School, Cornwall, and on leaving school after passing the Civil Service Examination he entered the Ministry of Labour and National Service in 1934.

Sgt Percy Keast. RAFVR

On the staff of the Employment Exchange, Falmouth, he was subsequently promoted and transferred to Aldershot then Bristol. On joining the RAF soon after war broke out, after basic training he was posted overseas to Canada to train as an Observer, he had just completed his training, been promoted and awarded his wings shortly before the fatal flight.

His school in St.Austell described him as a pleasant and quiet boy, and very conscientious in all he had to do and that he left many friends. He was interred in Campbeltown (Kilkerran) Cemetery on 30th July at 10:00 hours with full military honours. Division 4 Plot 587.

Civilian Wireless Operator Wilfred Bratherton, Civilian Technical Corps, was born on 27th September 1917 at Powell River, British Columbia, Canada. He was the son of Wilfred and Mary Bratherton (née Cole) of New Westminster, BC, Canada.

Though Wilfred was born and raised in Canada, his father was from Salford, Manchester, England, where his grandfather Alderman Bratherton JP, had served with Manchester Police for 58 years since the age of 17.

Wilfred's father had emigrated to Canada in the early 1900s and lived in Vancouver, BC. Here he met and courted Mary Cole and the pair were wed on 1st November 1912 and later had four children, John, Wilfred, Muriel and Kathleen.

Having some knowledge of electronics and wireless, in 1941 Wilfred heard that the British were forming an organisation called the Civilian Technical Corps with the aim of repairing vital radio, electrical and mechanical equipment for the Army, Navy and Royal Air Force.

The main office for the CTC was on Broad Street, New York, but another branch was situated on Pine Avenue, West, Montreal. Though the recruits mainly consisted of Americans, a small number of Canadians, including Wilfred applied and following a rigorous technical exam, those who passed were accepted for training courses at RAF Cranwell, Lincolnshire.

All these men, though still civilians, wore RAF uniforms but then with black buttons and CTC shoulder patches.

On 3rd May 1941 Wilfred, was given the licence number 4087 and accepted for test and training, and having passed was on his way to take up a place at Cranwell when the Hudson crashed.

Wilfred was interred in Campbeltown (Kilkerran) Cemetery, Kintyre, with full military honours in division 4, grave 588, next to the Observer Sergeant Percy Keast.

Wireless Op Wilfred Bratherton

Photo: Jack Bratherton and Pam Davies Via Alan Clark

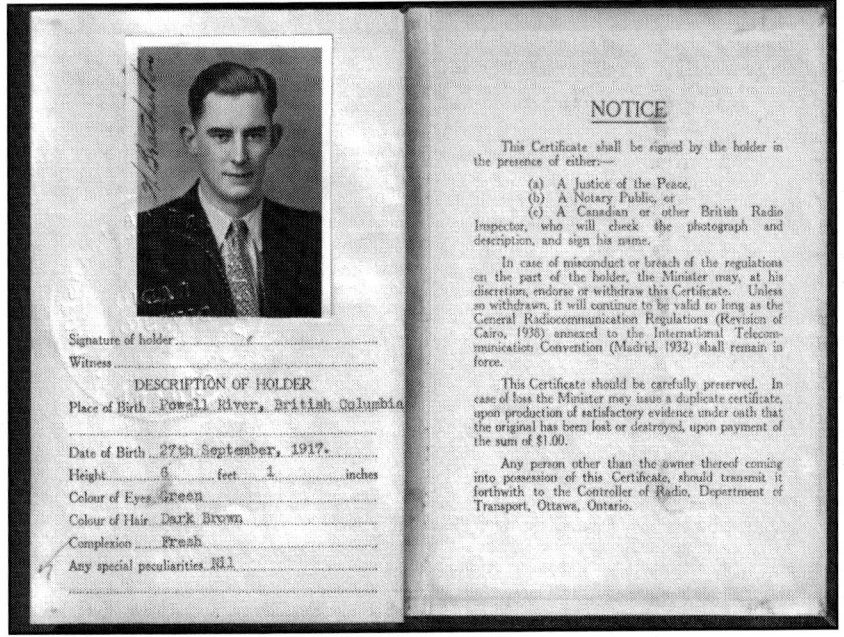

Wilfred Bratherton's Radio Operator's licence

Photo: Jack Bratherton and Pam Davies Via Alan Clark

TRAGEDY AT LOW SMERBY - MARTLET AL259

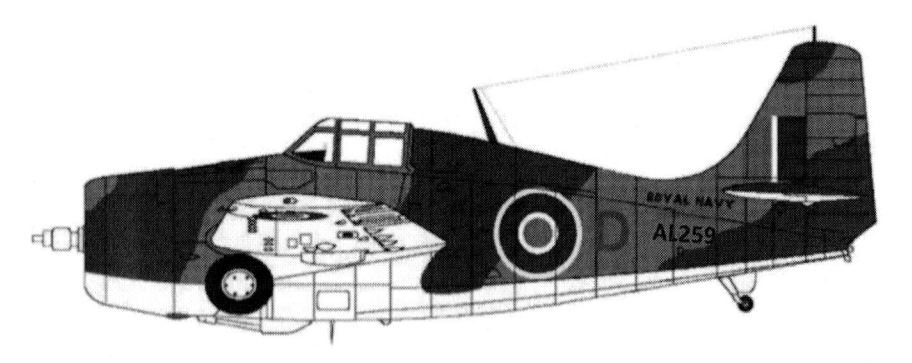

Originally an order for eighty one Grumman G-36A Martlet Mk.I aircraft had been placed to form part of a French consignment, but with aircraft having not been delivered by the time the Armistice between France and Germany was signed at Compiègne, north of Paris on 22nd June 1940, the order was quickly diverted to Britain under contract number F292.

This particular model differed from later versions in that it had non-folding wings, also it was armed with four 0.5in machine guns and powered by a Wright-Cyclone G-205A (R.1820) 1,200hp radial piston engine.

The aircraft in this account AL259, was just one of a production batch of 32 Mk.1s delivered on 3rd September 1940 to the British Purchasing Commission, arriving at Scottish Aviation Prestwick on 15th November. Nearly 12 weeks later on 4th February 1941, the Martlet was allocated to 802 Squadron Royal Navy Fleet Air Arm at RNAS Donibristle (*Merlin*) Fife.

On 8th June 1940 802 Squadron ceased to exist when the aircraft carrier HMS *Glorious* was sunk in the North Sea by the German battleships S*charnhorst* and *Gneisenau*, taking with her all the squadron's Sea Gladiators.

In November a section of 804 Squadron personnel was detached to reform 802 Squadron at Hatston, Orkney under command of Lt/Cdr John Milnes Wintour with a compliment of 12 Martlet Mk. Is. The squadron moved to Donibristle the following month then transferred to Machrihanish (*Landrail*) on 22nd June 1941.

On Monday 18th August 1941 RN pilot Midshipman (A) John Maurice Down was taking off from *Landrail* in AL259 when his aircraft suffered engine trouble at the most crucial stage of the flight, leaving the young pilot no choice but to attempt a forced landing in a small field ahead, just to south of Low Smerby Farm, between Campbeltown and the hamlet of Peninver off the A842 east coast road.

Grumman Martlet

Mary Campbell of nearby Ballymenach observed the Martlet approaching, she said that it appeared the pilot was turning the aircraft in an effort to avoid the farmhouse and out buildings, but in doing so he failed to line up with the field properly and it subsequently crashed to the ground and disintegrated. Farmers rushed to the scene but it soon became obvious that there was nothing they could do for the poor young airman.

Though thrown from the aircraft when it hit the ground, it was discovered later that Midshipman Down had suffered injuries to the effect that death would have been instantaneous.

This accident came eight months after another Martlet Mk.1 from the same production batch, AL251, crashed at Bheinn Bheula, near Inverary, Argyll, on 13th December 1940.

Wreckage from Martlet AL251. Photo: John Finch-Davies

The field where the Martlet crashed 76 years later. Photo: Author's Collection

AL251 had been on a delivery flight from Aldergrove to Donibristle when it flew into the hill in low cloud killing the pilot Lt. (A) Godfrey Frederick Russell. RN.

John's C.O. Lt/Cdr. Wintour operating from the carrier HMS *Audacity* (D10) escorting Convoy HG 76 from Gibraltar also lost his life later in an attack on a four engine Fw.200 C-3 Condor F8+ZL of 3/KG40, near Bordeaux on 8th November 1941, when his Martlet BJ516 was shot down by the Condor's gunners.

Shortly afterwards this enemy aircraft was destroyed by fellow squadron pilot Sub/Lt D.A. Hutchinson. The Condor pilot Oberleutnant Karl Krüger and five crew were reported as missing presumed killed.

Pilot Midshipman (A) John Maurice Down, RNVR, born 1921 in Hertfordshire, was the son of Charles Maurice and Florence Alice Down (née Walthew) of Harpenden, Herts. John had two sisters Barbara and Felicity of St. Albans, Hertfordshire.

John's father Charles was born in Woolwich and had served from 1908 as a gunner with the 1st Herts Bty, Territorial Army until 1912. By 1916, having progressed to the rank of Major he transferred to the RFC as a Lieutenant and joined a Kite Balloon Training Wing in October but was hospitalized after an accident on 1st December 1916.

On 14th July 1917 Charles was awarded the Croix de Guerre and in December that year he was honoured with a Mention in Dispatches by Sir Douglas Haig.

Lt Charles Maurice Down

When the war was over he married Florence Alice Walthew and the family lived in Harpenden. Charles went back to his old job as a journalist and the couple had three children. In the 1930s John's father was editor of the local paper `The Magnet` and this accorded the family a good education.

John was educated at Aldenham School, Elstree and played cricket for the Aldenhamians Cricket Team. In 1938 the team was mentioned in the Public School Cricket journal as: winning 4 matches, drawing 6 and losing five. It stated: `This was not so good a record as expected, but in view of the inexperience, it was by no means a bad one` It goes on to say that: `On the whole, the fielding was sound and few reasonable chances went begging. Mence and Hickson were outstanding and J. M. Down kept wicket in a safe and stylish manner`.

Aldenham, established in 1587 by Richard Platt, was one of oldest schools in Britain, which stood John in good stead for entering the RN college and training as flight cadet pilot later on.

Having joined the RNVR late summer of 1940, After his basic training he was posted overseas for flying training and navigation in Canada. Having graduated as a pilot and gained his wings, because he was still only 19, such was navy regulations that he was commissioned at the lower rank of Midshipman, rather than Acting Sub-Lieutenant, which would have been his rank at the age of $19 \frac{1}{2}$.

On arrival back in the UK in spring 1941, John was sent on a short operational training course, prior to joining 802 Squadron in June at Machrihanish

John was interred with a guard of honour in Campbeltown (Kilkerran) Cemetery, Kintyre, Division 4. Grave 586.

Midn. John M. Down in Kilkerran

Photo: Author's Collection

65

THE ARINARACH FERRY PLANE - LIBERATOR AM915

In 1939 the British government had placed an order with American aircraft manufacturers Lockheed, for 200 Hudson light bombers, 78 of which by the time war broke out in September, were already in service with 224 Squadron at RAF Leuchars, Scotland, and 220 Squadron at Thornaby.

Eighteen months later and with funds having been stretched to the limit, the United States president Franklin T. Roosevelt signed a document that would enable Britain to import arms and aircraft under a lend-lease agreement, which in effect meant that these materials could be used until at such time they could be returned, or were written off, and would be paid for by the British government at the end of hostilities.

It soon became apparent that shipping these aircraft and supplies to Britain with the threat of the dreaded U-boats was very risky, and also it took much longer than anticipated, therefore a plan was devised to ferry the aircraft over by air to Canada, thence across the Atlantic to Scotland.

In North America the ferry group was operated by the Canadian Pacific Railway Air Services Dept and staff recruited from MAP, BOAC, Dept of Transport and the RCAF, and in addition, although America was neutral at that time, US pilots were used to ferry aircraft to the Canadian border prior to them being flown to the UK.

On 10th November 1940, Captain Don Bennett, a former RAF pilot with BOAC, who was very skilled in navigation and had pioneered long flights, left Gander, Newfoundland, as Flight Commander of seven Lockheed Hudson`s, for the first successful Transatlantic ferry flight to Aldergrove in Northern Ireland.

Other flights soon followed on a regular basis and so was born the Atlantic Ferry Organisation or ATFERO, as it later became known.

With the development of the Consolidated LB-30A Liberator four engine heavy bomber, the first six would arrive by air on 14th March 1941, though the RAF decided that the lack of self-sealing fuel tanks meant that

One of the LB-30 Liberators at Prestwick running up for a return flight to Canada

the aircraft could not be used in combat over Western Europe, so all six were assigned to Ferry Command.

Their guns were removed and cabin heaters and a passenger oxygen supply were installed These LB-30s would now be used to transport ferry crews and mail etc back and forth across the Atlantic, and this was daubed the Return Ferry Service. RAF Ferry Command with its HQ based in Montreal, Canada, was established in July 1941, and under command of ACM Sir Frederick Bowhill, it merged with ATFERO.

At 17:26 local time (22:26 GMT) on 31st August 1941, one of these LB-30 Liberators serial AM915, took off from Montreal on a ferry flight to Scotland though at that time Prestwick, the usual port of call in Glasgow, was undergoing redevelopment in order to expand the airfield to accommodate more aircraft, so nearby Heathfield in Ayr was being used.

Captain and first pilot that day was Capt. Kenneth D. Garden, an experienced pilot who had already made over a dozen Transatlantic flights since 26th June, and perhaps even more? (Records for the first seven weeks since the formation of the organisation have been lost).

Forming Garden's crew were Co-Pilot F.O. Geoffrey L. Panes, Radio Operator Samuel Sydenham and Flight Engineer F/E Charles A. Spence plus six passengers: Count Guy De Baillet-Latour, Lt/Col Louis H. Wrangham, RM, Captain Sherwood Picking USN, Professor Robert B. Mowat, Dr. Mark Benjamin and Mr Eric Taylor.

ETA at Heathfield was planned as 07:59 (GMT) on 1st September and contact was made with ATC at 05:35, when an updated weather report and course to steer was transmitted to the aircraft.

Weather at Ayr was given as 9/10 cloud cover at 2,000ft, with visibility of 12 miles below cloud. Normally in such conditions the aircraft would be guided in from west to east over the field until it was heard by ground staff, then it would continue heading east for 2 to 3 minutes, after which the pilot would be instructed to turn on a heading of 250° for a further 3 minutes, descend through cloud on a bearing of 075° then land.

Around 08:15 the aircraft was heard above Heathfield and given instructions to head west, however, Capt. Garden appeared not to be happy with conditions at Ayr and asked for a weather report for Squires Gate, Blackpool, so he could divert to there, but there was some problems with the teleprinter either at Prestwick or Squires Gate so the report could not be read.

Prestwick tried again to contact the Liberator at 08:35 but there was no reply and at this point the aircraft appeared to be making for Squires Gate, but it was later found that this airfield was closed in by fog.

At 09:20 Prestwick sent another message to Capt.Garden asking what his intentions were and he was heard to reply: *"I'm making for Ayr"* he was then provided with a new heading and was last plotted flying on a north-westerly heading. No further contact was made with AM915 and when it failed to arrive over Ayr, aerodrome staff feared the worst.

An LB-30 Liberator AM920 of RAF Ferry Command

At approximately 10:10 on the 1st September 1941, AM915 flew into a hill at the head of Balnabraid Glen, three miles south-east of Campbeltown, all on board perished.

Having had no further contact with the crew since 09:20, a large scale search was initiated and continued throughout the day and the following morning, but reports came in that the aircraft had been found by a local shepherd and the search was called off.

Kintyre author and historian Angus Martin, when inquiring about the Liberator for his book `A third summer in Kintyre`, discovered a few accounts of what happened that day.

The first appeared in `The Scotsman` newspaper two days after the event, and is understood to be a definitive account of the events at Achinhoan (Also spelt Auchenhoan) by a local shepherd :

`I heard the drone of a 'plane on Monday morning but I could not see it. I next heard a loud bang and felt certain that the 'plane had crashed. As soon as dawn came next day I sent another shepherd out on the hills while I remained working at the hay and told him to search for a crashed 'plane.

He came across the 'plane about three miles from our house and hurried back and told me the news without even waiting to examine the wreckage. Word was sent to the nearest house with a telephone, and the occupant instructed his wife to inform the police. When the police arrived at mid-day on Tuesday I took them to the wrecked machine.'

It may seem odd that the shepherd said he had heard the sound of the aircraft, followed by a bang on Monday morning', yet for some reason didn't decide to investigate until dawn the next day. On speaking with John Bannatyne, son of Callum who lived and farmed at Achinhoan during the war, Angus Martin was offered some explanation as to why the shepherd wasn't so hasty in climbing the hill:

The crash was heard at Achinhoan, but there was a war on, and distant explosions, such as from military exercises, weren't so exceptional as to cause alarm. His father and the other Achinhoan shepherd had intended to bring in the hay and stack it, but the day was too wet – and misty with it – and so he had decided instead to whitewash the byre.

Around mid-day, they stopped work and had lunch. While listening to the wireless, they heard a report that an aircraft was missing. Calum fetched his dogs and went into the hills to look for signs of a 'plane crash`.

As the shepherd approached the head of Balnabraid Glen, he saw an unusual object on the top of the hill which he knew as 'Glenmurril Hill', an old ruin of that name on the south side of the glen. This hill formed part of his beat and he knew it well, in fact John said that the sheep stock was generally gathered on that hill before being herded down for clipping and dipping. At first Calum thought he was seeing a horse on the skyline, but as he approached closer he realised that the object was the tail of an aeroplane and he returned to Achinhoan at once.

Above left: Sandy McSporran with Liberator exhaust in Balnabraid Glen in 1995
Photo: Angus Martin

Above right & below: The same exhaust still on site in 2017. Photos: Mark Sheldon

'John believes it was his mother who was despatched to find a telephone and since Achinhoan at that time had no such link with the outside world, she would have walked, or run, about two-and-a-half miles, before she found a telephone at Davaar House. Once the ten bodies had been recovered, the work of removing the wreckage began. John wasn't allowed near the hill for several days, but when he did get there, he was amazed not only by the extent of the wreckage, but also by the incongruity of some of the other stuff lying about.

He particularly recalls seeing packs of playing cards strewn around, and big hams; the civilians on board had been in America, and may have seized on the opportunity of taking home commodities that were scarce in wartime Britain, which was subject to strict rationing'.

John remembered that the military presence at Achinhoan continued for months as the wreckage was transported off the hill by a 'Caterpillar' tractor towing a sledge. The wreckage was removed on 'low-loaders' which were sometimes parked overnight at the farm steadings. Another man, Duncan Purcell, a mining engineer in Australia, was an eight year old boy at the time and living at Davaar House when a knock came at the door just before he set off for school on Tuesday 2nd September.

'He answered the front door and saw a 'short, dark-haired man' whom he recognised as one of the Achinhoan shepherds. Duncan led the 'visibly shaking' shepherd into the kitchen and heard him mention an 'explosion' and a 'flash.

Duncan also recalled hearing that the shepherds had 'sat up all night with their shotguns', a detail with which his sister, Iona MacNeill, agreed. One of Duncan's parents telephoned the commanding officer of HMS Nimrod, Captain Farquhar, who was actually billeted at Davaar House and for whose use the phone had been installed. Soon afterwards, Duncan recalled, Naval personnel and 'flatbed lorries' were passing by Davaar House.

His older brother Bill in Canada, recalled that the road at Davaar Cottage had to be 'modified' to allow these large vehicles to get around the corner. They were loaded with wreckage in a quarry on the hill before Achinhoan farmhouse, and Bill remembered that for months afterwards the lorries would pass Davaar House with 'cut-up plane parts'.

The crash site of AM915, according to the accident report is Achinhoan Hill, but according to locals there was a brown scar and a shallow depression 10-15 feet from the heather-clad summit of nearby Arinarach Hill, with a debris trail down Balnabraid Glen, it would appear the aircraft had turned too late for a return to Ayr and while heading in an north-easterly direction, had struck the near top of the hill in cloud and momentum would have taken it over to Achinhoan Hill.

A former Radio Officer with BOAC offered an explanation as to why communication with the aircraft broke down: He said that the R/Op if speaking to the Captain via intercom, would block all incoming messages and so it could just have been that they never heard ATC?

71

A memorial that was found at the site in 2003, alas the bead welded steel plate was nowhere to be seen in 2017. Photo: Geoff Bland

1st Pilot Captain Kenneth Dardanelles Garden, BOAC, born in 1915, was the son of Frank Alexander and Mary Elsie Garden, (née Jarrett) of Coogee, New South Wales, Australia.

Kenneth grew up in Googee, a coastal suburb of Randwick, SE of Sydney, where his father was a salesman. Kenneth was educated at Sydney Boys High School, but despite living on a coast with a glorious beach and sea surf, he was more attracted to the air and aspired to becoming a pilot.

Learning to fly with the Australian Aero Club at Mascot Aerodrome on Tiger Moths and the like, amazingly by the time he was 20, Kenneth had both his Commercial and Instructors licences and was at that time the youngest Instructor in Australia.

In 1935/36 he became a pilot for the Ward Williams gold prospecting expedition operating out in New Guinea. Then later when this contract ended he became chief pilot for Guinea Airways, flying a weekly service between Adelaide and Darwin, and for a short time from Adelaide to Sydney.

In 1939 he resigned from his post at GA to join the staff of Imperial Airways and arrived in England in June. However, when war broke out on 3rd September he told the airline that he wanted to return to Australia to join the RAAF, but he was retained and given a post in the Air Communications Branch of the Air Ministry.

As a transport pilot he often flew between South Africa and Great Britain, ferrying supplies and troops, and on a number of

Captain Kenneth D. Garden. BOAC

occasions was involved in transporting wounded across the English Channel from France.

Having arrived in Canada around August 1940 he became part of the newly formed Atlantic Ferrying Organisation (ATFERO) and in November Kenneth became one of the first pilots to ferry aircraft, a twin-engine Lockheed Hudson, across the Atlantic.

In a letter to his parents just before Christmas, he told them that he was the present record holder for the number of bombers ferried across the Atlantic by one pilot.

On 20th July 1941 ATFERO began to operate using RAF Officers and the organisation became known as RAF Ferry Command. Civilian pilots such as Kenneth still flew with the unit but now wore uniforms.

Following the accident on Kintyre, Kenneth's body was recovered for cremation in Glasgow Crematorium. He is commemorated on the 1939-1945 memorial at Glasgow Crematorium. Column 1.

Co-Pilot First Officer Geoffrey Llwellyn Panes, BOAC. Born in Frome, Somerset on 29th January 1909, he was the son of Edward Llwellyn and Winifred Florence Panes, (née Hobbs) of Tonbridge, Kent. He had one older brother Philip.

F.O. Geoffrey Llwellyn Panes. BOAC

When Geoff was born the family lived at Manor Farm, Leigh-on-Mendip, Bath, but later moved east to Great Hayesden Farm in Tonbridge.

Geoff was educated first at Judd School in Tonbridge, then Sexeys Boarding School, Bruton, Somerset and finally Reading University where he studied agriculture and gained a BSc and MSc in that subject. He also studied agricultural economics and took a surveyors course, passing exams in both subjects.

After spending a number of years as a lecturer in the Estate Management Dept at Cambridge University, he became interested in flying, took lessons with Cambridge Flying Club, and carried out his first solo in a Gypsy Moth in January 1935, and was awarded his Pilots Certificate on 3rd February.

By the late 1930s Geoff had both his pilot and navigator certs, and was also a Sergeant in the RAF Reserves. He had decided to make a career of flying and like Kenneth Garden joined Imperial Airways and began flying continental routes, though when war broke out he began operating on the Egypt-India route, but was called back to England just prior to Italy entering the war and sent to Montreal, Canada, then USA to ferry the bombers over to the UK.

The Liberator that crashed on Kintyre was to be his third and final ferry trip. Following a service at Tonbridge Parish Church, officiated by Rev. F. Child, he was interred in Tonbridge Cemetery. Section A. Grave 6038.

R.O. Samuel Walter Sydenham. RAFFC

Radio Operator R.O. Samuel Walter Sydenham, RAFFC. Born 4th July 1916 in Melevel, Saskatchewan, he was the son of Samuel and Emilie Sydenham of Swift Current, Saskatchewan, Canada. He had four sisters, Norma, Audrey, Faye and Emily and was husband of Elizabeth 'Betty' Sydenham .

Sam was educated at schools in Swift Current and Moose Jaw, Saskatchewan and on leaving school worked for a few years with the Ministry of Transport in Edmonton. In the mid-1930s he studied radio via a correspondence course, then completed a course at a Radio School in Toronto where he graduated in 1938.

After graduating as a Wireless Operator he was employed in the Canadian Arctic by the Hudson Bay Company, but returned to Edmonton after about a year.

In the spring of 1940 Sam married his fiancée Elizabeth from Edmonton whom he called Betty, then on the 7th January 1941 he joined the Atlantic Ferry Organization as a Radio Operator and was at that time living in Montreal.

Following the accident Sam was interred in Campbeltown (Kilkerran) Cemetery with full military honours. Division 4. Grave 594.

Flight Engineer F/E Charles Alvan Spence, RAFFC. Born 1st July 1908, he was the son of William Wallace Mary B. Spence (née Graff) of North Charleroi, Washington, Pennsylvania. He had one older sister Bessie T and five older brothers Robert T, Henry L, Joseph O, William W and Edward E. Charles was also husband of Mary Hughes Spence.

From a young age Charles had been interested in aviation. He graduated as a Flight Engineer at the Park Air School in East St.Louis and also the Pittsburgh School of Aeronautics.

Prior to becoming an instructor for the RAF, he was employed by Pan American Airways at La Gardia Field, New York and at that time was living in Little Neck, Long Island.

Charles was a well known aviation enthusiast in the Monongahela Valley region, and after war broke out he volunteered his services and joined the Army Air Force in January 1941. He was noted to have been the first Washington County man to have died in the war in Europe.

His mother thought that he would have to be buried in England, but arrangements were later made for Charles' body to be returned home for interment in Monongahela Cemetery, Pennsylvania with a full guard of honour in Section/ Lot 223. Grave/Block 7.

Count Guy Comte de Baillet-Latour

Passenger. Count Guy Comte de Baillet-Latour, born 30th May 1905 in Brussels, was son of Count Henri Compte de Baillet-Latour and Elisalex Alexandrine Marie Edmée Sophie Felicie von Clary-Aldringen of Brussels, Belgium. Guy had one sister Thérèse Comtesse de Baillet-Latour.

Guy's father Count Henri was President of the International Olympic Committee (1925-1942) Guy was on board the aircraft after a trip to Washington. He was the assistant military attaché of the Belgian Embassy in London and had been in the capital on business as a member of staff of the minister of colonies of the émigré Belgian government. A former admin director of a mining company, Guy had been educated at Eton, Berkshire.

F/E Charles Alvan Spence. RAFFC

Passenger. Lieutenant Colonel Louis Harris Wrangham. MC. RM. Born 28th December 1897 in Hampstead, London, he was the son of Thomas Harris and Louisa Wrangham (née Sennett) of Bournemouth, Hampshire. He had one brother John Basil, a sister Joan and was husband of Mary Bellingham.

Louis was educated at Hailey School, Bournemouth from 1908 to 1912 then Dulwich College until 1914. He joined the Royal Marines on December 20th 1915 as Temporary 2nd Lieutenant and from June 1916 to the end of the war he served with the Royal Naval Division in France.

He was wounded on three occasions and awarded the M.C. on September 28th 1918. Having transferred to the permanent list after the war, he served for a short period on the Renown class battlecruiser HMS *Repulse*, then went to HMS *Renown* in September 1921 for the Prince of Wales tour of the Far East.

Louis later served as a Lieutenant in the 11th Royal Marine Battalion in the Mediterranean and soon after his return home in December 1924, he was seconded for employment under the Sudan Government.

Promoted to Captain in October 1926, altogether he served for seven years in the Sudan being G.S.O III, Sudan Defence Force, during 1927 and 1928, and Deputy Assistant Adjutant General during his remaining three years there.

Subsequent service included periods with HMS *Berwick, Colombo* and *Glorious* and it was while serving aboard the latter in the Mediterranean that he decided to retire.

Lt/Col Louis H. Wrangham. MC.RM

Having been placed on the retired list at his own request on 25th November 1936, Louis was recalled for service in June 1939 and appointed to the Admiralty for duty in the Naval Intelligence Division, where he served until the accident on Kintyre.

Louis had married his fiancée Mary Bellingham whilst serving in Cairo, Egypt. Back in England his usual residence at the time of his loss was in Middleton-on-Sea, Sussex.

After the accident. Following a service in his hometown, he was cremated at Golders Green Crematorium, Barnet, London where he is commemorated on Panel 3 of the memorial.

Passenger. Captain Sherwood Picking, USN. Born 21st February 1890, was the son of Rear Admiral Henry Forry Picking and Laura Sherwood Picking of Baltimore, Maryland, USA.

Sherwood's early school days were spent in Baltimore, but when his father passed away in 1899 he was sent abroad to be educated in Europe, spending four years at `Real-Schule` in Cassel, Germany and `La Villa` Lausanne, Switzerland. On his return to the USA, he attended Cheltenham Military Academy where he graduated in 1911.

During the First World War Sherwood was a Submariner and while in Command of a USN Sub O10, he was awarded the Navy Cross and Victory Medal. His commands also included that of a German U-boat U-111 which had been surrendered on 20th November 1918, then later in 1925, he commanded V-1, the largest US Submarine at that time.

In June 1927 he married Miss Elizabeth Warner of Boston at Gerrish Island, Kittery Point, York County, Maine, the couple went on to have three children, two daughters Elizabeth and Frances, and a son Henry Forry, honouring his father.

During the early 1930s Sherwood served three tours of duty in China and the Philippines. Then in 1936 he went to Harvard University as assistant professor of naval science, practicing here for three years.

In 1939 Sherwood became Captain and Commander of Submarine Squadron 3

Captain Sherwood Picking. USN.

at Coco Solo in the Panama Canal zone, but was detached from here in July when he became the assistant US Navy attaché for Washington, he was on his way to London in that role when the accident occurred.

Services were held in Glasgow and London and he was cremated at Glasgow Crematorium prior to his remains being returned to the USA. Later a service was also held in the United States at Falmouth, Portland by his family and arranged by Rear Admiral William T. Tarrant. His ashes were, in compliance with his widow, taken on board the submarine USS *Grenadier* then scattered at sea.

Professor Robert B. Mowat. M.A. Litt.D.

Passenger. Prof. Robert Balmain Mowat, M.A. Litt.D. Born 26th September 1883 in Edinburgh, he was the son of Robert and Mary Mowat and husband of Mary G. Mowat (née Loch) of Edinburgh.

Robert was educated at George Watson's College and Merchiston Castle School where he gained a scholarship for Edinburgh University. He later obtained a first class honours degree in the final school of modern history.

In 1910 Robert married Mary Loch, the daughter of Sir C.S. Loch and the couple were later blessed with five sons and one daughter.

Assistant Master at Eton, (1905-1906) a Fellow and member of the Naval Dept and Secretariat of the War Cabinet (1916-1919) Tutor at Corpus Chriti College, Oxford, (1907-1928) Professor of History at the University of Wisconsin, he was always kept busy.

After WW1 Robert was a member of the Secretariat of the Peace Conference and in 1928 succeeded Prof Leonard in the Chair of History at Bristol University. He later became a Honorary Fellow of Corpus Christi, Oxford in 1938.

During his time as a Professor of History, aside from the many lectures, he also wrote 40 books including: *A history of Great Britain*; *A history of European Diplomacy* and *The Diplomatic Relations of Great Britain and the United States*.

Prior to the tragic accident Robert had been in America for several months, lecturing at universities on international affairs under the auspices of the Carnegie Trust. On Monday 15th September 1941, a memorial service for Robert was held in Bristol Cathedral in the company of family, friends and associates. There was a large congregation with the University and many associations with which Prof. Mowat identified himself. Even the Prime Minister, who himself is Chancellor of the University, sent a telegram of condolence in which he said:

"I heard with sorrow of the death of Prof. Mowat. His loss will be a great blow to the University, where his contribution to the School of History has been so outstanding. Please accept my deepest sympathy. - Winston Churchill."

It is believed Robert was cremated in Glasgow, though it is not known where his ashes were scattered. His name is in the book of remembrance at St.George's Chapel, Westminster Abbey, London.

Passenger. Doctor Mark Benjamin. BSc. Hons, Ph.D. Born 13th March 1909, he was the son of Mrs H. Benjamin of Hammersmith, London and husband of Elizabeth `Betty` Benjamin of Wembley Park, Middlesex.

The eldest son of a Russian immigrant, Mark was one of seven children. His parents were Jewish Taylors and ran a shop in London. Mark worked in the store but attended night school where he studied Science and Physics and eventually gained his Ph.D and BSc.

Mark had been based in America with the Central Scientific Office in Washington, his specialist field was valves and transistors, which would provide the power needed for a new type of miniaturised radar set, the cavity magnetron, which was planned for use in aircraft to provide navigators with essential data for safer journeys over land and sea, and in effect would provide locations of potential enemy aircraft, ships and land masses en route. The tragic irony being that if AM915 had been fitted with this new radar, the accident could have been avoided.

Sir Clifford Patterson. OBE. FRS. was a former Director of GEC Research Laboratories in Wembley from its formation in 1919 until his death in 1948. Sir Clifford kept diaries which were later published in a book `A Scientists War` in which he mentions Mark Benjamin:

"He was a Physicist of great promise who had begun to make his mark in pure science as well as in applications to the industry. His most recent work brought out his qualities to the full, with results that will be far-reaching.

That his colleagues in the Laboratory feel his loss to be most grievous goes without saying, but there will be many elsewhere who will miss him and will know the reasons for these feelings".

Another project Mark was involved with was remote or radio controlled fuses and the production of small valves and circuits, small enough to fit into anti-aircraft shells and withstand the immense acceleration of these projectiles.

Mark`s mission in America was considered to have been a great success. His work on the radar paved the way for his successors. The US adopted the circuit which had been evolved for the British fuse, and America went on to produce 22 million proximity fuses during the Second World War.

Grave of Mark Benjamin. B.SC. PH.D

Mark was returned home for burial by the family and interred in Willesden United Synagogue Cemetery, Willesden, London Borough of Brent. Section FX. Row 11. Plot 493.

Passenger. Civilian Technical Officer Eric Taylor, B.Sc Hons. Attached to the RAF, was born in Leeds in 1896, he was the only son of Frederick William and Lucy Hannah Taylor (née Sugare) of Leeds, West Yorkshire.

Eric was educated at Cockburn High School in Leeds, and a former student at Leeds University. When war broke out he joined the West Yorkshire Regiment but later held a commission in the Tank Corps.

He took his Bachelor of Science degree in 1922 and obtained first class honours in mechanical engineering. That same year he married Renee Sugare, the daughter of a local doctor.

Having arrived at the Royal Aircraft Establishment at Farnborough in 1926 as a junior technical officer, by the late 1930s he had become principal technical officer, working alongside some of the country's leading scientists and specialists in the field of aviation.

Working in conjunction with a fellow Yorkshireman W/Cdr. R.L.R. Atcherley, Eric helped develop a method of in-flight re-fuelling for bombers. He was also co–inventor of an oxygen regulator and with Sir Robert Davies and Prof. J.S. Haldane, he developed pressure suits worn by pilots on high altitude flights.

Grave of Eric Taylor. B.Sc.

Photo: Author's Collection

Eric, was described by those who worked alongside him as a brilliant technician. He left a wife and three young children, who at that time were living in Leeds, but later moved to the village of Cove, Farnborough, Hampshire.

Eric, in accordance with personnel serving on attachment to HM Forces, was accorded a full military funeral in Campbeltown (Kilkerran) Cemetery. His name also appears in the Civilian War Dead Book of Remembrance at St. George's Chapel, Westminster Abbey, London.

NIGHTMARE NAVEX - BLENHEIM Z6350

No 5 Air Observers School (AOS) RAF Jurby, situated on the north west coast of the Isle of Man, was formed on 18th September 1939 under control of 25 Group Flying Training Command with a compliment of Bristol Blenheim, Fairey Battle and Hawker Henley aircraft.

However, within a period of just three months it became No 5 Bombing & Gunnery School, but then reverted to its original title of 5 AOS on 19th July 1941 and added the Handley Page Hampden, Avro Anson, Hawker Hurricane and Westland Lysander to the training syllabus.

In addition, the unit acquired a large number of Handley Page Herefords (a variant of the Hampden but powered by the unreliable 24 cylinder Napier Dagger) which proved to be unpopular with pilots, trainee observers and ground crew, mainly due to the number of engine failures and overheating problems which frequently occurred.

On the morning of Sunday 21st December 1941, Pilot Sgt John E. Orton with fellow pilot as Obs Sgt Arthur J. Gearing and a crew of two trainees:

U/T Observer Cpl Robert S. Cohen and an U/T W/AG AC2 Peter G. Gibson, were airborne in Bristol Blenheim Mk.IV Z6350 engaged on a cross country navigation exercise.

The Irish sea and in particular the Sound of Mull and Kintyre peninsula, are subject to very changeable weather as low pressure systems rush in from the Atlantic, bringing wind, rain, low cloud and mist. Standard instructions that were issued by the C.O. of 5 AOS to all pilots stated:

"Return to base immediately, if weather conditions become unsuitable for flying, and if employed on a navigation exercise remain below cloud level if the cover is more than 6/10ths."

Setting course for the low lying Isle of Tiree in the Inner Hebrides, they began to enter intermittent cloud as the aircraft approached Kintyre.

As conditions began to quickly deteriorate with the cloud ceiling down to 300 metres, Sgt Orton decided to land as a precaution at the nearby Fleet Air Arm base of Machrihanish.

A Blenheim IV undergoing maintenance by the ground crew

However, prior to entering the circuit of the airfield, the Blenheim, still in low cloud and coastal fog, collided at 11:30 hours with the ridge of a 329 metre hillside approximately three miles south east of the small village of Taigh an Lòin (Tayinloan) on the west coast of Kintyre, where it immediately caught fire resulting in the loss of all on board.

It was considered by the board of inquiry that the pilot thought he was over the sea, and this lead to his let down through the overcast, where it is thought he expected to break clear and begin his approach for the airfield at Machrihanish.

Following the removal from the wreckage of the four unfortunate airmen, an RAF salvage team arrived at the scene, and although there was little left of the aircraft following the fire, the two Bristol Mercury XV engines were recovered. According to the late Duncan McArthur and fellow researchers on Kintyre, parts of the aircraft were said to still remain at the crash site in 2005.

Above: The control column that was found at the crash site in the 1960s

Bristol Blenheim IV cockpit

The area of the crash, just south of Killean on the west coast is heavily afforested, so the site today would be very difficult to locate.

Captain and Pilot Sergeant John Edward Orton. RAFVR, was born in Douglas, Isle of Man in 1917, he was the only son of Reginald and Mabel Orton of Woodland Terrace, Douglas, Isle of Man.

Educated in Douglas, John joined the RAF in 1940 and following basic training he was selected for pilot training. He attended No.22 E.F.T.S at Caxton Gibbet and Bottisham, Cambridge, then 4 EFTS at Brough, East Riding, Yorkshire, where he finally graduated as a Sergeant pilot and was presented with his pilots wings on 10th May 1941.

That same year, likely after the training course ended, John was given leave and returned to his hometown of Douglas, where he married his fiancée Dorothy at St.Ninian`s Church.

At the time of the accident on Kintyre, John had flown a total of 265 hours on various types, this included 98 hours on the Blenheim and 167 on the Tiger Moth and other training aircraft, which probably included the Anson or Oxford as 54 hours were duel control.

John was interred in a family grave in Douglas Cemetery, Isle of Man, Block. N.G. Grave 315. He is also commemorated on St.John`s War Memorial, in the island`s west coast parish of German, (Manx: Carmane) .

The Orton family grave in Douglas Cemetery

Pilot/Obs Sergeant Arthur John Gearing. RAF, born in Liverpool in 1919, was the eldest son of Bertrand John and Winifred Gearing (née Smith) of Wallasay. He had one younger brother Ronald who was also in the RAF and another brother Eric in the army.

Arthur's parents had married in West Derby, Liverpool in the summer of 1917 and their three sons attended local schools here and in Wallasey. Arthur must have developed an interest in flying from an early age, for he joined the RAF shortly after leaving school in 1935.

Arthur was interred in Wallasey (Rake Lane) Cemetery, Wallasey, Cheshire. Section 1.R, Grave 37.

Sadly, younger brother AC2 Ronald Phillip James Gearing, was serving with No.26 Air School as an Under Training pilot when he was killed in Airspeed

Sgt Arthur John Gearing. RAFVR

Photo: Author's Collection

85

Translation: *"It is sweet and proper to die for the fatherland. May he rest in Peace"*

U/T Observer Corporal Robert Sydney Cohen. RAFVR, born in 1915 in Fulham, London, was the eldest of three children of Jack and Marie Cohen (née Darsa) of Fulham.

Robert, his brother Samuel and sister Tova, were all born in Fulham and attended Jewish schools in London and Middlesex.

Robert was interred in Golders Green Jewish Cemetery, Chiswick, Middlesex. Row 46, Grave 5.

Gearing family grave in Wallasey

Photo: Author's Collection

U/T Wireless Operator & Air Gunner AC2 Peter Gibson Woodward RAFVR, born in Wandsworth, Surrey in 1920, was the son of Harold Victor and Agnes Annie G. Woodward (née Croal) of Surbiton, Surrey. He had one older brother Victor and a younger sister Angela.

Oxford 3712, when it collided with another Oxford 3649, also from this unit.

His aircraft was on approach to Pietersburg airfield in South Africa. The Instructor pilot F/O K. Allen survived the crash and was injured, but AC2 Geoffrey S. Adams the U/T pilot from the other aircraft was killed.

He was buried at Polkowane (or Pietersburg) Cemetery, Limpopo, South Africa. Reference: Military Sec. Grave 12.

Peter's parents had formally lived in Wandsworth, where they were married in 1914. All the children were born here and attended local schools.

At the time of his death the family were still in Surrey, but later lived in Surbiton, hence Peter was interred there in Surbiton Cemetery. Section 12, Grave 5106.

The Inscription reads:
"DULCE ET DECORUM EST PRO DEO ET PATRIA MORI"
REQUIESCAT IN PACE"

IN THE DRINK - SWORDFISH W5982

Throughout March 1944 various squadrons of the RN Fleet Air Arm had busied themselves with dive bombing exercises, in preparation for an attack on the mighty German battleship *Tirpitz* berthed in Kaafjord, Norway in April 1944.

The assault on the ship would later become known as Operation *Tungsten*, and decrypted German signals indicated that *Tirpitz*'s trials had been delayed until 3rd April, so it was hoped that an attack on this date would catch the battleship away from her usual well protected mooring.

One man who remembered the attack well was Arthur Towlson, a Sub/Lt pilot serving at the time with 829 Squadron flying Barracuda aircraft from HMS *Victorious*.

Sub/Lt Towlson had taken off from the 35,000 ton Illustrious class carrier with other members of his squadron, and he recalled in an interview with a local newspaper shortly before his passing the events of that day over seventy years ago:

"The Tirpitz was huge. I don't think we had a ship as big as that. We were briefed to attack the centre line of Tirpitz from stem to stern. The bombing practice runs had shown that we could be much more accurate attacking in line than sideways. In fact when it became my turn to bomb, the ship was partially covered by smoke".

Arthur said that he was not nervous during the raid and didn't encounter any German fighters defending *Tirpitz*, but they did have to contend with the shells from anti-aircraft guns. Though the raid didn't sink the ship, it was put out of action for months until it was eventually destroyed in a raid by Lancaster bombers in November 1944.

This was not the first time Sub/Lt Towlson had stared death in the face, for he had twice been stationed at Machrihanish with 823 and 829 Squadrons in 1942 and 1943 and it was in fact during his first tour from the station that he almost met his end.

87

Swordfish of 823 Squadron had arrived at Machrihanish from Fraserburgh on 30th January 1942 and Sub/Lt Towlson arrived a few days later.

On the evening of Tuesday 17th February, detailed for a night flying exercise, Sub/Lt Towlson took off alone in W5982 on what should have been just a local familiarization hop, but soon after leaving the airfield his engine failed and being unable to make it back he was forced to ditch the aircraft in Machrihanish Bay, just off Westport, north of the airfield.

Fortunately he was uninjured save for a few bumps and bruises, and with the Swordfish sinking fast, he pulled the emergency hand release for the dinghy in the top of the wing, this popped the hatch and activated a CO_2 cylinder to inflate the craft, he then clambered aboard and began drifting away from the wrecked machine.

However, the breeze and tide were not on his side and the dinghy began drifting out to sea. There had been no time to send out a distress signal, but when he failed to return from the flight a search was soon initiated.

In the darkness it was difficult to spot the tiny yellow inflatable, but finally after drifting for almost six hours in an icy sea, the dinghy was spotted by a Merchant Ship the SS *Busiris* and the pilot was hauled aboard.

In 2005 it was reported that parts of this Swordfish, were on found on the beach in the sand dunes near Westport, it is not known specifically what was found, but probably just alloy panels, nor is it known if anything still remains today, though heavier items such as the engine and undercarriage are likely to be at the bottom of the sea.

Fairey Swordfish

W5982 had been with the squadron for just six weeks. Built as a Mk.1 by Blackburn Aircraft Ltd at Sherburn-in-Elmet, under contract No. B31192/39 from a production batch of 100 on 14th December 1941, it had been delivered to the squadron on 1st January 1942.

Pilot Sub/Lt (A) Arthur Robert Towlson, RNVR, born 1921, was the son of Herbert G and Lillian V. Towlson of Norwich, Nottinghamshire. He had one brother Geoffrey and was a married man with two children James and Kate.

Arthur, who had studied to be an accountant before the war, joined the RN FAA in 1940 and had conducted his early flying training at Lee-on-Solent and at HMS *Grebe*, a shore station at Dekheila, Egypt, where he was commissioned an Acting Sub-Lieutenant (A) on 27th September 1941.

Having been posted in May to 828 Squadron aboard HMS *Eagle*, Sub/Lt Towlson and his crew consisting: Observer Midshipman M.W.S. Jones and Telegraphist Air Gunner L/A V.R. McBride, flying Swordfish V4561, got lost while returning from an anti-sub patrol from Gibraltar and were forced to ditch when the aircraft ran out of fuel off Cape Trafalgar. Luckily they all survived and were picked up by A/S trawler *Lady Hogarth*.

Arthur was posted to Tanga to join HMS *Illustrious* on 11th August 1942, after the ship he was serving on HMS *Eagle* at Hal Far in Malta, was sunk by torpedoes. Aboard *Illustrious* he served with 829 Squadron for the next year, before another posting took him to Tain, Ross-shire on 10th September 1943 for DB training on the Barracuda.

A/S trawler Lady Hogarth

Whilst on an exercise from Tain on 25th November, Arthur, flying a Barracuda Mk.1 P9890 'Q' was forced to make a precautionary landing back at base due to hydraulic problems. He made it down OK and the aircraft was deemed Cat. X, repairable and put back into service within a few days.

Another lucky escape came on 31st January 1944, when again stationed at Tain, he landed 160 degrees into the wind in P9854 with no brakes, the aircraft ground looped causing Cat. X2 damage, putting it out of action for a couple of weeks.

On 25th March 1944, Arthur was awarded the DSC with the citation in the LG:

'*For bravery, leadership, skill and devotion to duty whole operating from, or serving in HM ships Victorious, Furious, Emperor, Pursuer and Searcher, during successful strikes at enemy shipping off the coast of Norway*'

Two days later he was promoted to the rank of Lieutenant (A) and posted to Crail (*Jackdaw*) in Fife to join 896 Squadron. Thence to 831 Squadron in October where on the 6th he was taking off from Victorious in Barracuda BV941, when his aircraft suffered a bird strike, the starboard wing stub was badly damaged and Arthur was forced to return to the ship, where thankfully he landed safely.

Arthur was in Orkney in March 1945 with 835 Squadron at Hatston (*Sparrowhawk*) where just a couple of days prior to the squadron disbanding, on the 28th he was airborne in Barracuda MD615 when the aircraft's engine caught fire, somehow he managed to get back to the airfield, and after hitting a wire fence causing the undercarriage to collapse, he made a successful belly landing downwind and escaped unhurt.

Fairey Barracuda

Finally Arthur went back to Crail to join 711 Squadron on 15th June and served here until the squadron disbanded on 21st December.

He left the Royal Navy in 1946 as a Lieutenant Commander and in civilian life worked as an architect until retirement in 1986.

In 2013 Arthur, already a holder of several awards during his military service, including the Africa Star, Atlantic Star, Defence Medal and the General War Medal, was awarded the Arctic Star for his involvement in helping to provide safe passage for the Russian convoys, protecting the Merchant ships with supplies for allied forces. Arthur Towlson, at the age of 90 passed away peacefully on 26th August 2016.

CAMPBELTOWN ANNIE - ANSON R3344

No 3 Radio School was formed at Prestwick (Glasgow Airport) on 27th December 1940 as an AI/ASV school, with the purpose of training Observers and Wireless Operators on radar.

Initially the unit had 9 Blenheims for Airborne Interception training and 9 Bothas equipped with Air Surface Vessel radar sets, but later took delivery of a number of Avro Anson Mk1`s.

Courses for pupils here would generally last four weeks, during which they would be introduced to the AI radar (Still a highly secret piece of equipment) which would be carried by aircraft to show aircraft or ship targets as blips.

Initially the Nav/Radar Operator would have had two three inch radar scopes, but later the sets were modified to use just one. It would be the job of the navigator to direct the pilot to change his heading until the blip was in the centre of the one scope, and at the same time have him also change height until the blip was centred on the other. Then, with both blips centred on both scopes, the navigator would then advise the pilot as the range decreased and visual contact was made. It was then the job of the pilot to decide if the target was friend or foe and act accordingly.

These exercises were vital work and although a lot of the instruction was carried out in the classroom for the first couple of weeks, the second part of the course saw pupils take to the air to see how the radar really performed.

Weather conditions did often hinder progress and on a number of occasions aircraft failed to return, either they diverted to another airfield or were perhaps unlucky enough to hit a hill or be forced down in a field somewhere.

The aircraft in this account falls into the latter category, though fortunately without loss of life.

On Sunday 15th March 1942, Sgt Frank Scandiffio, a Canadian staff pilot for 3 Radio School, along with Navigator/Radar Operator F/Sgt Charlie Strandling and four pupils, took off from Prestwick on a cross-country training flight off the west coast of Scotland.

Avro Anson 1

With a large low pressure system drifting north-east across much of the British Isles, came low cloud and rain squalls causing poor visibility for pilots.

Sgt Scandiffio, though an experienced pilot, had been airborne in N3344 for over an hour and tried to get under the cloud base but the weather just got worse, and on nearing Kintyre, had realised there was a high risk they would fly into a hill, therefore as soon as a decent field presented itself, he decided to attempt a landing.

What appeared to have been flat from the air however, was not so flat once the aircraft put down and the Anson, although relatively intact ended up being badly damaged, but the crew all managed to escape unhurt.

The Anson had crash landed on the outskirts of Campbeltown and when first inspected by the RAF Maintenance Unit the it was thought to have been a write-off, but after being recovered and transported back to the station it was deemed repairable.

N3344, one of a production batch of 200 built by Avro at Woodford, Cheshire, following repairs was put back into service and flew with 62 OTU at Usworth, 63 OTU at Cheddington and finally 7 OAFU at Bishops Court, eventually being S.O.C here on 31st December 1945.

Pilot Sergeant Frances Michael Scandiffio, RCAF, born 24th November 1913, was the son of Ralph Raffaele and Maria Guiseppa Scandiffio (née Lattarulo) of Toronto, Ontario, Canada. He had two brothers and three sisters.

Frances, or Frank as he was referred, was born in Canada, but his parents both Italian were from Pisticci, Matera, Basilicata, Italy, having emigrated to Canada in 1905, arriving on the SS *Prinz Albert* on 7th April.

The Scandiffio's had six children, all born in Canada. Michael was the eldest, then Anna, Esther, Mildred, Thomas and Frank. The family lived in Albany Avenue and the children were educated in Toronto, but after his father died in 1941, the family moved and lived at Yarmouth Gardens.

Frank left school to become a clerk, but also served for five years in the Del La Salle Cadet Corps and Gov. Gen Horse Guards Band for two years, prior to enlistment as an AC2 in the RCAF at Toronto Recruitment Centre on 24th February 1941.

Following basic training at 1 ITS he became a U/T pupil pilot and was promoted to LAC on 6th June, he was posted to 14 EFTS at Portage la praire, Manitoba, training on Tiger Moths and Fleet Finches, then 12 SFTS at Brandon where he the flew Cessna Crane from 10th August - 17th October.

Promoted to Temp Sergeant on 25th October 1941, Frank was then given leave prior to embarkation from Halifax to the UK on 12th November. He arrived at 3 PRC, Bournemouth on the 23rd and was posted to 3 RS at Prestwick on 6th January. A further promotion to F/Sgt came on 25th April, followed by a posting to 63 OTU at Usworth, near Sunderland, for Airborne Interception radar test flights.

Sgt Frances M. Scandiffio. RCAF

Next came 55 OTU at Annan, Dumfriesshire, on 22nd September 1942 and following a few circuits and bumps in the Miles Master to get used to the base, he flew his first solo in a Hawker Hurricane on 8th October and continued to fly the type here until July 1943 when he was posted to ATC. Poona, India, flying and delivering Hurricanes with 21 Ferry Control, 320 MU where aside from Hurricanes he would fly Vengeance, Defiant, Harvard and P-47 Thunderbolts. Alas, it would be the latter that would end his flying career on 15th July 1944.

Frank, by this time a Warrant Officer, had taken off at 08:22 from Mauripur in Thunderbolt HD163 on a delivery flight with five other aircraft to Nagpur.

Thunderbolts at Chittergong, India. HD173 in foreground is from same production batch as the one in which Frank Scandiffio was lost. Photo: USAAF

The ferry flight, described as a routine affair, should not have presented any problems, but due to a communication error only half the weather report was submitted by phone prior to taking off, and around 70 miles from Jodhpur, the convoy ran into heavy cloud.

The flight leader P/O Edward Keith Hender, broke cloud to find he was in an area of high ground and so climbed above the overcast, followed by the others, and after a couple of minutes they were clear, but it was soon noticed that W.O. Scandiffio was missing from the No6 position on the starboard side, and at that point No2 reported having seen a thin plume of black smoke and that No6 was gone.

All the others safely made it to their destination. A Court of Inquiry was opened the following day and as the investigation progressed, it was established that the port wing of Frank's Thunderbolt at 10:00 had clipped the top of a mountain, causing the aircraft to swing round the curve of the peak and crash further on killing the pilot almost instantly.

An officer was reprimanded for failing to pass weather conditions received by him on to the W/Cdr in charge at Mauripur.

Described as a good average pilot, Frank had logged over 1,000 hours flying time, 623 of which were solo on various aircraft types in India and according to his logbook, apart from the Anson on Kintyre and the fatal Thunderbolt crash, he had never lost another aircraft.

Frank's mother must have been devastated when she heard the news, for she had already lost her husband in 1941 and her other son Thomas, an Observer on Wellingtons had gone missing from operations in Malta in LB195 of 458 Squadron on the night of 15/16th June 1943. These certainly were bad times for the Scandiffio family.

Warrant Officer Frank Scandiffio was eventually recovered from the mountain and interred with military honours in Delhi War Cemetery. Ref: 5 B 15. His brother Warrant Officer II Thomas Peter Scandiffio, RCAF, was never found and is remembered on the Alamein Memorial to the missing in Egypt. Column 272.

Footnote:

It may be of interest to fellow historians that Frank Scandiffio recorded in his log just six days prior to the Thunderbolt crash, that he flew a `Twin Jet VI Vampire` number `52249` and what could be `100 AF` below? In his duty notes alongside he added that the he was flying from `Bolpol to Kalyan` and that the `Motor conked out over the Malayans on re-approaching. Time 48.00. Miles Per Hour 629`. Was this a secret test? It seems very fast for a Vampire and a little early for one to be with a squadron.

Navigator & Radar Operator Flight Sergeant Charles Stradling, RAFVR, born 1st December 1910, was the son of Solomon and Ada Stradling and husband of Lilian Dorothy Stradling of St.Paul's, Bristol.

Only sparse information was found on Charles. He was a Private Detective at the time of his marriage to Lilian in 1939 and his wife hailed from Merton and Morden in Surrey. Soon after the couple married they lived in Seymour Avenue. It is believed Charles joined the RAF when war broke out.

He arrived at 3 RS around the same time as Frank Scandiffio in January 1942 and flew as Frank's navigator on numerous occasions in Ansons, both at 3 Radio School and at 63 OTU.

Sadly he lost his life in a Blenheim accident whilst serving with 54 OTU at Charterhall, Berwickshire. He was returning from a night exercise in Blenheim Mk.1 L8720 when the aircraft, running low on fuel, on 7th November 1942, crashed into trees during a forced landing in the grounds of Nisbet House, Duns, in the parish of Edrom, Berwick. His pilot F/Lt William Alfred Maurice. AFC was also killed.

Bristol Blenheim Mk.1

Charles is buried in Morden Cemetery, Surrey, Sec. S.B. Grave 1058. His epitaph: *"To live in the hearts of those we leave behind is not to die".*

The cemetery, in the North West corner of Morden Parish, is south of Raynes Park Station and East of Motspur Park Station. A Cross of Sacrifice is erected near the chapel in the middle of the cemetery and a Screen Wall records the names of those graves which are not marked by a headstone.

TOO MANY FISH IN THE HARBOUR
V4312, V4489 & V4441

Monday 31st August 1942 was a marginal day for flying as a North Atlantic front swept across the Kintyre peninsula, bringing mist, low cloud and heavy rain across the airfield at Machrihanish. The Swordfish crews of 836 Squadron RN Fleet Air Arm, had earlier been briefed to undertake an anti-submarine bombing exercise over the Skipness range to the east, but had expected the flight to be cancelled and were looking forward to a day of rest.

However, staff in the control tower had decided otherwise and declared that flying would commence despite the rapidly deteriorating weather conditions.

First to take off was the squadron Commanding Officer Lt/Cdr. Ransford W. Slater. DSC with TAG P.O. A.D. 'Robbie' Robertson, swiftly followed by three other Swordfish Mk I's, V4312 coded 'C' with Pilot Sub/Lt Jack Lisle and Observer Sub/Lt John Cartwright,

Fairey Swordfish in formation

In the drink - A ditched Swordfish

V4441 'B' Pilot Sub/Lt Bob E. Barrett, Observer Sub/Lt Jim Palmer and L/A Marriott and finally V4489 'G' Pilot Sub/Lt Phil W. Blakey, Observer Sub/Lt Gordon M. Robertson RNZN and L/A Farrant. RN.

As a fifth Swordfish taxied and turned into the wind ready to get airborne, a multitude of red Very pistol signal flares were fired and a red Aldis warning light prevented this last aircraft from taking off, much to the relief of its New Zealand pilot Sub/Lt Owen Johnstone and crew who hastily returned to the dispersal. Meanwhile, the four airborne Swordfish had now reached Campbeltown and encountered thick fog and with visibility down to almost zero, Lt/Cdr. Slater ordered the aircraft to adopt a line astern formation for safety.

Suddenly, he had to take immediate evasive action as a grass covered hillside appeared out of the mist ahead, turning to starboard over the harbour his formation rapidly followed.

Sub/Lt Bob Barrett however, still at low speed after completing the line astern manoeuvre, stalled and V4441 crashed into the harbour, soon followed by Sub/Lt Jack Lisle and finally Sub/Lt Phil Blakey whose Swordfish V4489 overturned during the process. Fortunately there was only three feet of water which allowed the crews to await rescue or wade ashore. with the exception of Sub/Lt`s Lisle and Cartwright who scrambled into the aircraft`s dinghy and with difficulty paddled to the beach.

Phil Blakey recalled: *"Robbie called to me that Bob had gone in. I had no time to tell him that a similar fate was on hand; as I levelled the wings the undercarriage hit the water and we somersaulted head over heels. On such occasions one's past life is supposed to pass before one's eyes. I cannot substantiate this claim as on this and another occasion when a booster malfunctioned in India in 1953 the water entered in like fashion".*

Lt/Cdr. Slater, described as an exceptional pilot, had managed to return to Machrihanish and land safely, but was extremely annoyed that the exercise had been allowed to proceed in such atrocious conditions in the first place, and with the subsequent loss of three aircraft and possibly nine airmen.

Thankfully, unbeknown to Slater, all the men had survived the crashes, and although John Cartwright was slightly injured, all managed to make their way to the shore. The three Swordfish were all deemed Cat. Z write-off's, and were later salvaged for scrap by the Admiralty.

The precise location of this incident is not known as documents found only state that the aircraft came down on a beach in Campbeltown harbour in 3ft of water. So there's no doubting that this was at low tide and it seems likely to be on and around the sandbank of The Doirlinn, which stretches across Kildalloig Bay to Daavar Island.

This aerial shot of the harbour and sandbank shows roughly where the 3 Swordfish crash landed in August 1942. Photo: Author's Collection

Pilot Lieutenant Commander Ransford Ward Slater. OBE. DSC. RN, was born in Guilford, Surrey in 1914, he was the son of Sir Alexander Ransford Slater, GCMG, CBE and Lady Dora Waterfield Ward Slater of White Parish, Wiltshire. He had two sisters Beatrice Marion Slater MBE and Nancy Waterfield.

Ransford enrolled as a cadet at the Initial Officer Training establishment the Royal Naval College Dartmouth in 1927. He became the Chief Cadet Captain prior to joining HMS *Nelson* at Greenwich as a Midshipman in 1934, and HMS *Excellent* (Whale Island shore station, Portsmouth) in 1935, where he was promoted to Temporary Sub/Lt on 1st May.

On 13th September 1936, now a full Sub/Lt he was sent for pilot training with the RAF at Leuchars. Here he was given the temporary RAF rank of F/O in November 1937, before going on to serve at Gosport, HMS *Furious* and *Glorious* until Jan 1940 flying Swordfish. In April Ransford married Miss Katherine Mayson King in the Parish Church at Knutsford, Cheshire.

Happiness soon turned to tragedy, for sadly just two weeks after the wedding his father passed away after suffering a long illness. His last appointment had been as Captain-General and Governor-in-Chief of Jamaica from 1932-1934, but he had to retire owing to ill health.

Late summer 1940, Ransford was posted to Lee-on-Solent for torpedo trials, then went on to Crail in Fife as an Instructor for pilots on bombing and torpedo courses. The following year he was posted to Malta with 830 Squadron flying Swordfish from Hal Far, mostly carrying out night bombing and torpedo attacks.

Lt/Cdr. Slater and bride Katherine on their wedding day

On 15th December he flew on a general reconnaissance of Malta. At 05:55 hours on the 16th he took off for a torpedo attack on enemy shipping, touching down at 04:45. On the 18th he carried flares for another attack (4 hrs 40 mins) and on the 26th flew another 5 hrs 5 mins on night operations. By 2nd May he had totalled 84 hours on night ops.

Ransford on 24th January flew his CO Lt/Cdr. H. Hopkins through some of the dirtiest weather for 5.5 hours to locate a convoy. On landing Hopkins ordered another strike, taking off with a fresh pilot half-an-hour later to press home the attack. Hopkins was given an immediate DSO for his outstanding determination, while Ransford's exploits in Malta later earned him a DSC.

On 9th July 1942, Ransford took over from Lt/Cdr. J.A. Crawford RN as C.O. of 836 Squadron and after working up at St. Merryn, Thorney Island and at Machrihanish, he led 'A' flight in the first attachment to MV *Empire MacAlpine*, a Merchant Aircraft Carrier, known more commonly as a MAC ship, where he made the first deck landing on 7th May 1943.

With a flight of Swordfish IIs for each of the 19 MAC ships, plus a few spares for training and relief, 836 Squadron eventually grew to a strength of 91 aircraft, certainly a record for the FAA and Ransford was awarded the military OBE for his efforts on 4th April 1944.

Having survived a landing on a MAC ship, carrying two depth charges after his arrester hook had been torn away, his luck as a pilot and an excellent leader finally ran out during a routine flight from RNAS Maydown Northern Ireland on 28th June 1944, when his Swordfish LS182 hit power cables at Enagh, around 1 mile from the airfield, then crashed to the ground and burnt out, Ransford along with two others on board, Lt (A) Anthony Wyndham Evans Lawrie and Lt Harold Denis Hodkinson were killed.

Owing to the destruction of the aircraft Lt/Cdr. Ransford Slater's body was never recovered and he is commemorated on the Lee-on-Solent Memorial. Bay 5. Panel 1.

It was such an impression that Ransford had made on his fellow aviators that after the war, Sub/Lt Reg Singleton and members 836 Squadron, got together and decided they should form a club dedicated to all members of the squadron who had served from Spring 1943 to Autumn 1943 under his command.

Letters were sent out and various suggestions put forward as to who should be president and where they should meet etc. In the end, Lt/Cdr (A) Jim Palmer MBE was nominated as club secretary and Ransford's widow Katherine was delighted to accept the role of President. The club was affectionately named 'The Ransford Club'.

V4312 Pilot Sub-Lieutenant (A) John 'Jack' Lisle. RNVR, born 1920, was the son of Frank E and Ann G. Lisle (née Slade) of Basingstoke, Hampshire, he had one older sister Doreen.

Jack joined the RN Fleet Air Arm shortly after war broke out and was commissioned Temporary Sub/Lt (A) on 3rd May 1941. Describing Jack, an ex-836 Squadron mate once said: *"His noisy half-wellington boots and raucous laugh caused heads to turn in the wardroom, especially at breakfast, which we discovered in naval tradition should be a silent meal".*

Jack never seemed to have much luck, for only 6 weeks prior to the Swordfish ditching at Campbeltown, he and his crew had been involved in another incident, when on 17th July with 836 at Lee-on-Solent, his aircraft V4414 suffered an engine failure. He returned to base but landed heavily at the airfield with a torpedo on board, the Swordfish was a total wreck, though fortunately Jack and crew escaped uninjured.

On 3rd March 1943, Jack and his crew Obs. Sub/Lt (A) Roy Stuart Allen and TAG L/A Pat Slowey, had been out mine laying from Lee off the northern coast of France when their Swordfish HS272 was shot down. They crashed in the sea 2ml off the mouth of the estuary at Le Havre, and sadly 21 year old Roy Allen of Newton Abbot, Devon, was killed and went down with the aircraft.

Jack Lisle and his TAG were picked up by the Germans and taken prisoner. The pair being an officer and rating, were soon separated and Jack spent the rest of the war as POW no.250 in the infamous Stalag Luft III at Sagan & Balaria.

V4489 Pilot Sub-Lieutenant Philip 'Phil' William Blakey, RNVR, born 1st March 1922 in Wakefield, West Yorkshire, was the son of William and Florence Blakey (née Hudson) and husband of June.

Phil Blakey had joined the RN at the beginning of the war and was commissioned Acting Sub/Lt (A) on 1st March 1942 whilst serving at Lee-on-Solent, then after further training on Swordfish, he became a full Sub/Lt on 24th June.

He then joined 836 Squadron, also based at Lee, and served from 9th August at Machrihanish. Next came Crail, St. Merryn and Thorney Island under command of Lt/Cdr. Slater. During which time he had the prang in the Swordfish at Campbeltown.

Promotion to Temporary Lt (A) came on 20th September 1944 and soon after he became a full Lieutenant while serving at Inskip (*Nightjar*) in Lancashire. He managed to see the end of the war without further incident.

Phil married his fiancée June Common in Settle, West Yorkshire in 1946 and the couple later had three children, William, Virginia and Philippa. He remained in the Navy and flew Seafires with 1831 Squadron at Stretton, where he suffered one minor taxi prang in SX285 on 22nd April 1951.

Hawker Sea Fury FB.II VW551 of 804 Squadron

In 1953 Phil flew Hawker Sea Fury's with 804 Squadron from HMS *Theseus* and *Indomitable,* surviving three more minor accidents in VW668, WJ230 and WJ292 between January and March.

Phil ended his RN career flying Jets, in particular the Sea Hawk FGA.6, and a though placed on the RAF Emergency List in 1957, he finally retired the following year and emigrated to New Zealand, travelling from Glasgow with his wife and three children, First Class aboard the T.S.S. *Captain Cook.*

V4441 Pilot Sub-Lieutenant (A) Robert Edward Barrett, RN, born 1921 in Wandsworth was the son of John Wilson and Helena M. Barrett (née Marsh) of Tooting, South London, Wandsworth.

Known to all as Bob, his parents were married in August 1919 at St. George's Church, Southall, Middlesex and his father was employed as an engineer.

Bob joined the Royal Navy early in the war, trained as a pilot and became an Acting Sub/Lt (A) in the Fleet Air Arm on 16th November 1941 Lee-on-Solent (*Daedalus*).

In the summer of 1942 he was flying Swordfish with 836 Squadron and on the 17th June in aircraft 'B' he was involved in a minor landing accident on the escort carrier HMS *Biter* (D97) in the Firth of Clyde. Luckily Bob, his Observer Jim Palmer and TAG L/A Woodhams were all uninjured.

Staying with 836 Squadron, promotions to Temporary Sub/Lt and full Sub/Lt came on 24th June and 16th November, respectively, and throughout 1942 and 1943 he flew the Swordfish II.

In the spring of 1944 Bob married his fiancée Peggy Mary Rosina Collins in Wandsworth, and on 17th May was serving at *Shrike,* Northern Ireland when he was promoted to Lieutenant.

With the war over a posting to 762 Squadron came on 4th October 1945, the squadron was based initially as a twin engine conversion unit at Yeovilton, with the Airspeed Oxford and Bristol Beaufort, but later moved to Dale and Halesworth where it switched to Mosquitoes until 1949.

821 Squadron came next where he flew the Fairey Firefly AS.6 and FR.5 from various stations such as Arbroath, Machrihanish and Eglinton flying exercises over the North Sea and Atlantic, to Hal Far and HMS *Glory* operating in the South Atlantic and Mediterranean.

Bob suffered a minor prang aboard *Glory* on 1st November 1952, when landing in a Firefly he clipped a wire and 'pecked the deck' with his prop. There was little damage and he escaped injury.

He was not so fortunate the following month when on Christmas Day, at the height of the Korean War, flying Firefly FR.5 VT471 of 821 Squadron, again from *Glory,* he was engaged with another aircraft in attacking a railway bridge when his aircraft was hit by flak west of Haeju, it was seen to spiral out of control from around 1,000 feet and crash to the ground where it exploded.

Sadly, Bob has no know grave and is commemorated on both the Armed Forces Memorial at the National Arboretum, Staffordshire, and on the Commonwealth Memorial at the United Nations Memorial Cemetery, Pusan. South Korea.

The memorial for Commonwealth Armed Forces at Usan, South Korea

BOMBER ON TORR MOR - BEAUFORT N1180

While on detachment from RAF Abbotsinch near Glasgow, the crew of a Bristol Beaufort Mk I N1180 TU-S arrived at Girvan, on the Ayrshire coast, overlooking the rather spectacular granite island of Ailsa Craig situated on the Firth of Clyde, for Torpedo Training at the TTU RAF Turnberry and would shortly be briefed to undertake night navigation exercise No3 over the sea.

The purpose of the exercise was to prepare new crews fresh from OTU`s, low level torpedo bombing techniques and navigational skills, which were imperative for operational sorties to Norway and the like for attacking axis vessels, flying under cover of darkness or cloud, often surrounded by mountainous terrain and in harsh elements.

At the pre-flight briefing on the evening of Wednesday 2nd September 1942, the crew consisting: Two New Zealanders Pilot P/O Albert A. Haydon, Pilot P/O Leonard P. Booker, Observer Sgt Francis J. B. Griffin RAFVR and Canadian Wireless Operator & Air Gunner Sgt Tom H. Grasswick, were warned to expect deteriorating weather conditions by Turnberry's Meteorological Staff.

Taking off at dusk, P/O Haydon eased the twin-engine bomber into darkening sky and flew on a reciprocal course towards their first navigation point.

As the flight progressed the forecast weather conditions changed rapidly in excess of the information supplied during the briefing, and the Beaufort began to drift off course.

Warnings of the increase in velocity and a westerly wind direction were transmitted by the weather station, but not acknowledged, so it remains uncertain that W/Op received the messages.

Presumably unaware of their true position, and whilst flying at a height of a little under 1,300 feet, at 22:40 hours, N1180 collided with the 414 metre hill of Tor Morr, approximately 1½ miles ESE of the 330 year old lighthouse on the Mull of Kintyre. It burst into flames as fuel tanks ruptured on impact and sadly all the crew perished.

The aircraft was only slightly off course, so it's possible that the navigator became aware of the wind change and was trying to correct when they crashed.

Small pieces of the aircraft still at the site today. The Mull lighthouse road can be seen in the background. Photo: Dave Ramsey

N1180 was not the only aircraft from this unit that failed to return that night, for just twenty minutes later F/Sgt Ronald Lutes RCAF in Beaufort L9803 'Y' with a crew of three consisting: Obs. Sgt Clive Hammond RAFVR, and two W/AG's F/Sgt Bruce Frances. RCAF and F/Sgt John Hargreaves. RCAF, crashed into the north-east side of Mull's highest mountain Ben More, once again there were no survivors.

The crash site of N1180 today looks pretty much the same as it did 20 years ago, with only sparse pieces of wreckage lying in a peat hollow on the heather clad moor, in particular aluminium panels, some being recognisable as engine cowl.

Pilot. Sergeant Albert Augustine Haydon, RNZAF, born in Wellington, New Zealand on 1st November 1915, was the son of Edward Francis and Celia Julia Haydon (née Brady) of Albert Street, Palmerston North, NZ.

Albert being a Catholic was educated at Marist Brothers' School, Wellington and later St. Patrick's College Silverstream, Upper Hut, where he was a cross country running champion. After college he became a commercial traveller for Benn Beauty Supplies in Auckland. An interest in flying later led him to the Wanganni & Auckland Aero Club where he became a U/T pilot in November 1937.

On 17th August 1941 Albert became a U/T pilot with the RNZAF and he arrived at the Initial Training Wing at Levin, thence to 4 EFTS on 28th September and 3 FTS on 8th November where he graduated as an air force pilot on 20th December and was awarded his wings, swiftly followed by promotion to Sergeant on 31st January 1942.

After a period of leave Albert and other fellow countrymen embarked for the UK on attachment to the RAF. He eventually arrived at No3 Personnel Reception Centre, Bournemouth on 15th April, but had to wait until 12th May before being allocated to 11 (P) AFU at Wheaton Aston, Staffordshire, where he was attached to 1521 BATF flying Oxfords.

Next came 5 (Coastal) OTU at Turnberry on the Ayrshire coast on 1st July. Here he would fly the Beaufort on operational training sorties with a newly formed crew, prior to joining a TTU at the same base for torpedo training in August.

At the time of the accident on Kintyre Albert had logged a total of 269 flying hours, including his training in New Zealand, but had just 35 hours on the Beaufort with only 4 hrs on the type at night.

Following the accident he was accorded a full military funeral in Brookwood Cemetery, Woking, Surrey and was interred in Grave ref. 2.H.1.

Albert had a brother who was also a pilot. P/O Edward Leonard Haydon who had served in England with 75 NZ

Sgt Albert A. Haydon. RNZAF

Photo: NZ Press

squadron and flew Wellington bombers on numerous raids over France and Germany. On several occasions he had cheated death as he battled through flak and night fighters.

On one occasion he had been on a night training exercise in Wellington Mk.III X3538 on 27th August 1942, when on approach to the airfield he crash landed in a field at 21:30 hours around a mile west of Mildenhall, luckily he and his crew were uninjured, but the aircraft was a total write-off.

Unlike his brother, Edward survived the war and for a time lived in Palmerston North, before work took him to Manurwa, and finally to Papakura, Auckland where he passed away in 1981.

Len then went to the Initial Training School at Levin, Rongotai on 19th April 1941, after which he remustered as a U/T Air Gunner with the Initial Training Wing on 12th May, then embarked to undergo further training in Canada on 18th June.

After 12 days at sea and a long rail journey, Len arrived at No3 Wireless School in Winnipeg, Manitoba on 5th July. He was attached to the RCAF under the British Commonwealth Air Training Plan where he spent the next twenty five weeks learning wireless telegraphy and became proficient

Sgt Haydon's grave in Brookwood

Photo: Author's Collection

Wireless Op / Air Gunner Pilot Officer Leonard Percy Booker, RNZAF, born 25th April 1913 in Christchurch, New Zealand, was the son of John and Mary A. Booker of New Plymouth.

Len was educated at New Plymouth Boys High School, after which he was employed as a carpenter with Hunter & Party Coal Mining Company at Rewanui on South Island's west coast.

Having joined the RNZAF as an Aircraftman on 4th November 1939 and been sent to New Plymouth on the 17th, he was assigned to General Duties, but remustered as a Flight Rigger on 1st September 1940.

P/O Leonard P. Booker. RNZAF

Photo: NZ Press

enough in the use of both radio equipment and Morse code for operational flying duties.

Having graduated as a W/AG in December 1942, he would normally be promoted to Sergeant, but had put in for commission which was granted on 22nd December so he became a Pilot Officer.

Leaving Canada for the UK on 8th January and arriving on 21st, following an eight week course at 3 Radio School, he arrived at 5 (C) OTU Turnberry on 30th June and the TTU in August.

Following the accident Len was interred in Campbeltown (Kilkerran) Cemetery, Kintyre. With full military honours. Div.4. Grave 600.

Sgt Jack Griffin's grave & CWGC stone in Harrow (Pinner) Cemetery

Observer Sergeant Francis John Bliss Griffin, RAF, born 1909 in Aylesbury, Buckinghamshire, was the only son of Francis George and Mary Griffin of Aylesbury and husband of Doris Griffin (née Young) of Pinner, Harrow.

Very little is known about Sgt Griffin, who appears to have been referred to as Jack by family and friends.

His parents Francis and Mary had been married in Aylesbury 1901 and it would appear his grandparents also hailed from that area. Jack married Doris Young, in St.Paul's Church, Hounslow in 1933, she was the eldest daughter of Mrs F. Woodruff Young of Hounslow. Jack was interred in a family grave in Harrow (Pinner) New Cemetery Middlesex. Cemetery. Sec. F.5 Grave 125.

P/O Booker's grave in Kilkerran

Photo: Author's Collection

Wireless Operator / Air Gunner Sgt Tom Henry Grasswick, RCAF, born 23rd March 1921 in Calgary, Alberta, Canada, was son of Tom Henry and S. Vernetta Grasswick (née Marsh) of Calgary.

Tom's parents were American, his father was from Minnesota and his mother a native of South Dakota, but soon after being married they moved to Canada where his father was a car mechanic and owned his own garage business.

Tom attended Balmoral Public School for academic studies from 1927-1933, then Western Canada High School from 1934-1937 where his main subjects were Drafting, Woodwork, Metalwork and in his final two years he studied Electrics.

Sgt Tom Henry Grasswick. RCAF

On leaving school at 16 Tom became a junior clerk for a local firm, but was made redundant. He then went to work for his father as a driver and mechanic, and later worked as a driver for Crossland & Beagle Union Milk Co, prior to being drafted into the army on 27th January 1940 where he served until 16th July when he was discharged to attend a Radio School. At the end of the course he enlisted in the RCAF an AC2 at Calgary, Alberta on 16th October.

After basic training Tom was sent to No1 Wireless School in Montreal where he learned Morse, telegraphy and signals and was promoted to LAC in May the following year.

Bombing and Gunnery School was next and arriving at 4 B&GS at Fingal on 15th September, Tom attended a four week course and was awarded his gunners badge on 13th October 1941 and promoted to a Temporary Sergeant Wireless Operator & Air Gunner.

Tom endured further training in the air at 31 OTU in November and December, then after being on leave over Christmas, he reported to Ferry Command at Dorval for embarkation via Bermuda to the UK on 7th January 1942.

On arrival on 11th February he reported to 3 PRC Bournemouth and was posted to 3 RS then 3 RDFS at Prestwick for further training in British weather conditions prior to being crewed up at 5 (C) OTU at Turnberry and finally 1 TTU at the same station.

After the accident Tom was interred in Campbeltown (Kilkerran) Cemetery, Kintyre with full military honours. Division 4. Grave 601.

NO PLACE TO LAND - ANSON K6309

Constructed by A.V. Roe & Company Limited at their Woodford plant from a batch of 174 Mk.1s, Anson K6309 was a multi-role aircraft powered by two 350-hp Armstrong Siddeley Cheetah IX, seven cylinder radial engines.

Delivered to 61 Squadron at RAF Hemswell, Lincolnshire on 24th March 1937, the Anson formed part of a re-equipment schedule from their aging Hawker Audax biplanes.

K6309 remained with this unit until 7th February 1938 when the first of the Bristol Blenheim Mk.I's arrived and the Anson, by then surplus to requirements, transferred to 48 Squadron based at RAF Manston in Kent. The idea was for the squadron to assist in the formation of the School of Air Navigation (SAN) under the RAF expansion scheme.

However, the Air Ministry required a further reconnaissance squadron and 48 was requested to transfer on 1st September 1938 to nearby RAF Eastchurch, situated on the Isle of Sheppey off the north Kent coast, but for some reason K6309 remained with the Navigation School.

On the afternoon of 27th May 1941 the Anson was damaged in a minor accident, but was it quickly repaired and continued with the unit's busy training program.

In June K6309 moved north to RAF Cranage near Middlewich in Cheshire to join No 2 School of Air Navigation, nine months later on 9th April, it was sent to Martin Hearne Ltd, RAF Hooton Park, Wirral, for overhaul and repairs

Upon completion of the necessary work a move further northwards followed on 22nd June 1942, this time to RAF West Freugh, in Wigtownshire to join No 4 Air Observers School (AOS) Some sources give No 5 AOS RAF Jurby, Isle of Man as the unit for K6309, but 4 AOS ORB and the 78 movement card state it only ever served at 4 AOS.

These observer schools provided detailed instructions in navigation and the use of various weapons and gunnery tactics employed by the Royal Air Force. Alas, despite its lengthy service this would be the last unit to accommodate the aircraft.

At 14:35 on Saturday 14th November 1942, Temp F/Sgt Anthony Lambert Perrett, RAF, eased K6309 off West Freugh's main runway and slowly climbed into the cold grey sky, with his

Anson 1 K6309 is seen here with 61 Squadron at North Coates in 1937

three trainees likely taking turns to manually hand crank the Anson's retractable undercarriage into the stowed and locked position. This took up to 160 turns of the handle to achieve.

From all accounts the exercise proceeded normally until on the last stage of the homeward flight over the sea, with the cloud base constantly reducing K6309 began to develop problems with one of the normally reliable Cheetah engines, and when the unit failed completely, F/Sgt Perrett in the prevailing darkness at approximately 18:00, unable to maintain height, was left with little alternative but to ditch the aircraft off the west coast of Kintyre close to Machrihanish.

Having successfully achieved the ditching, unfortunately on hitting the water LAC Robert Kerr Somervaille, a Navigator under training, was thrown violently forward in the cabin and received an arm injury. After climbing into the dinghy as their aircraft slipped beneath the waves, the crew, seeing the dark shadow of a coastline to the east, began paddling towards the shore where they managed to get help.

After contacting the Duty Officer at Landrail the exhausted airmen were collected by a Royal Navy Ambulance, taken to the Station Sick Quarters for examination and provided with food, hot drinks and warm clothing.

LAC Somervaille upon examination of his injury was diagnosed as having a comminuted fracture of left humerus, he was later transported and admitted to HMS *Nimrod,* a RN Hospital located in the original Campbeltown Grammar School under Naval Surgical Specialist Surgeon Lieutenant Taylor, but on Thursday 19th November it was arranged for him to be transferred by air and road to the Emergency Medical Service Hospital, Hairmyers in East Kilbride, Lanarkshire, where after further treatment he eventually made a successful recovery. The following day an aircraft was sent to Machrihanish to pick up the crew and F/Sgt Perrett and the others returned to their station by air.

The cause of the engine failure could not be established due to the loss of the aircraft, but low cloud and winds that day had influenced the pilot to fly lower but when the engine cut out there was not enough height to find a suitable spot to on land to put down. The latter was emphasised by the Officer Commanding stating that that the accident was also attributed to a *"very small degree of inexperience"*, though F/Sgt Perrett at that time did have at total of 261 hours flying time with 111 on the Anson.

Pilot. Temporary Sergeant Anthony Lambert Perrett, RAF, born in 1918, was the only son of Anthony and Martha Elizabeth Perrett (née Lynn) of Pewsey, Wiltshire and husband of Gladys Perrett (née Catton) of Bournemouth, Hampshire.

Tony's parents had been married in Pewsey in 1914, where Tony was educated prior to joining the RAF in 1941. He married his fiancée Gladys Catton in Chatham, Kent, in 1943.

By summer 1944 he was a F/Sgt and having successfully passed his four engine training course at a HCU on the Avro Lancaster, he was posted to 90 Squadron based at RAF Tuddenham in Suffolk.

As a Captain and Pilot flying the Lancaster Mk.1 & III, from the beginning of August he flew many missions over enemy occupied Europe to such targets as Keil, Stettin, Le Havre and Rüsselsheim and had his fair share of hair-raising moments.

On 11th August Tony and his crew took off in Lancaster HK602 'U' for a bombing raid on Keil, a city in the north German state of Schleswig-Holstein, he and his crew reached the target area OK, but during the bombing run a 1000lb GP bomb hung up, unable to shake it loose they were forced to bring it back to base. Luckily they had a smooth landing.

Having applied for a commission, this was granted on 19th August when he was promoted to Pilot Officer.

A few days later on the 23rd, Tony and his crew in HK604 'G' were flying ops to the city of Rüsselsheim, their Lancaster was caught in a cone of searchlights at 00:54 and was peppered with flak, Tony took evasive action by corkscrew manoeuvre, but in doing so missed the target markers, he returned and released his bombs but not accurately due to a u/s computer box. They finally made it back but the aircraft was damaged.

On the 31st he took off at 16:05 in HK608 'T' for a raid on Pont Remy, an occupied village in northern France, but one of his starboard engines failed, and after feathering and jettisoning his bomb load at 5,000 feet over the Channel, he was forced to return and landed back at base at 17:33.

A few successful daylight ops to Le Havre followed on Sept 5th and 10th, but the following day, during a night mine-laying sortie over the Baltic Sea, his Lancaster for reasons unknown, failed to return.

An Avro Lancaster of 90 Squadron

He had taken off from Tuddenham at 19:40 in ME838 `D` for mine-laying in the Pomeranian Bay area but sadly never came back. One of his crew F/Sgt Francis Graham Barrett-Lennard RAAF of Beverley, Western Australia, was found washed ashore near Kristianstadt, Sweden on 16th October and interred with honour and respect in Malmo Eastern Municipal Cemetery, Sweden. The other crew members including Tony have their names inscribed on the Runnymede Memorial at Coopers Hill, Surrey. Panel 212.

Pupil Navigator Leading Aircraftman Robert Kerr Somervaille, RAF, born in 1921 at St. Faith`s, was the son of Mr & Mrs Somervaille (Mother nee Kerr) of St.Faith`s, Norfolk and husband of Marjorie Somervaille.

Robert joined the Royal Air Force in 1941 and became a trainee Navigator at No4 AOS. After recovering from his injuries sustained in the ditching of Anson K6309 and on completing his course, he was promoted to Flight Sergeant and sent for training on Mosquitoes with 30 year old pilot F/O Basil Henry Francis Templer.

F/O Templer (nicknamed Simon, based on the fictional character by Leslie Charteris) had joined the RAF as a VR when war broke out. He had gained his private pilots certificate in a DH Gypsy Moth with London Air Park Flying Club in January 1939, and was commissioned in the RAF on 28th December 1940 as a Pilot Officer, so was already a veteran flyer by the time joined `B` Flight in 540 Squadron on 16th May 1944. This was a photo reconnaissance unit based at Benson, Oxfordshire, operating with de Havilland Mosquito IX`s.

Operations for Templer and Somervaille from May to July were fairly routine, though still dangerous, flying photo-recon` missions to railways in Ambieux, Lyons, Corbieres and Salvuza.

On 5th August the pair had been briefed for a photo sortie to Konigsburg – Gdynia-Stattin-Lubeck and Rostock in Germany, but 30 miles SW of Bremen their aircraft LR433 was attacked off the port beam by two FW-190s, the Mosquito swiftly turned on a southerly course, the fighter followed but after a few minutes broke away to head towards Bremen. Moments later, the crew found out why their pursuer had suddenly given up. Six USAAF P-47 Thunderbolts had appeared on the scene, but relief soon turned to horror as the US fighters split into three groups, dropped their long range fuel tanks and homed in for an attack, and despite the Mossie firing off the friendly recognition colours of the day, they continued to pursue for five minutes before breaking away when another two FW-190s appeared in the area.

Having eventually lost the P-47s, LR433 set a course for Lubeck, but after receiving heavy flak the crew decided to return to base and landed back home at 14:30, a little shaken but unscathed.

Robert and his pilot Templer, for their daring photo sorties, both received DFCs on 8th May 1945. They remained with the squadron, but Robert flew with other pilots mainly on transit flights. Staying in the RAF after the war he reached the rank of F/Lt. Robert married his fiancée Marjorie Dor`e in Aylesbury in 1952 and the couple lived at Elstree, where he sadly passed away in 1967 at the young age of just 43.

SOLE SURVIVOR - ALBACORE N4330

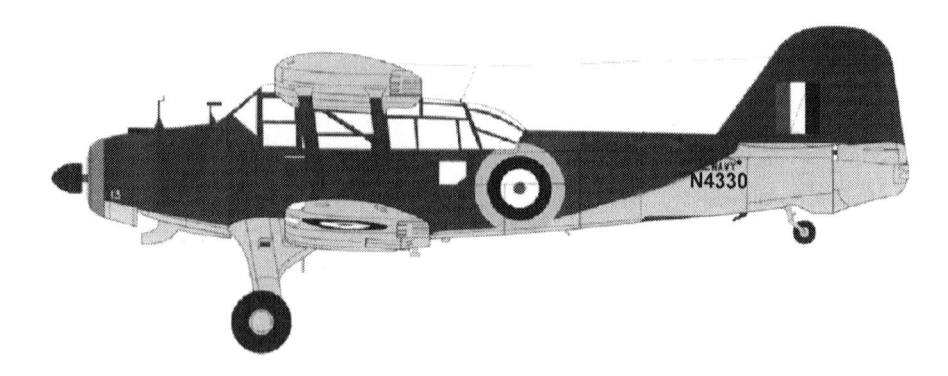

With the German attack on the Soviet Union known as Operation *Barbarossa* commencing on 22nd June 1941, Royal Navy Fleet Air Arm strikes on Petsamo and Kirkenes were decided at the highest level by Prime Minister Winston Churchill himself, in an effort to support his new found ally Stalin.

The initial plan was intended to strike at enemy lines of communications in Northern Norway and Finland and this would become known as Operation "EF" that would include the passage of the high-speed minelayer, HMS *Adventure* to Archangel with a large cargo of mines, while the air groups of the two carriers HMS *Furious* and *Victorious* attacked a concentration of shipping in the two northern ports used by Nazi Gebirgs Korps Norge.

These strikes on Petsamo and Kirkenes and took place respectively on 30th July 1941, but losses on the side of the allies were so heavy, that the whole of 827 Squadron was almost obliterated.

Joining *Victorious* from the shore station at Hatston, Orkney, were 21 Fairey Albacores of 827 and 828 Squadrons with 12 Fulmars of 809 Squadron, and among the Albacores was the one in our story N4330, which on this occasion was being piloted by Lt J.C. Reed along with the squadron C.O. Lt/Cdr. J.A. Stewart-Moore and P.O. H.J. Lambert.

Sadly, any chance of a surprise attack on the 30th under the cover of darkness was thwarted, as the Arctic midnight sun made it easy for the German forces to spot the fleet before they could effect a launch from the carriers.

During the Petsamo raid the allies found the harbour virtually empty and the flak was heavy. The aircraft claimed the sinking of a small steamer and the destruction of several jetties, but paid the price with loss of one Albacore and two Fulmars.

Kirkenes was a complete disaster, for despite sinking one 2,000ton vessel, setting a further one on fire and N4330

114

Fairey Albacore

claiming one Bf.110 probably damaged and a Ju.87 damaged, the Luftwaffe had shot down 15 allied aircraft from the two carriers, in which 13 airmen had been killed and 25 taken POW.

However, out of all this carnage, among the aircraft that made it back to HMS *Victorious* was Albacore N4330, and though badly damaged, after carrier returned to Scapa Flow, it was flown back to Hatston on 8th August 1941 for repair, but was involved in an accident on the 27th with Sub/Lt H.J.M. Pike.

Once repaired at Donibristle the Albacore lay in storage for some time, before being assigned to 766 Squadron at Machrihanish in October 1942 for use in bombing training exercises.

On the evening of Saturday 6th February 1943, New Zealand pilot Sub/Lt (A) Raymond Jamieson, RNZNVR, and his two crew Observer Sub/Lt Graham Ewart Thomas, RNVR and Telegraphist Air Gunner Leading Airman Reginald Nigel Willcock, RN, took off in N4330 from Machrihanish for a night bombing exercise at the offshore bombing range at Crossaig, situated on the east coast of Kintyre between Grogport and Skipness.

Flying through rain squalls as darkness fell the aircraft was spotted by the observation post at Crossaig, whose job it was to monitor the results, but soon after its arrival, the Albacore suddenly disappeared from view. It was later found to have crashed into the sea.

The pilot, Sub/Lt Jamieson somehow managed to release his harness and scramble clear of the sinking wreck, but his two crew sadly never made it and must have been trapped in the aircraft and drowned, possibly having been rendered unconscious by the impact.

Pilot Sub-Lieutenant (A) Raymond Jamieson, RNZNVR, born in Auckland on 20th January 1920, was the son of Charles John and Eva Vyse Jamieson (née Orange) Puhinui, Auckland, New Zealand.

Educated in Auckland, Raymond attended Seddon Memorial Technical College prior to becoming a clerk for the Radio Dept of the Post & Telegraph Office in Wellington.

He joined the NZ Army Territorial Force, 2nd Field Ambulance Division of the NZMC on 25th August 1939 for 18 months prior to joining the RNZN at HMS *Philome*, Auckland.

On loan to the RN/FAA as U/T aircrew, Raymond embarked for the UK on 19th June 1941 and on arrival on the 31st, he was attached to RNAS Gosport (*St.Vincent*). In November he was posted to Puckpool (*Medina*) a shore station on the Isle of Wight, mainly for classroom work.

Next came 24 EFTS at Lee-on-Solent for pilot training in Tiger Moths and the like, and having achieved good results, he was selected for training in Canada, embarking on 21st March 1942 with other cadets for 31 SFTS HMS *Saker*, where at the end of July he graduated, received his pilots wings and was promoted to Temp Sub-Lieutenant.

Following graduation leave, he eventually sailed for the UK and arrived on 7th September where he was posted to No 9 (P) AFU for further training and assessment on Swordfish and Albacore

Sub/Lt Raymond Jamieson. RNZNVR
Photo: *NZ Weekly News*

types before joining other Torpedo Bomber Pilots at Crail for Deck Landing Trials prior to arrival at 766 Squadron Machrihanish on 25th January 1943.

On 19th March, following a period of survivors leave after his accident on 6th February, Raymond joined 827 Squadron flying Barracuda IIs, first from Machrihanish, and later, Dunino, Lee-on-Solent and HMS *Furious*,

It was while operating from *Furious* on 15th November 1943, Raymond lost his life when his aircraft BV765 collided over the Clyde with P9797. His crew: Obs. Lt. (A) Charles Frederick Kirby RNVR and TAG L/A Stanley Douglas

Bridges, RN also died, as did the crew of the other Barracuda Pilot Sub/Lt (A) Montague Gordon Christopher Mathew, RNVR, Obs. Sub/Lt (A) George Ridsdale Bleasby, RNVR and TAG L/A Fred Anderson. RN.

Observer Acting Sub-Lieutenant Graham Ewart Thomas, RNVR, was born in 1922 in Pontypridd, Glamorgan. He was the son of William Ewart Thomas and Margaret Janetta Thomas (née Bebb) of Llantwitfardre, Glamorgan.

Graham had only recently joined 766 Squadron. Sadly, even though a widespread search was conducted following the accident, he was never found and is commemorated on the Lee-on-Solent Memorial to the missing. Bay 5. Panel 1.

Telegraphist Air Gunner Leading Airman Reginald Nigel Willcock, RN, born 13th July 1923 at Newbury, Buckinghamshire, was the son of Sidney J and Kate A. Willcock (née Skinner) of Newbury, Bucks.

Reg as he was known, came from a large family of four brothers: Norman, Eric, Alan and Colin, and two sisters Alice and Dorothy. His father was a greengrocer and his parents had been married in Paddington in the summer of 1912.

Reg joined the Royal Navy in 1942 when he was 18, he qualified as a TAG 3rd Class on Course 43A. He is commemorated on the Lee-on-Solent Memorial. Bay 4. Panel 3.

Aside from the Lee-on-Solent Memorial, the Fleet Air Arm Memorial at the National Arboretum in Staffordshire honours all those who served with the RN FAA.

Photo: Author's Collection

Above: The main FAA memorial feature at the National Memorial Arboretum
Below: The plaque honouring the sacrifice made my the men of the FAA
Photos: Author's Collection

This memorial commemorates the outstanding courage professionalism and sacrifices made by all those who have flown, maintained and supported naval aircraft with selfless devotion to the nation
We pay tribute to the men and women of the
FLEET AIR ARM
who have given their lives in the service of their country

TARGET TUG TURMOIL SKUA L2907

Earning the nickname `Clapham Junction` with Fleet Air Arm aircrew arriving there, RNAS Machrihanish was one of the busiest of all the Royal Naval Air Stations during the Second World War.

The airfield, situated on the south west coast of the Kintyre peninsula and nestled in a hollow, was surrounded by hills on three sides with sand dunes and a bay and golf links to the west, it consisted of four tarmac runways. One at 1000 yards running NNW/SSE, a NNE/SSW and a NE/SW each of 1030 yards as well as a longer runway of 1190 yards stretching WNW/ESE.

Needless to say this was a poorly sited airfield by all accounts, and the weather dictated how flights would operate, and as one FAA Observer once said: *"It would be hard to imagine a more idyllic spot scenically, but for aircrew operating at night and in poor visibility, it was a death-trap".*

Strategically placed to enable protection of the Western approaches to Liverpool and the Clyde, providing cover for both inbound and outbound Atlantic convoys, the position of this airfield, albeit not ideal, had obviously been well thought out, for aside from providing shipping cover, the base would house training squadrons that would take off from here to practice deck landings on HMS *Argus* out in the Clyde.

Twenty four year old Sub/Lt (A) John A. Quigg, RNZNVR, was based at Machrihanish with 772 Squadron in 1943 and almost ended his flying career before it had even begun, when the Skua Mk II he was piloting was involved in a dramatic accident on the 9th.February.

That Tuesday afternoon Sub/Lt Quigg had just taken off in L2907 coded `M8L` adorned with a target-towing aircraft colour scheme of all-over yellow with black diagonal stripes, when, for reasons unknown, he was forced to return to base.

On the ground, three Swordfish crews of 835 Squadron had been briefed to carry out dummy torpedo attacks on HMS *Cardiff,* and aircraft were queuing up at the end of the runway awaiting a take off signal.

One of the Swordfish with its crew of three consisting: Pilot Lt (A) Harry C.K. `Hank` Housser, RCNVR, Observer

HMS Cardiff

Sub/Lt (A) Edward E. 'Barry' Barringer RNVR and Telegraphist Air Gunner L/A Alec Thompson. RN, was first in line for take off and whilst positioned with engine ticking over, the crew were to witness at close quarters the whole event and its miraculous, yet near tragic outcome.

The Observer Barry Barringer, recalled what happened next in his excellent autobiography 'Alone on a wide, wide sea'

"Instead of being cleared for take off by the expected flash from the green Aldis lamp, we were given an ominous red. And we soon saw why. A Blackburn Skua which had just taken off in front of us had got into difficulties and, instead of making an emergency landing dead ahead with wheels up, the pilot decided to try and get back to the airfield and land with his wheels down.

Skua L3007 with its TT paint job, but the roundel was different on L2907

red Very lights started shooting up from all directions as the Skua came hurtling back downwind, out of control and straight towards us. Hank tried to swing our Swordfish out of its path, but about 50 yards short of us, the Skua tipped on its nose. Its engine was torn clean away and went sailing over our heads, then the rest of the plane, with a terrible screeching of metal and fabric, slithered along the runway and smashed straight into us.

If its engine had still been in place that would have been the end of us all. As it was, the fuselages of both planes had collapsed in a shattered heap, but there was no seepage of petrol, no explosion or fire. I grabbed the fire extinguisher, struggled out of the cockpit, then came face to face with the Skua pilot dangling upside down, but by some miracle not seriously injured. I was just wondering how to free him so that he didn't drop head first on to the runway, when the crash-tender and ambulance came screaming to a halt beside us, and within seconds we were all extricated, more or less intact, then helped to a safe distance from the shattered planes".

After treatment at the SSQ, the airmen were all discharged with only minor cuts a bruises and were very lucky indeed to have avoided a tragedy.

The Skua after examination by the salvage team was deemed Cat. Z and later Struck Off Charge. However, it is believed the Swordfish was repaired and later put back into service.

Skua Pilot Sub-Lieutenant (A) John Alphonsus Quigg. RNZNVR, born 14th December 1918 in Oamaru, NZ was the son of Henry and Jane 'Diamond' Quigg of Clareville, Carterton District, Wellington, New Zealand.

The Skua/Swordfish accident at Machrihanish

John and his sister T.J. sadly lost both parents while they were still at school, their father passed away on 3rd August 1924 and their mother 21st August 1932.

Brought up by relatives, John became an office clerk after leaving school and worked for a local firm. He joined the RNZNVR as a naval airman in June 1941 and following training in both New Zealand and Canada, he was commissioned a Sub/Lt pilot in July 1942.

Whilst overseas John met and courted a girl in the Canadian army, and the couple were married just prior to him having to leave for England to join a Fleet Air Arm squadron.

As we know he served for a time with 772 Fleet Requirements Squadron at Machrihanish, but not long after the accident he was posted to 813 Squadron and later served aboard the aircraft carrier HMS *Campania* flying Grumman Wildcat Mk V fighters.

Not uncommon with other pilots landing on carriers in rolling seas, John had his fair share of minor prangs in the Wildcat. The first occurred on 1st May 1944, when he was landing in JV575 the hook missed the wire and he went into the barrier, and did the same again in that aircraft later that day. Next was a landing in JV577 five days later, when the hook pulled out and caught the trickle wire, the Wildcat again ending up in the barrier.

The third incident involved JV590 in which he was returning to *Campania* after target-towing, but found he was unable to lower the hook. Again this resulted in a collision with the barrier, though no injuries were sustained in this or any of the other two accidents.

On 10th February 1945, still serving with 813 Squadron, John, now a Lieutenant, was flying with wingman Sub/Lt (A) Peter J.W. Davies. RNVR when they spotted an enemy aircraft and closed in for an attack.

The pair had been involved in providing escort for Convoy JW-64, a consortium of 28 ships leaving the Clyde and bound for the Kola Inlet near Murmansk in Northern Russia.

During an interview prior to his passing Peter Davis described the events of that day in which he and fellow pilot John Quigg were awarded the Distinguished Service Cross:

'It wasn't long before I spotted a Ju88 low over the water coming towards us. Lieutenant Quigg, just as I saw this, reported six more. We dived on the leader and the rest broke up and went into cloud.

We carried out several attacks and the 88 disappeared into cloud, the starboard engine smoking ... I saw an 88 right down over the water with a Wildcat in hot pursuit.

The aircraft had evidently been hit and its starboard engine was smoking. I saw Lieutenant Quigg finish his attack and on the breakaway heard him report he'd run out of ammunition and had been hit.

I came in on the starboard quarter and from above and broke off almost dead astern. It was in this attack that my aircraft was hit. I'd seen a lot of tracer coming from the 88 and suddenly there was a bump and a flash.

Grumman Wildcat

As the aircraft had not been badly damaged I came in once more from the starboard quarter and the 88 pulled up into cloud, its starboard engine on fire. As my ammunition had run out I was told to return 'home' where I was rather too warmly welcomed [by our own fire] ... By this time the engine was coughing unhealthily, especially after I was waved round the first time, so I made a pass at the deck.

The second time I came in the engine cut twice on the approach, so I reckoned this time I'd land or be picked up out of the 'oggin'.

At least, I'm glad to say the aircraft was unserviceable before I hit the barrier."

Lt John Quigg managed to ditch his aircraft JV686 near the carrier HMS *Nairana* and was picked up 15 minutes later by the O-class destroyer HMS *Opportune* (G80). That day Lt John Quigg had claimed one Ju88 probably destroyed at 72.38N -13.35E and another possibly destroyed at 73.02N - 20.56E, shared with Sub/Lt Davies` in Wildcat JV755.

HMS Opportune

John Quigg returned to New Zealand with his wife after the war and settled in his hometown of Clareville. He passed away on 1st May 1996 and was laid to rest in a family grave in Clareville, Carterton Cemetery, Wairarapa, New Zealand. Plot 120.

Swordfish pilot Lieutenant (A) Harry Cron Kennedy `Hank` Housser. RCNVR. BA Hons, born 10th December 1915 in Vancouver, Canada, was the son of George Elliott and Nan Housser (née Kennedy) and husband of Martha Louise (née Farris). The couple were married at All Saints Church, Kingston, Ontario, in August 1941 and they later had four children. Bruce, Kathie, Stephen and John. Hank passed away on 13th July 1995 in Victoria, British Columbia.

Observer Sub-Lieutenant (A) Edward E. `Barry` Barringer. RNVR, born 1921 in Mitcham, Surrey, was the son of Frank and Rose Barringer (née Wadsworth). He had four brothers Frank, Charles, Victor and Arthur, and a sister Minnie.

Barry volunteered for RN Fleet Air Arm in June 1939 and joined as a Naval Airman 2nd class in Sept 1939 to train as an Observer. He graduated in Aug 1940 as a Midshipman (A) was assigned to HMS *Illustrious* in the Med and sailed to Alexandria. Whilst serving with 813 Sqn aboard HMS *Eagle* in 1941 he was involved in the destruction of 6 Italian destroyers and also the capture of a German supply ship *Lothringen* during a search for the battleship *Bismarck*. For his actions he was Mentioned in Dispatches. He left the service as a Lt/Cdr. In civilian life was the Chairman and Managing Director of Cadbury`s and Chairman of Thomas Cook before retiring in New Zealand.

Lt (A) Hank Hausser & wife Martha

Sub/Lt (A) Barry Barringer. RNVR

SGREADAN HILL WELLINGTON HX420

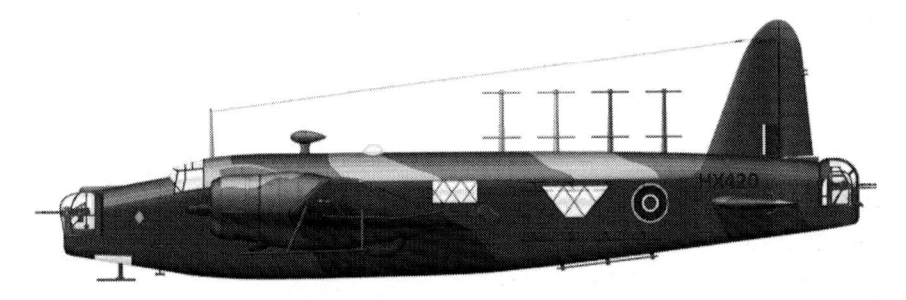

Built by the Vickers aircraft factory at Weybridge, Surrey, Wellington HX420 a Mk.VIII arrived at 32 MU, St.Athan, Glamorgan on 5th May 1942 where it was briefly housed at 51 MU Lichfield, Staffs, prior to delivery to 7 (Coastal) OTU at Limavady, Northern Ireland a few weeks later on 7th June.

One of the first pilots to fly this aircraft was an American serving in the RCAF P/O Paul Albert Hartman. On 30th June he took off mid-afternoon for a low level bombing exercise in the Firth of Clyde, but having misjudged his height on the run-up to the target, in conditions that were described as bright sunlight and a glassy sea, at 15:45 the aircraft struck the top of a target mast, however, Hartman managed to keep control, return to base and land safely.

On inspection later, damage to the Wellington was deemed to be only minimal and it was soon repaired and put back into service, but in February 1943 it would be lost in a more severe accident in the hills of Kintyre.

HX420 continued throughout 1942 with navigation and low level bombing exercises, then, on 19th January 1943 it was flown to Weybridge for modifications to accommodate two torpedoes, the aircraft then returned to Limavady for use in torpedo bombing practice prior to the crews going overseas.

On 13th February Sgt Jack Pool and crew took off in HX420 for an attack on a target with dummy torpedoes, on this occasion the flight went without a hitch and they returned to base an hour later.

The morning of Wednesday 17th February saw Sgt Pool and crew take off again on the first of two dummy torpedo attacks that day. The target was found, cargo released and after a duration of 35 mins, they returned to base.

The aircraft was re-armed with two more dummy torps and later that morning, Sgt Pool and crew took off again from Limavady on another torpedo bombing exercise, but this time they failed to return.

It would appear that the aircraft missed its navigation point and was a little too far north of track, when at an altitude of just over 1,000ft, climbing and heading eastwards, it crossed Lussa Loch, flew up a cul-de-sac glen, struck Easach Hill and crashed just below the summit of

7 (C) OTU Wellington VIII on dispersal at RAF Limavady

Sgreadan Hill. Navigator Sgt Harry Hoyle was killed the pilot Sgt Pool died shortly after. According to W/AG Sgt Jack Jones, the navigator had just changed places with him prior to the crash Jack recalled to his son in later years that Sgt Hoyle had been in the radio operators position where Jones normally sat and the switch took place shortly before they hit the hill at 12:00 after a flight duration of just 20 minutes.

Of the five crew, the Co-Pilot and two Wireless Operator Air Gunners had survived, but all had been injured. Sgt Jones had been knocked unconscious and awoke to find himself lying under one of the broken wings, meanwhile, the less injured of the other two (names not known) made his way southwards and eventually reached Drumgarve farm at the head of Glen Lussa, where he alerted the daughter of the tenant Sandy Wilson.

The crash survivor managed to give details of where the aircraft hit, and eventually word got through to the authorities and rescue services were on their way.

Once at the scene, the two remaining survivors were bought down to Drumgarve and treated for their injuries before being taken to hospital in Campbeltown.

Alex Coleville, a former member of Campbeltown Fire Brigade during the war, recalled in a Kintyre journal bringing down one of the two airmen who had died and said that both were taken to the nearby Albyn Distillery, where the cellar was used as a temporary mortuary.

At a Court of Inquiry the accident was considered to be due to an error in navigation, the reason for this was described as 'Obscure', though poor weather at the time and inexperience on the type, undoubtedly contributed to the loss of this aircraft.

Unlike the scene today where much of the hill is covered in trees, the route was a little more accessible in 1943 and the recovery of the wreckage was accomplished with the use of tractors.

Captain & Pilot Sergeant John Pool, RAF, was born at Toxteth Park, Liverpool in 1920, he was the only son of Capt. David Oswald and Alice Pool (née Wentzel) of Toxteth, Liverpool, Merseyside.

Known to all as Jack, his father was a Second Officer and later a Captain in the Merchant Navy and his Grandfather was a book keeper for a steam ship company. His parents were married at the Presbyterian Church in Park Road, Toxteth Park on 13th June 1916.

Being a Merchant Seaman Jack's father was often on board ship and away from home. When Jack was born they lived in Rosslyn Street, East Toxteth, but later moved to Garston, Lancashire where he attended primary school, before the family moved house again.

At the age of eleven, Jack attended the new Wirral Grammar School for boys, on Cross Lane, Bebington, which had a grand opening by the Lord Lieutenant of Cheshire, Brigadier-General Sir William Bromley-Davenport on 26 September 1931, and is perhaps notable today for a former pupil by the name of Harold Wilson who attended 1932-34 and became the school's first Head Boy, and of course Britain's Labour Prime Minister 1964-76.

While a vast number of sports were played and encouraged at the school, some of the boys, including Jack became interested in aeronautics and joined the local Air Training Corps, which in turn eventually led to training as a pilot in the RAF soon after war broke out.

Sgt John Pool in Plymyard Cemetery

Photo: Author's Collection

It is understood that Jack arrived at Limavady at the beginning of November 1942, and following a few local familiarisation flights and Navex's, from mid-December onwards, he and his crew would be engaged in dummy torpedo attacks on various targets off Kintyre.

At the time of the accident Jack had logged a total of 394 flight hours on various aircraft, but only 20 hours on Wellingtons, so although an experienced pilot, he was not familiar with the type. He now rests in Bebington, Plymyard Cemetery, Wirral, Sec. A. (C of E) Grave 344.

Navigator Sergeant Harry Hoyle, RAFVR, born in Leeds in 1920, was the only son of Sam and Lily Hoyle (née Fletcher) of Leeds, West Yorkshire. He had one older sister, Lily and was engaged to Miss Peggy Green of Cross Gates, Leeds.

His parents, both from Yorkshire had been married in Leeds in 1917. The family lived in St.Michael's Lane, Headingley and Harry was educated at Leeds Modern School. He was always keen on sports and distinguished himself at athletics.

Harry had been a former employee of George Mann & Co. Ltd, a printing machine manufacturers specialising in lithographic machinery based in Leeds, and was later employed by the Yorkshire Electric Power Company prior to joining the RAF. Harry was also a member of the 18th NW (Burley) Group of Boy Scouts and became a King's Scout and Assistant Scoutmaster for the troop.

Sgt Harry Hoyle. RAFVR
Photo: *Yorkshire Evening Post*

He joined the RAF in May 1941 and following basic training Harry was selected for aircrew and trained to be a navigator, both in the UK and overseas in Canada at Trenton, Ontario under the British Commonwealth Air Training Plan, after which he received his navigators brevet and was promoted to Sergeant before returning to England in a bomber of RAF Ferry Command in October 1942.

It is understood Harry arrived at Limavady around the same time as Sergeant Pool in November 1942, so like the others had only served here for a few months prior to the accident.

At 3.15pm on Tuesday 23rd February, a service was held in Burley Church, Leeds, attended by family, friends, former employers and service representatives, with interment at Lawnswood Cemetery at 4pm. Sec. V. Grave 255.

Wireless Operator & Air Gunner Sergeant John 'Jack' Jones RAF, born 21st December 1920, was the son of Fred and Emily Jones (née Carrington) of Higher Bebington, Wirral. He had four brothers: William, Arthur, Fred and Alf and two sisters Alice and Kate. Jack was also husband of Margaret Jones and the couple had four children.

128

Sgt John `Jack` Jones. RAF

Photo: Mark Jones

Known to family and friends as Jack, he joined the RAF on 16th January 1941 and after completing basic training, was posted to No.4 Signals School at RAF Madley, Hertfordshire, where he learned Morse code and Wireless, but aside from classroom work, he also got to fly in Percival Proctor and de Haviland Dominie aircraft.

Jack completed the course and qualified as a Wireless Operator on 25th August 1942. It may be of interest that the well known British actor and comedian Eric Sykes also trained here as a Wireless Operator during the Second World War and Jack and Eric may well have crossed paths?

Next came armament and he was sent on a gunners course to No 8 Air Gunnery School at Evanton, Ross-shire. This airfield was based 16 miles north of Inverness and here Jack would have practiced firing at ground targets and aerial drogues from Blackburn Bothas. As an LAC he qualified here on 25th September and would have been promoted to Sergeant.

He then went on No 3 Radio Direction Finding School at Prestwick, Glasgow, for a course on radar and often flew in Avro Ansons. Here he finished the course and qualified as a Radar Operator on 4th November and a two week gap in his flying logbook suggests he may have been given leave prior to joining 7 (C) OTU at RAF Limavady, Northern Ireland.

Jack was to spend quite some time in hospital and convalescing following the accident on Kintyre, but eventually was deemed fit for flying duties and made his first post-crash flight on 3rd June 1943.

On 1st January 1943, No1 Torpedo Training Unit had been formed at RAF Turnberry, Strathclyde, for advanced torpedo bombing training for ex-OTUs. This unit used a variety of aircraft, Beauforts, Hampdens, Beaufighters etc, but on 11th March 6 Wellington Mk.VIII/TBs arrived, followed a week or so later by 30 Wellington TB/XIs.

Jack arrived at Turnberry on 11th June and again flew on Wellingtons attacking dummy targets in the Firth of Clyde. He remained here until 3rd July.

A Short Sunderland at Castle Archdale in the summer of 1944

A posting to 303 Ferry Training Unit at RAF Talbenny, Pembrokeshire, came next on 30th July. Here Jack joined other crews in preparation for ferrying aircraft overseas. The course lasted until 9th September when he was posted out to Egypt.

On 23rd February 1944, he joined 201 Squadron flying Short Sunderlands from Castle Archdale (Lough Erne) County Fermanagh, Northern Ireland, and Pembroke Dock, where in June the squadron, under command of W/Cdr. Guy Van der Kiste DSO, was heavily involved in anti-submarine patrols to provide protection against the dreaded U-boats during the D-Day landings.

During his time with 201 Squadron Jack regularly flew in Sunderland U-Uncle with F/Lt M.H.A. Fearnside and crew, often as the rear gunner.

Jack remained with 201 Squadron until February 1946, making his last flight on the 2nd. He was by this time a Warrant Officer and was demobbed on 30th March after five years service.

Returning to civilian life he was employed in a variety of jobs including bricklayer and fishmonger, but later became a Pub Landlord in Liverpool.

He married his fiancée Margaret and the couple had four sons, John, Mark, Brian and Malcolm, with Mark eventually following in his father's footsteps by joining the RAF in 1983 and finishing as a Squadron Leader in 1999.

Jack finally retired from the Brewery business in 1983 and lived in Bebington, Wirral, where he sadly passed away on 1st February 2009 at the age of 89.

Despite several attempts to find information on the Co-Pilot and other Wireless Operator Air Gunner who survived the crash in HX420, their names do not appear to be listed for the date of the accident in the station log for Limavady or in 7 (C) OTU record book, so it can only be hoped that both these men recovered from their injuries and survived the war.

In May 2018 Wireless Operator Sgt Jack Jones' two sons Mark and Malcolm, arrived on Kintyre with hopes of finding the crash site of their father's Wellington.

Mark Jones gave his account of a memorable trip with his brother:

'We travelled over by car on the Thursday to our hotel for the next three nights - the Argyle Hotel at Bellochantuy on the A83 road to Campbeltown run by Nick and Ian - it turned out to be an excellent decision....

On the Friday Recce Day, we took a route up the side of Lussa Loch until we got to a locked Forestry Commission gate by the farmhouse. We parked the car there and then walked up the side of Sgreaden Hill towards the radio mast via a stone fire break just off the track. Hoping that was near to the top, we got to it only to find still a bit of a yomp over marshy boggy land, the weather closed in and it started to rain. So we called it a day and hoped for better weather on the Saturday!

Back at the hotel, Nick, the co-owner, said that there was a much easier route to the fire break as he has walked the area with his dogs, in that turning left out of the hotel and then right on a track not far up the A83 that was once part of the Kintyre Way, and would see us drive on a great

One of the firebreak trails leading up Sgreaden Hill. Photo: Mark Jones

Looking westward from Sgreadan Hill

Photo: Mark Jones

track road through the forest to Bord a Dubh, bypassing the locked gate and enabling us to drive right up to the fire break saving an hour of walking!

So with an early start and blue skies, we set off and drove to the fire break within 10mins, then yomped through the marsh to top of Sgreaden Hill - being overweight and unfit, both of us didn't realise how hard it would be walking over that terrain having to watch every step, a real slog!

Given that this is the type of land all around we thought then it would be highly unlikely without specialist tools i.e. a metal detector, that we would find anything! From the trig point, we then followed the fence posts down to Earsach Hill and had a look around the cairn, again to no avail.

We then cut the corner back to the fire trail using the radio mast as a reference point, never ever going through the forest as that looked a difficult trek.

Overall, it was a great and emotional experience for my brother and I to visit the area where our late Dad could have perished 75 years ago and we would not be here today! It was a bonus that overall the weather was kind, the hotel brilliant and scenery Campbeltown to Glasgow amazing`.

It had been a gallant effort by the boys even though they failed to find the site, they were not alone. In the Kintyre Aircraft Crashes booklet in 2003, it describes the site as still having some remains on the hill just below the cairn, and it was mentioned that large amounts of ammunition were to be seen, though the latter could well have been removed?

A disturbed area on Easach Hill—Could this be the crash site?

Photo: Mark Jones

Based on the Kintyre crash list locations, others have tried to locate the site in recent times but without success.

There must still be some remains on the hill, but the area is very marshy and likely whatever is still there is hidden by the tufts of grass or has sunk beneath the marshy surface?

The cairn mentioned in the Kintyre crashes book, below Sgreadan Hill trig

Photo: Gary Nelson

Mark Jones, son of Sgt Jack Jones at the trig point on Sgreaden Hill, Kintyre

Photo: Mark Jones

WAY OFF COURSE - WELLINGTON HX779

Originally based at Hawarden near Chester in order to train fighter pilots, 7 OTU was disbanded on 1st November 1940 to become 57 OTU, but this unit eventually reformed at RAF Limavady, Londonderry on 1st April 1942 as 7 (C) Operational Training Unit under control of 17 Croup.

Largely equipped with the Vickers Wellington Mk. VIII and manufactured at their Weybridge works, in order to combine and enable individual aircrew trades intent on becoming part of an efficient fighting force, training would involve general reconnaissance missions and torpedo attacks, the latter being performed from Abbotsinch near Glasgow, using state of the art Airborne Surface Vessel (ASV) radar for detection of enemy shipping and submarines.

Late evening on Friday 26th February 1943, Canadian pilots F/Sgt Donald Frank Sutterby and W.O. II John Noble Mitton, eased their heavily laden Wellington VIII HX779 off Limavady's main runway. Their duty that night, a flare dropping exercise off the west coast of Scotland.

As far as can be asserted the flight proceeded normally, although the weather conditions rapidly began to deteriorate.

At 01:35 hours on the 27th the Wellington, having now drifted 60 miles off its intended route, flew into dense cloud over Kintyre and impacted with a hill south of Balinakill at a height of approximately 500 feet. It had crashed close to Loch Ciaran and above the east coast village of Clachan where it immediately burst into flames with the loss of all on board.

With no radio contact and its failure to return to base, HX779 was declared overdue and an air and sea search was organised. In addition, the following day alarming reports began to circulate with regards to another Wellington having come to grief. HX737 had crashed on a navigation exercise near An Fál Carrach (Falcarragh) a township in north west Donegal, Eire. Sergeant pilots. Leonard Ashby Court and John D'arcy Wall along with crew: Sgts John S.Campbell, James Gilmour, Ronald Gutteridge and James S. Farthing all lost their lives.

134

Wellington VIII HX419 from the same production batch

A double tragedy for the unit in less than 24 hours. Both these accidents occurred just ten days after the loss of HX420 at the head of Lussa Glen bringing the casualty total to thirteen dead and three survivors.

Pilot Sergeant Donald Frank Sutterby, RCAF, born in Toronto, Canada on 11th July 1920, was the only son of Walter Everett and Beatrice Alice Sutterby (née Gosling) of Toronto, Ontario, Canada.

Donald's father was an American from Buffalo, New York, and his mother was from Dover, Kent, England. His father, a former Marine met and courted his mother in England and the couple were married at Elam, Kent in 1916 but had emigrated to Canada in 1919.

The family lived in Hiltz Avenue, Toronto, where his father worked as a lineman for the Bell Telephone Company.

Donald attended the Duke of Connaught Primary School 1925-1934 and the Eastern High School of Commerce until 1939 where he took a general business course. His main Sports at college were rugby, swimming and basketball, but he was also a keen amateur photographer.

After graduation Donald found employment as a Junior Bookkeeper, Stenographer and Shipper with the Canadian Electric Box Company in Queen St, East Toronto, where he worked for 18 months prior to joining the RCAF as an AC2 on 10th March 1941.

Following basic training at 6 I.T.S, where he obtained good marks on all his courses, he was recommended for pilot training with 20 EFTS at Oshawa, Ontario, arriving on 18th December 1941.

Sgt Donald Frank Sutterby. RCAF

Photo: Veterans Affairs Canada

Here he flew 66hr 35min on Tiger Moths and was graded a good average pilot and recommended for twin-engine training at 16 SFTS at Hagersville, Ontario, where he completed the course on 19th July 1942, graduated as a pilot and was promoted to Temporary Sergeant.

Following a spell of leave after graduation, Donald reported to 1 GRS for a reconnaissance course prior to embarkation for the UK on 28th October where he eventually joined 7 (C) OTU on 30th November for operational training on Wellingtons.

After the accident on 3rd March 1943, Donald was interred in Campbeltown (Kilkerran) Cemetery alongside three of his crew. Division 4. Grave 605. He was posthumously promoted to Flight Sergeant.

Pilot. Flight Sergeant John Noble Mitton, RCAF, born 14th May 1917 at Moncton, New Brunswick, Canada, was the son of Arthur Wellington and Jessie Violet Mitton (née Horseman) of West County, New Brunswick, Canada and husband of Ada Clarabel Mitton (née Duffy) also West County, NB.

John attended Georgetown Public School 1923-1932 and Shediac Superior until 1935, after which, with aims of becoming a primary school teacher, he took a teacher's course for a year, then a correspondence course in bookkeeping, typing, filing and business administration with the Success Business College from Jan—May 1939.

Grave of Sgt John N. Mitton. RCAF

Photo: Author's Collection

In order to earn his keep and fund his business course, John found himself a job at a local electrical store J.J. Lutes, selling radio licences, before becoming a school teacher in 1939.

John enlisted as an AC2 in the RCAF at Moncton Recruitment Centre on 27th February 1941 and following basic training and assessment, he was recommended for a navigation course with No2 Air Navigation School.

However, his grades lacked substance and he really wanted to become a pilot so remustered as a U/T pilot and was posted to 21 Elementary Flying School at Chatham on 3rd July, then 9 SFTS at Summerside on 2nd September where he faired much better, and even his navigation grades were good.

Promoted to LAC at 21 EFTS, with permission from his Commanding Officer he was given leave to marry his fiancée Miss Ada Duffy at Hillsborough, Albert County, NB on 13th September 1941.

On 21st November that year John was awarded his pilots wings and promoted to Temporary Sergeant. Further navigation courses followed with 2 ANS and 1 ANS at Penfield Ridge and Rivers, respectively, then on to 1 GRS at Summerside in August 1942 before leaving Halifax on 25th October arriving in the UK on 4th November to join 7 (C) OTU on the 30th.

After the accident John was interred in Campbeltown (Kilkerran) Cemetery. Division 4. Grave 607.

Sgt William Evans Davies. RNZAF

Photo: *NZ Weekly News*

Navigator Sergeant William Evans Davies, RNZAF, was born in Port Chalmers, NZ on 11th April 1921. He was the son of Samuel Evans and Margaret Naismith Davies (née Lattimer) of Tainui, Dunedin, Otago, New Zealand.

William attended Otago Boys High School in Dunedin, after which he was employed as a Warehouseman for Kempthorne Prosser & Co, a drug and fertilizer manufacturing firm in Dunedin.

On joining the RNZAF as a U/T pilot on 17th August 1941, he was sent to the Initial Training Wing at Levin, thence to

1 EFTS at Taleri for flying training on Tiger Moths, but a reverse of John Mitton, his flying wasn't up to standard and he remustered as a U/T Air Observer on 7th November 1941 and was sent overseas to Canada on 8th January on attachment to the RCAF for observer training with 9 AOS at Saint-Jean-sur-Richelieu, Quebec on 4th February.

A bombing and gunnery course came next with 4 B&GS at Fingal, Ontario on 10th May, then finally 1 CNS at Rivers, Manitoba on 21st June, where he graduated, got his Navigators brevet and was promoted to Sergeant on 4th Aug 1942.

Leaving for England on 21st August, on arrival William reported to No 3 Personnel Recruitment Centre, Bournemouth and was posted 3 SGR at Blackpool, Lancashire on 3rd October, prior to operational training with 7 (C) OTU at Limavady on 1st December 1942. After the accident William was posthumously promoted to Warrant Officer II and interred in Campbeltown (Kilkerran) Cemetery on 3rd March 1943. Division 4. Grave 604.

Wireless Operator & Air Gunner Sergeant Herbert Gordon Brooks, RAFVR, born 19th February 1915 in Liverpool, was the son of Thomas and Helen Mary Brooks (née Robins) of Chesterfield, Derbyshire. Herbert was the youngest of four children.

Bert's father was originally from Staffordshire and his mother Lincolnshire. His parents had married in Burton-Upon-Trent, Staffs in November 1893 and moved to Liverpool shortly after their first child Gertrude was born.

Bert and his brothers William Thomas, Sidney and Stanley Hiram were all born in Liverpool and attended local schools there, but sadly Bert's mother passed away in 1927.

His father Thomas, a potter by trade, was remarried in 1932 to Sarah Hughes of Hasland, Chesterfield, Derbyshire and the family moved here where Bert worked at Barker Lane Potteries in Chesterfield.

Bert joined the RAF in 1940 and arrived at No 3 Recruitment Centre at Padgate on 20th October and having been selected for training as a Wireless Operator, the following day he was sent to 10 Signals Recruitment Centre

Sgt Herbert Gordon Brooks. RAFVR

Photo: Lesley Cooper

at Blackpool, Lancashire, this was a reserve base used for wireless training and Morse code etc, after which he was sent to Yatesbury in Wiltshire on 25th July the following year joined 2 Signals School for theory of wireless telegraphy, electrics and Morse studying both in the classroom and in the air flying in de Haviland Dominie or Percival Proctor aircraft.

Three months later Bert arrived at RAF Snaith, Yorkshire for further experience of using radio in the air. He spent several weeks here and at the Service Wireless School, after which he was promoted to Leading Aircraftman.

Next came a gunners course with 1 AGS at Pembrey, Wales, on 11th July 1942, where he finally graduated and was awarded his Air Gunners brevet and a promotion to Temporary Sergeant.

Bert's last course before operational training was at Prestwick, Ayr, with 3 Radio School on 25th August, flying in Avro Anson and Blackburn Botha aircraft on cross country training flights, ending in September when on the 30th he joined 7 (C) OTU at Limavady, Northern Ireland.

Along with three other members of his crew, Bert was laid to rest with full military honours in Campbeltown (Kilkerran) Cemetery, Kintyre. Division 4. Grave 606.

Wireless Operator & Air Gunner Sergeant James Michael Wilson, RAFVR, was born in 1918. No information has been found on Sgt Wilson,

Grave of Sgt Herbert G Brooks. RAF

Photo: Author's Collection

other than after the accident and following a service, he was cremated at Edinburgh (Warriston Road) Crematorium, but his name is not recorded in the book of remembrance so presumably he was not from Edinburgh?

According to a research group on Kintyre in 2003, the crash site was reported to have been 600 yards north of the east end of Loch Ciaran, but the scene has not been visited by the authors or associates, so it is not known if there are any pieces of the aircraft still remaining, but it does seem likely.

LOW LEVEL HELL - ALBACORE X9165

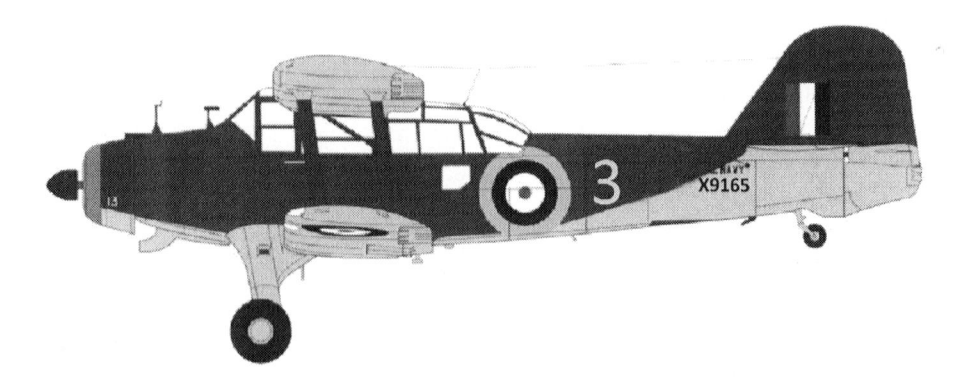

The Fairey Albacore biplane was designed to specification S.41/36 for a three-seat torpedo/spotter/reconnaissance aircraft for the Fleet Air Arm as a replacement for the Fairey Swordfish, though in reality the Swordfish outlived its intended replacement.

The Albacore did offer more advantages for crew comfort, an enclosed cockpit with heating, an automatic dinghy release in the event of a ditching and a variable pitch 3 bladed propeller connected to a Bristol Taurus XII 1130-hp, 14 cylinder radial sleeve valve engine.

It would appear that initially the Albacore suffered from reliability problems with the Taurus engine, but the failure rate was deemed to have been no worse than the Pegasus equipped Swordfish, nevertheless, it remained unpopular with pilots as it was less agile, with controls being too heavy for a pilot to take effective evasive action after releasing an 11,100lb torpedo.

Despite its pitfalls, the aircraft would eventually operate with 15 front line Fleet Air Arm Squadrons and various other training units throughout the war.

Formed at Machrihanish on 15th April 1942, as a Night Attack Light Torpedo Course unit under command of L/Cdr R. Edgar Bibby DSO. RNVR, 766 Squadron was initially equipped with Swordfish but received several Albacore's later that month.

X9165, one of a production batch of 250, was delivered to Worthy Down on 23rd December 1941 after completion by the Fairey Aviation factory in Hayes, Middlesex, under contract B35944/39. In March 1942 the aircraft was taken on charge by 823 Squadron at Lee-on-Solent, serving briefly before transfer to 766 Squadron in July 1942.

On Saturday of 3rd April 1943, X9165 now displaying the unit code number '3' was engaged in a night anti-submarine formation exercise off the north west coast of Kintyre. The crew detailed to carry out the task that evening consisted: Pilot. Temp Sub/Lt Maurice W.H. Squire (A) RNVR, Observer. Temp Sub/Lt Alan H. Campion. (A) RNVR and Telegraphist Air Gunner L/A Denis Callnon RN.

Fairey Albacore

Having formed up with other aircraft the squadron proceeded to the Ballure bombing range to carry out dummy runs on sea targets, however, it was during one of these low level runs that the aircraft hit the water at 55:43N - 05:40W just to the south of Ardpatrick Point.

In the prevailing darkness, the true fate of the crew all listed as missing, would not be known for several hours as a search went underway. Sadly, it was realised that all had perished in the crash and that the Obs. Sub/Lt Campion and TAG L/A Callnon were found washed ashore but it seems likely the pilot went down with the aircraft.

Next of kin were notified of the tragic circumstances on 6th April, and funeral arrangements were made for the interment of the two airmen in Campbeltown (Kilkerran) Cemetery, Kintyre.

Pilot Sub-Lieutenant (A) Maurice William Hilary Squire, RNVR, born in 1918, was the son of Sir John Collings Squire and Lady Harriet Anstruther Squire (née Wilkinson) of Chelsea Gardens, London.

He had two elder brothers Raglan and Jack and a younger sister Julia. Their father Sir John Squire was an accomplished author, writer and poet associated with the old 'Western Daily Mercury' and most notable editor of the 'London Mercury' newspaper.

Maurice was educated at his father's old school, Blundells in Tiverton, Devon, where he was on the school rugby team and also played cricket for the Old Blundellians from 1936-1938.

His main subjects were history and English and he later won a scholarship for Sidney Sussex College, located in the very heart of Cambridge and founded

141

in 1596 by Lady Frances Sidney Sussex, prior to him becoming a Royal Navy cadet at Gosport and later Portsmouth until 29th December 1939.

Having trained initially as a NA1 at Worthy Down, Hampshire, as a Midshipman he eventually won his wings and a promotion to Temporary Sub/Lt on 22nd December 1940.

Maurice was posted to 753 Squadron under command of Lt/Cdr. A.C.Mills. RNVR. The squadron operated mainly Swordfish and Albacore aircraft and had been based at Arbroath since 22nd August 1940.

Having been posted to 766 Squadron at Machrihanish, Maurice regularly flew Albacores on training exercises in preparation for operations.

His brother Jack was in the RAF serving as a pilot on flying boats with Coastal Command. He survived the war and stayed in the service as a reserve until June 1959 when he left having reached the rank of Flight Lieutenant.

In civilian life Jack was known as Anthony Squire and was a well known writer and film director responsible for work on 'The Sound Barrier' (1952) and several TV series for ITC including Robin Hood with Richard Green.

Maurice's brother Raglan was in the Royal Engineers during the war and later became an architect. He also wrote and published a book 'Portrait of an Architect' in 1984.

Their sister Julia was a costume designer for film and theatre, she married actor George Baker (Inspector Wexford) in the 1950s.

Having never been found after the accident Maurice had his name inscribed on the Lee-on-Solent Memorial, Bay 4. Panel 6. He is also remembered on the Sidney Sussex college Roll of Honour.

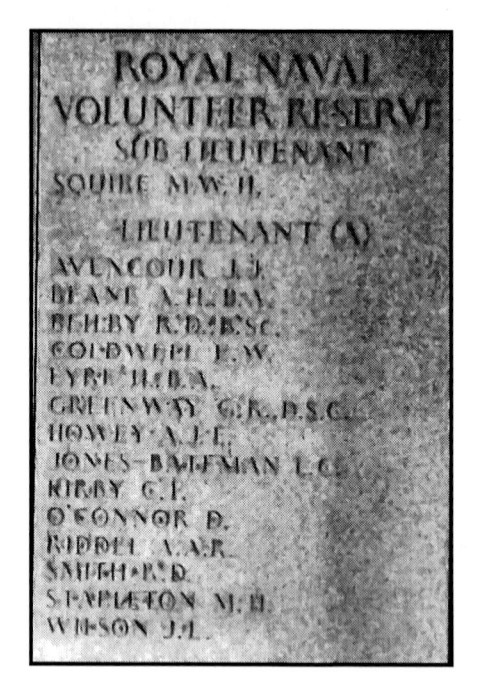

Lt (A) Maurice W.H. Squire. RNVR

Top of Panel 6 of the Lee-on-Solent Memorial to the missing in Surrey.

Photo: CWGC

Observer Sub-Lieutenant (A) Alan Hubert Campion. RNVR, born in 1923 was the son of the Reverend William Ashton Campion. M.A. and Mary Wilhelmina Campion of The Rectory, Skerries, Co.Dublin, Irish Republic.

Glasgow with his grandfather James Callnon, (formally spelt Callanan) in order to seek work in dockyards.

At the time of the accident Denis' mother was living in Ibrox Street, Glasgow, so it is presumed that this was the usual residence of Denis prior to joining the Royal Navy Fleet Air Arm.

At the time of the accident Denis was with 766 Squadron at *Landrail*, but during training he passed his TAG's course 43A in the UK and served aboard the aircraft carrier HMS *Formidable*. He was interred in Campbeltown (Kilkerran) Cemetery. Div.4 Grave.608.

Sub/Lt Campion's grave in Kilkerran

Photo: Author's Collection

Alan was interred in Campbeltown (Kilkerran) Cemetery, with full military honours. Division 4. Grave 609.

Telegraphist Air Gunner Leading Airman Denis Callnon. RN, born in Glasgow on 15th October 1922, was the youngest son of Denis and Jane Callnon of Glasgow. He had one brother James Adair and a sister Catherine Currie Callnon.

Denis was born and educated in Glasgow, but it is understood that the family originated from Cork in Ireland and that his father came over to

L/A Callnon's grave in Kilkerran

Photo: Author's Collection

143

FLAT CALM CHAOS - SWORDFISH DK744

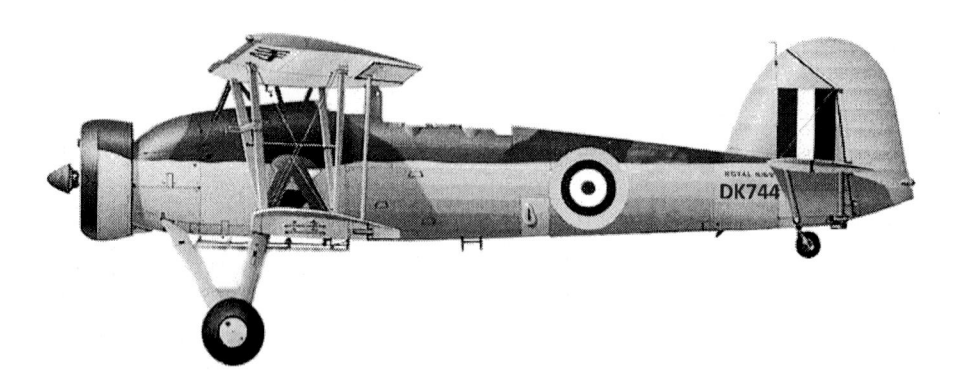

The plan Originally in 1939 was for 766 Squadron at Lee-on-Solent to become a Royal Navy Seaplane School Pool, but further discussion and proposals eventually led to its formation on 15th April 1942, as a Night ALT (Attack Light Torpedo) course for operational training in Swordfish and Albacore aircraft which would now be based at Machrihanish.

All the naval airmen, Pilots, Observers and Telegraphist Air Gunners, were fresh in from various training units and it would be here they would form into individual crews. Most of the Pilots and Observers were commissioned officers, but with the odd young Midshipman thrown in at the deep end.

As the war progressed most of the latter had trained overseas, either in Canada or the USA, so Machrihanish with its very inclement weather, narrow muddy roads and leaky Nissen huts for accommodation, must have been quite a culture shock for these young naval aviators.

Arriving on the 27th April was Sub/Lt (A) John Henry Reeves, RNZNVR, a twenty year old New Zealand pilot from Haumoana, Hawkes Bay, NZ. He been in the navy since September 1941 and flown Albacores and Swordfish from squadrons at Arbroath and Crail.

Joining him as a crew were a 22 year old Observer Sub/Lt (A) Ronald S. Hamlet, RNVR, from Overton Bridge, Flintshire and Telegraphist Air Gunner Leading Airman Peter Pritchard RN, aged 21 from Altringham, Cheshire.

Exercises at the base usually consisted of formation flying practice, night and day navigation flights, dive bombing, torpedo bombing, and anti-sub warfare tactics, and though the majority of flights were carried out successfully, there were times when things just went horribly wrong.

One such occasion involved Sub/Lt Reeves and crew on the night of Saturday 1st May 1943. The crew had been briefed, along with another Swordfish crew, to carry out an attack on a mock

Fairey Swordfish loaded with a torpedo

enemy submarine target at Skipness bombing range in Kilbranan Sound off the North East coast of Kintyre.

The target was a floating conning tower made of wood, representing a German U-boat and the plan would been to have one of the aircraft drop a flare, which in turn would allow the other Swordfish to bomb the silhouetted target.

Sub/Lt Reeves and crew in Swordfish DK744, had been detailed to carry out the low level attack, while the other aircraft dropped the flare from a higher altitude.

It was a relatively calm night, which is all very well for sailing vessels, but for such an exercise it can be treacherous as the calm sea makes it very difficult for the pilot to judge his height, which proved to be the case on this occasion, for as Sub/Lt Reeves made his approach in the twilight sky, at 23:50 he hit the sea with such force that the machine tore almost in half, and it is believed the pilot was killed instantly but the two crew may have survived the initial impact and been knocked unconscious.

An ASR launch was quickly dispatched, but whilst rushing to the scene, the crew of second aircraft thought they could help by dropping a flare to light up the area, but sadly the parachute on the flare caught fire and it dropped into the ocean, now awash with fuel from a ruptured tank of the crashed aircraft, it immediately caught fire and the ASR had to stay back until the flames died down.

Tragically, by the time the launch reached what was left of the machine, it was too late and all they could do was recover the bodies for burial, save for the pilot who was trapped in the cockpit and went down with his aircraft.

Sub/Lt (A) John H. Reeves. RNZNVR

Photo: *NZ Weekly News*

Pilot Sub-Lieutenant (A) John Henry Reeves, RNZNVR, born in Napier, NZ on 22nd August 1922, was the son of George Frederick and Elizabeth Wilkins Reeves (née Kaye) of Haumona, Hawkes Bay, New Zealand.

John was educated at Hastings Boys High School, Hawkes Bay and on leaving became a Mercer`s Assistant for the gents outfitters H.W. Blackmore, Established 1924 in Hastings and Hawkes Bay, until he joined the 1st Battalion of the Hawkes Bay Regiment of the NZ Army Territorial Force on 22nd April 1940.

On 2nd September 1941 John joined the NZNF (Later re-designated RNZN 1/10/41) at Auckland (*Philome*) and on 5th September, he embarked for the UK on attachment to Gosport (*St.Vincent*) as U/T aircrew, arriving in England on 17th October.

Posted first to Puckpool Camp (*Medina*) at Ryde on the Isle of Wight, then RNAS Lee-on-Solent for basic training, John was then attached to 14 EFTS at Elmdon, Birmingham, with the RAF, where as an under training pilot, he flew Tiger Moths and the like from 5th April until early June 1942.

Returning to *Daedalus* on 12th June, the following day he embarked for advanced training in Canada, with 31 SFTS at Kingston, Ontario, where on completion he was awarded his pilot`s wings and a commission to Temp Acting Sub-Lieutenant on 23rd October.

On returning to the UK and following a few weeks at Naval Air Torpedo School, John was attached to 9 (P) AFU at RAF Hullavington, Wiltshire, on 21st December, where he would familiarize himself with the Fairey Swordfish and Albacore prior to joining a squadron.

A posting to Scotland came next and he arrived at Crail, Fife, on 5th February 1943 to join 785 Squadron flying Swordfish Is, then six weeks later 769 Squadron at Arbroath, for Deck Landing Trials with HMS *Argus*.

Finally, just four days prior to the accident, John joined 766 Squadron at Machrihanish. He is commemorated on the Devonport Naval Memorial. NZ.

TAG L/A Peter Pritchard (Centre) in Canada on TAGs Course 47A at Yarmouth in March 1943. Pictured front row 2nd left is Alec Boar who was killed in a Miles Martinet on Rousay, Orkney in May 1944

Photo: TAGs Assn Via Ken Sims

Observer Sub-Lieutenant (A) Ronald Standring Hamlet, RNVR, born 20th April 1921, was the son of Jesse and Eliza Ellen Hamlet (née Lester) of Overton Bridge, Flintshire.

The family lived at Rose Hill Lodge on the banks of the River Dee, where Ron's father was a gardener and also a Police Constable during the war.

After leaving school Ron became a Drawing Office Junior in Wrexham but left to join the RN. He conducted part of his basic training at RNAS Eastleigh (*Raven*) in Southampton, before graduating as an Observer in Canada. He is buried in Erbistock (St.Hilary) Churchyard Ext. NW Part. Row 1.

Telegraphist Air Gunner Leading Airman Peter Pritchard, RN, born 1921, was the only son of Peter and Lilian Pritchard of Timperley, Altringham, Cheshire.

Peter's father was born in Sheffield and his mother was from Stocksbridge, the couple had been married in Sheffield on 28th June 1919, and they later moved to Timperley where his father was employed as a universal miller for a local engineering firm.

Having joined the RN in 1942, Peter conducted his basic training in the UK before going overseas to Canada to train as a TAG. Following the accident he was interred in Sale Cemetery with a full guard of honour. Sec. A.E. Grave 95.

LOST AT SEA - BARRACUDA P9748

Designed to meet the requirements of the Air Ministry specification S.24/37, calling for a single engine monoplane type with the combined duties of a dive bomber, reconnaissance aircraft and torpedo bomber, the Fairey Barracuda would go into production and begin operating primarily from aircraft carriers from Jan 1943, gradually replacing the Fairey Albacore biplane with Royal Navy Fleet Air Arm squadrons.

One such aircraft, Barracuda P9748 had been constructed by the Fairey Aviation Company Limited at their Heaton Chapel works in Stockport, Cheshire.

This Mk. II built from a production batch of 250, was a high wing monoplane design fitted with a V-12 Rolls Royce 1640-hp Merlin 32 engine and four bladed airscrew, was delivered to the storage section at RNAS Worthy Down near Winchester on 6th April 1943, but soon transferred to 810 Squadron at Lee-on-Solent, Gosport, Hampshire prior to joining a carrier.

Here it received the code letter 'H' and became one of 12 Barracudas to join the squadron, which would be a Torpedo Bombing Unit under command of Lt/Cdr. (A) A.J.B. Forde. DSC.RN.

HMS Illustrious (87)

Between March and the end of May, the squadron carrier was being refitted with new radar equipment and two additional arrestor wires, so all aircraft disembarked for the shore station on Kintyre.

Arriving at RNAS Machrihanish on 21st May 1943, the squadron began working up for operations off Norway with the 23,000 long ton carrier HMS *Illustrious (87)*.

On Friday 25th P9748 was airborne with 24 year old Sub/Lt (A) Michael Longford Beresford-Jones. RNVR, having been briefed to undertake a dive bombing practice exercise over the range off Crossaig on the east coast of Kintyre.

Normally the type would accommodate a crew of three, but on this occasion the young Sub-Lieutenant would be on his own. Soon after arriving over the target area his aircraft was observed to go into a steep uncontrollable spin and with the pilot unable to effect a recovery, it crashed into the sea and broke up leaving debris and fuel littering the surface.

A sea search was immediately initiated, but sadly there was no sign of the poor pilot and it is believed he died instantly and went down with his aircraft.

Sub/Lt Beresford-Jones was quite an experienced pilot with a good safety record. Early in the war he flew Swordfish from both shore based stations and aircraft carriers, so it is still unclear what went wrong that day. The Barracuda was a beast of an aircraft and pilot's either loved it or loathed it. There are several reports of hydraulics leaking and of some pilots

149

as a result, became asphyxiated by the fumes. Could this have been the case here? A question that after such a passing of time will doubtless ever be answered.

Sub-Lieutenant (A) Michael Longford Beresford-Jones, RNVR, born in the Cathedral City of Canterbury in 1919, was the son of Arthur and Evelyn Beresford-Jones and husband of Elizabeth Purefoy Beresford-Jones. He had one younger sister Susan.

Michael's father Arthur was a Doctor and ran a practice before the first war along with Dr. Richard Davies of Cheltenham. He married Miss Evelyn Freeman in May 1917 and finished the war as a Captain having served in the Royal Army Medical Corps. After the war he became an orthopedic surgeon for Kent and Canterbury hospital.

Michael attended primary school in Canterbury but in 1933 enrolled at Eastbourne College, East Sussex, founded by the Duke of Devonshire in 1867. As a boarder here it is understood that he joined the Combined Cadet Force, run by the college in preparation for future induction into military service, be it Army, Navy or Air Force.

The College said of him:

"Michael Beresford-Jones entered the School House in January 1933 and left in December 1936, having been a House Prefect in his last term. He will be remembered as an alert and friendly person, always busy and active about all kinds of pursuits".

In the RN List of 1941, Michael is noted as a Temporary Sub-Lieutenant on Probation and on the 12th December,

Dick Stark of Nottingham, a former TAG and Leading Airman at that time, noted in his logbook that he flew with Michael in a Swordfish coded 'A' based at a TAGs training School at St.Merryn, Cornwall.

The pair took off at 11am to practice stern defences with RN battleships and in his log Dick mentions that he fired off 200 rounds of ammunition, on a flight that lasted 65 mins. Michael was with 774 Squadron at that time.

Michael has no known grave and is commemorated on the Lee-on-Solent Memorial to the missing. Bay 4. Panel 6. His unit on the CWGC website is given as HMS *Blackcap* a shore station Stretton near Warrington, but at the time of his death he was serving at Machrihanish (*Landrail*).

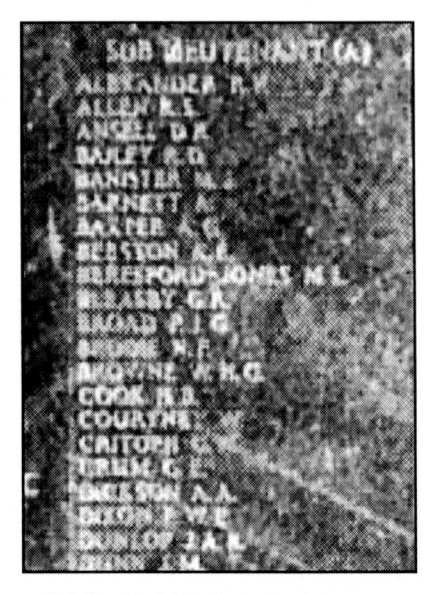

Sub/Lt (A) M.L. Beresford-Jones on the Lee-on-Solent Memorial panel

CLOSE CALL - HUDSON FK780

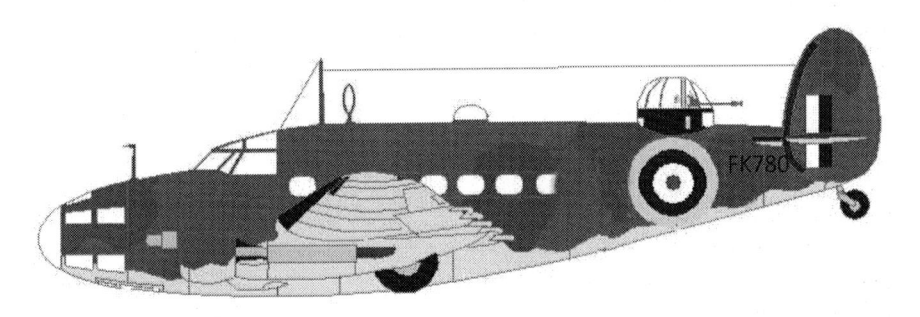

Shaken, yet still in one piece, the young Norwegian flyer and his three companions, must have been wondering how they had survived as they began to extricate themselves from the battered remains of a once proud aeroplane, now lying in a crumpled heap on a hillside in Scotland.

Once again, Sgt Nodeland had cheated death. For two years previous he and five others had escaped from Nazi occupied Norway in an open motor boat the M/B *Cathinka II* and braved the harsh elements of the North Sea to reach Great Britain, leaving Kristiansand on 16th August 1941 and arriving three days later in Scotland.

To recap on events leading up to the bomber's demise on the hill. It began with a brand new Lockheed Hudson twin engine bomber, serial number FK780 built under Lend–Lease contract as a Mk IIIA in a production batch of 80, that was to be delivered from the factory

Lockheed Hudson

in the United States, via Canada and the North Atlantic ferry route, to Prestwick in Scotland.

Elected to ferry this aircraft on 9th June 1943 was Sgt Thorleif Nodeland, now an experienced pilot having trained at Little Norway, Canada in 1942 under the British Commonwealth Air Training Plan.

On 10th June, having successfully made it to Reykjavik, Iceland, the Hudson had refuelled and set off for Prestwick, but due to poor weather conditions the aircraft diverted to RAF Limavady in Londonderry, Northern Ireland. Once the weather had cleared, at 08:45 the Hudson took off again and flew eastward, but just 40 minutes later, having run into sea fog, Sgt Nodeland became disorientated and despite a request from his Radio Operator Sgt Moe to change the radio frequency in order to get a fix, he began to climb in hope of reaching clearer air. It was at this point that the aircraft struck a hill nose up, just to the north of Machrihanish. Fortunately there was no fire.

Leaving their wrecked bomber behind, the four crew: Pilot Sgt Nodeland, 2nd Pilot Sgt Eric Swanston, Navigator Sgt Einar Pederson and Radio Operator Sgt Sven Moe, having suffered only abrasions made their way down the hill.

The precise location of the Hudson has so far not been located, but local sources are of the opinion it crashed

General cockpit layout of the Lockheed Hudson

to the east of Putechan Lodge, near the top of a hill in a now densely forested area. It has been said that because of the soft boggy ground the Hudson was not fully recovered by the RAF salvage team and that much of it sank in the marshy ground.

It was also recalled that the RAF arrived on Kintyre in 1978 to recover some aircraft remains here, but after a strenuous effort they failed to do so.

1st Pilot Thorleif Nodeland, RNAF, was born in 1920. He was the son of Tobias Oskar Endresen Nodeland and Elisabeth Hansdatter Nodeland. He had three sisters Helga, Thora and Esther.

The family lived in Kristiansand, Vest-Agder, a city in southern Norway. The old town of Posebyen, features traditional wooden houses and in the centre a neo-Gothic Kristiansand Cathedral, with the Sørlandets Museum nearby.

Sgt Thorleif Nodeland pictured here boarding a T-6 North American Harvard during training at Little Norway, Canada. Photo: Canadian Archives.

Thorleif as you will recall left Kristiansand in August 1941 for Scotland but encountered bad weather. Those who made this perilous voyage with him were Olaf Berge, Birger Fjellstad, Reidar Keim, Edvard Tallaksen, and Trygve Åsland.

The men had purchased an old pilot vessel for the journey, but when the Germans appeared to have become suspicious, this vessel was loaned to some young boys who went on vacation in the east, while her original intended passengers switched to another boat, the *Cathinka II*.

At the time of the accident Thorleif had logged a total of 325 flying hours with 140 on the Hudson, so he was a fairly experienced pilot.

On 1st November 1944 he joined 333 (Norwegian) squadron and his rank was 2nd Lieutenant. The squadron flew as part of a Strike Wing based at Banff, Aberdeenshire, with Mosquito VI`s for anti-shipping patrols off Norway.

Until January 1945, Thorleif flew mainly training flights, air to air firing and local navigation exercises, but on 12th January forming part of `B` Flight, Thorleif and his Navigator 2/Lt Øiulf Bjørnøe, took off in Mosquito VI `Q` at 07:45 for a armed recon` flight off the Norwegian coast in areas of Lindesnes and Marstein.

They made landfall at Lindesnes at 09:18 and flew NW along the coast. At 09:23 in Farsund harbour they spotted a MV of 4,000 tons heavily laden and stationary lying NW-SE of the bridge, and at 09:26 at Flekkefjord another MV of 2,000 tons was lying west of quay 8 where they experienced moderate accurate light flak.

At 09:30 in position 58.15N – 06.22E on a heading of 330 deg at 2,000 feet, they sighted a Ju.52, and turning to port they commenced an attack by spanning fire with very short bursts at 600 yards.

They then closed in and fired at 300 yards and again at 100 yards with 3 sec bursts with cannon, with strikes on fuselage, starboard engine and a fuel tank catching fire, the e/a then went into a diving turn, hit the sea, broke up and burned fiercely with no survivors.

The Ju.52 was confirmed as 7U+FL Wr.0006756 of Transportstaffel 3./TGr 20 from Sola N3 airfield flown by Oberfelwebel Kurt Näth with 3 crew which is reported by German sources to have crashed of the Lista Peninsula, Norway.

Thorleif and Bjørnøe continued with the reconnaissance patrol without further incident and returned to base at 11:10.

Promoted to Lieutenant on the 15th February 1945, Thorleif continued to fly with 333 Squadron, mainly operating as an outrider for the strike aircraft and recce missions, though he did manage to bomb a railway bridge, attack several navigation installations and a couple of MV`s before the war was over.

Thorleif passed away in 1964 and was buried in Kristiansand Cemetery, Norway, Square 02. Row 00E. Grave 032.

2nd Pilot Sergeant Eric Hanway Swanston, RAF, born 1922 in Chertsey, Surrey, was the son of Henry Eric and Dorothy Marion Swanston (née Cooper) of Watford, Hertfordshire. Eric had an older sister Rosalind Dorothy M and a younger brother Miles A.

Eric was flying as 2nd pilot in a B-25 Mitchell FV990 on a transatlantic ferry flight to Reykjavik, Iceland on 28th November 1943, when the aircraft went missing over the ocean soon after leaving BW1 Greenland. No trace of the crew or aircraft were ever found.

The other crew members were: Pilot 2/Lt Erik Bertil Palm, RNAF, Nav F/Lt Harold Alexander Wills RCAF and R/Op P/O Gerald Raymond Styles RCAF. All are remembered with honour on the Ottawa Memorial, Ontario, Canada.

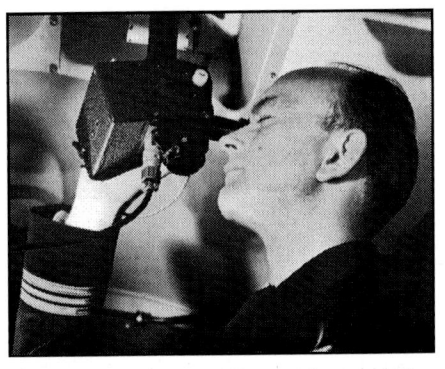

Navigator Einar Sverre Pedersen with astro navigation equipment with SAS

Navigator Einar Sverre Pedersen was born on 29th January 1919 in Trondheim, Norway, he was the son of architect Prof. Sverre and Edith Gretchen Pedersen (née Børseth) of Trondheim, Norway.

As a child Einar became interested in polar exploration and the Arctic. He was greatly influenced by the Norwegian Arctic explorer Roald Amundsen, and chose to educate himself greatly on the Arctic, meteorology, geography and navigation.

When the Germans invaded Norway in April 1940, Einar was a student at the Naval Air School, Horten, located on a peninsula along the Oslofjord in the county of Vestfold. He made his way through northern Norway and sailed aboard the Shetland Bus to Scotland, then eventually on to the Little Norway camp in Toronto, Canada five months later where he trained as a navigator.

During the war he flew as a navigator on the Catalina and Sunderland on anti-submarine patrols with 330 (Norwegian) squadron based at Sullom Voe, Shetland.

A Second Lieutenant by 1944, he was often crewed with Lt C. Johnson and Co-Pilot Qm. O. Lorentzen and crew flying Sunderland IIIs off the Norwegian coast. Flights were tedious, often 12-14 hours with very little but fishing boats, allied aircraft and vessels being sighted. A few of the aircraft Einar regularly flew in were: ML780, ML818 and NJ177.

After the war he returned to Norway and in 1946 he became a navigator on Transatlantic routes for Scandinavian Air Systems airline, and the following year set up a navigation course for his navigator colleagues to prepare them for flights over the Arctic when they became applicable.

This was a great navigation challenge in that, when operating in the polar region the magnetic North Pole makes an ordinary compass useless. Traditional observations are difficult when neither the sun nor the stars are visible in the Arctic "twilight" around spring and autumn equinox. This means that ordinary maps and compasses can't be used.

In the years 1953-75, Einar was the chief navigator of SAS's polar routes and an obvious choice for the historic flights by SAS on the world's first polar route Copenhagen to Los Angeles on 15th November 1954, and Copenhagen to Tokyo on 24th February 1957.

On 13th October 1967 when Einar and two Norwegian aviation enthusiasts, pilot Thor Tjontveit and Co-Pilot Rolf Storhavg were flying from Alaska to Scandinavia, one of the engines of their Piper Apache cut out over the Blow River in the Yukon territory of Canada, and they had to force land.

The radio equipment was broken and Einar had broke his right arm in three places. The three distressed aviators had to practice Arctic survival for 9 days before they were eventually spotted by a Wein Air Alaska F-27 Search aircraft from Anchorage and rescued by helicopter.

The wrecked Apache in October 1967

Photo: Daily News-Miner Paul Noden

Einar and his companions praised the hospitality of the hospital staff and were quite taken by the friendliness of the Alaskan people. In 1979 he and his wife settled in Anchorage and he continued with his exploration of the Arctic from the air, including Systematic observation of the sea ice.

During the early 1990s he became a consultant for Northern Forum, an international co-operation body which works to lay the foundations for air routes around the North Calotte region. In May 1994 he became honorary leader of the world's first commercial flight around the Arctic Ocean, made by using a chartered Boeing 727 in which the 80 paying passengers aboard landed at 13 different locations.

That same year the University of Alaska at Fairbanks, made him a honorary doctorate for his work on polar aviation, navigation and for his contribution to climate research in the northern hemisphere.

Einar went on to write numerous articles and books about the Arctic before passing away on 26th January 2008 in Anchorage, Alaska.

Radio Operator Sergeant Sven Brun Moe, RNAF, born in 1921, was the son of Johan Mangelson Brun Moe and Gudrun Brun Moe (née Juell) of Kristiansand, Norway. Sven had four siblings: Karen, Dorothea, Juell and Meyer.

Like the others Sven made his way to Canada to train as a Radio Operator in Little Norway, Toronto, and after qualifying became a R/Op for BOAC flying the Sweden to Scotland route transporting passengers between Bromma Airport in Stockholm to Leuchars. Between 1941 and 1945 the department transported more than 1,500 passengers, but lost eleven crews and eighteen passengers in accidents.

Regrettably Sven, his pilot Capt. Alf Kristian Hiorth and 1st Officer Lars Larsen Bergo, were one of the eleven crews that were lost.

They were aboard Lockheed Lodestar G-AGIH which had taken off from Bromma at 20:01 on 28th August 1944 with 12 passengers bound for Leuchars. The aircraft suffered radio problems and intended to return to Bromma, but having flown into bad weather the crew requested an alternative airport and were directed to either Såtenäs or Torslanda at Gothenburg, Sweden.

It is believed the pilot chose Såtenäs and was descending below cloud when at 00:30 on the 29th, the aircraft struck Kinnekulle, a ridge which at its highest point is 306m asl, and in fact the only high ground in the province of Västergötland,

The aircraft was totally destroyed and only four on board survived, but sadly Sven was not one of them.

Sven was buried in Minnesmerker Cemetery, Oslo, Norway, but he is also commemorated on the war memorial at Akershus festning, along with his crew and other Norwegian flyers the memorial bears the epitaph:

`The air is inviolably clean over the kingdom of the dead. It's like splitting a friendship if we wanted to mention one`.

Lockheed Lodestar replica of G-AGIH in BOAC colours, Armed Forces Museum, Gardermoen, Gardermoen, Oslo, Norway. Photo: Paaln—under CC Licence

INTO THE FOG - BEAUFIGHTER LZ156

Formed on 31st December 1942 as part of 15 Group RAF Coastal Command, 304 Ferry Training Unit based at Port Ellen, Islay in the Western Isles, as the name implies, flew various types of aircraft for the purpose of familiarizing crews in preparation for ferrying aircraft on long haul flights to various overseas bases.

The course normally took two weeks, flying various navigation exercises with fuel consumption and handling tests, though due to poor weather aircraft were sometimes grounded and the course would last longer.

Among the aircraft based at Port Ellen in the summer of 1943, were several Bristol Beaufort and Beaufighter Mk TF-X `s, the latter, a two-seat torpedo bomber was powered by two Bristol Hercules 14-cyl 1600-hp radial engines, boasting a top speed of 320 mph at 10,000 feet.

On Saturday 28th August 1943, Pilot F/O Ronald Arthur Thomas Buchman RAFVR and his Navigator P/O Thomas Norman Stockdale RAF, had been briefed to fly a night navigation exercise off the west coast of Scotland.

Having taken off at 19:17 in LZ156, the aircraft was returning to base a little over an hour later when it strayed off track in bad weather, and unbeknown to the crew was heading directly for the high ground obscured by sea fog, near the Mull of Kintyre.

At approximately 20:27, a large explosion rang out as the aircraft impacted with the hill and burst into flames killing the two crew instantly. Wreckage was scattered over a quarter of a mile and one of the engines buried itself deep in the marshy ground.

When the Beaufighter became overdue at Port Ellen, a widespread search was initiated by other aircraft from the base along with RAF Search and Rescue vessels. The wreckage was eventually located and the two unfortunate crew were recovered for interment in their hometowns.

The Beaufighter had crashed in a very remote spot and on rough moorland between Borgadelmore Point and Rubha Clachan, a location in the far south lying roughly 14 miles from Campbeltown by vehicle.

A Bristol Beaufighter TF-X LZ293 seen here with 236 Sqn

The location proved a very difficult job for the RAF salvage team detailed to carry out the recovery operation, who were plagued with bad weather.

Based at Carluke in Lanarkshire, the men of 63 Maintenance Unit that were assigned the task, hastily made their way to the crash site and a report on what they experienced was later described in the station log:

"Several difficult jobs have been encountered during the month. Outstanding amongst these was a Beaufighter which had crashed 2 miles from the nearest road, and the route between road and crash was made over a series of very steep ravines, which was impassable to either tractor or horse. The aircraft had to be dismantled and cut into small pieces to enable the party to manhandle it to the nearest road.

One engine and propeller was buried four to five feet and had to be dug out.

Three airmen in the party were laid up in a billet for 3 days with severe colds and strains, owing to harsh weather and strenuous working conditions. NCO i/c party states that this job was the most exacting and strenuous he had encountered in his two years on salvage work, and one that taxed the limits of human endurance. It took 25 days to complete the job".

The crash site is in a very isolated place, it lies on rough swampy ground, still often windswept by the North Atlantic gales. Very little of the aircraft can be seen, save for small pieces of melted aluminium, rusty nuts and bolts, badly corroded and hazardous ammunition. A crumpled oil tank and one of the carburettors also remains but both are in a poor corrosive state.

The crash site of LZ156 in 2017 Photo: Author's Collection

Above: Fuel shut off tap valve.

Photo: Dave Ramsey

Above: One of the carburettors

Photo: Gary Nelson

Pilot Flying Officer Ronald Arthur Buckman, RAFVR, born in Midhurst, Sussex in 1918, was the son of William and Edith Kate Buckman (née Terry) of Midhurst, Sussex. He had one older brother Victor William.

Ronald's parents had been married in Midhurst in the summer of 1911 and he and his brother Victor, three years his senior, attended local schools there.

He had joined the RAF in 1940 and worked his way through the ranks, he was a F/Sgt when he applied for a commission and became P/O on probation on 27th July 1942, thence F/O on probation on 27th January 1943.

Ronald was a very experienced pilot who at the time of the accident had amassed 1,050 flying hours on various aircraft types. He had however, only logged 25 hours on the Beaufighter with just 46 hours at night in total, though the latter would not be an issue as double British summer time meant it would be light until late.

After the accident, at the request of his family a private service was held in St.Mary Magdelane church, followed by interment in a family plot in the churchyard at West Lavington.,Sussex.

Wireless Operator & Air Gunner Pilot Officer Thomas Norman Stockdale, RAF, born 1922, was the son of Thomas and Hanna Stockdale of Bangor, Northern Ireland.

Thomas, who joined the RAF in 1942 reached F/Sgt and had flown 112 sorties before applying for a commission and was promoted to Pilot Officer on 28th May 1943.

Thomas was accorded a full military funeral on Saturday 4th September 1943 at Dundonald Cemetery, with a service conducted by Reverend J.R.W. Roddie. B.A. before interment in a family grave with his grandparent's John and Mary Scott. His cousin, SQMS Alexander Scott Brown, North Irish Horse also died, and he is commemorated on this memorial.

Also buried in this grave is army gunner John Thompson, from the same address as Stockdale's parents, though it is not known what the connection with the Stockdale family was.

P/O Thomas Stockdale's grave

Photo: Author's Collection

161

MID-AIR MISHAP SEA HURRICANES NF867 & NF701

In August 1942, Fleet Air Arm 813 and 824 Squadrons were serving aboard the aircraft carrier HMS *Eagle* as part of the escorting force during Operation *Pedestal*, this was the delivery of essential supplies to the Mediterranean island of Malta, but at 13:15 hours on Tuesday 11th the ship was hit by four torpedoes launched by Kapitänleutnant Helmut Rosen of U-73 a type VIIB U-boat, she sank within four minutes.

With the demise of *Eagle* there was no longer a requirement for two swordfish squadrons, therefore 824 was absorbed by 813 and the "new" 824 was reformed at Lee-on-Solent the same month with six Swordfish, and later they also received six Mk. IIc Sea Hurricanes.

Two of these Hurricanes NF687 and NF701 were built by Hawker Aircraft Ltd for the Admiralty under Contract Acft/2719 at their satellite airfield situated at Parlaunt Farm, near Langley Buckinghamshire

NF687 was shipped to the Aircraft Repair Section at RNAS Hatston (*Sparrowhawk*) up in Orkney during December 1942 and after testing was passed suitable or operations on 14th January 1943 and then transferred to 800 Fleet Air Arm squadron, Naval Air Station *Landrail*, serving here from March to July 1943.

The Hurricane was later transferred across the airfield to 824 Squadron, this new unit having moved to Machrihanish on 18th August 1943 from RNAS Donibristle. Fife. NF701 was taken on charge by the Storage Section of RNAS Yeovilton and flight tested on 13th and 14th May 1943 prior to joining the Squadron.

On the morning of Wednesday 1st September 1943 Sub/Lt Russell Byres Adams of the RNZNVR and Sub/Lt J.W. Hayes RNVR, were briefed to undertake mock dogfighting practice north of the airfield when at 12:00 noon

Sea Hurricane being fuelled up

at a height of 12,000 feet, the two aircraft collided with devastating results. Sub/Lt Adam's Hurricane NF687 immediately burst into flames, went out of control crashed into the sea off Bellochantuy, a small coastal hamlet around ten miles north of Machrihanish.

More fortunate, Sub/Lt Hayes was able to fly his damaged aircraft, NF701 back to Machrihanish, land safely and exit the cockpit just as clouds of smoke began to pour from the machine, a fierce fire erupted and eventually engulfed the aircraft and despite a strenuous effort by airfields emergency services, the Hurricane was completely destroyed. An air and sea search for Sub/Lt Adams was immediately put into effect, but sadly no trace of him or his aircraft was ever found and he was listed as missing, presumed killed.

NF867 Pilot Sub-Lieutenant (A) Russell Byres Adams, RNZNVR, born 24th July 1922, was the son of Jubilee Arthur and Hepzibeth Adams (née Byers) of New Brighton, Christchurch, New Zealand. He had three brothers Desmond, Maurice and Ngair.

New Brighton, where Russell was raised is a suburb of Christchurch which lies on the coast around 8 miles east of the city centre and is sparsely populated. Russell attended Christchurch District High School before leaving for employment as a storeman at the Para-Rubber Company.

Russell joined the Navy in summer of 1941 he embarked for the UK on 2nd September and arrived on the 17th to join other cadets as U/T aircrew at Gosport (*St.Vincent*), then on to Puckpool Camp (*Medina*) an overflow camp and shore station accommodation for the FAA on the Isle of Wight.

163

Sub/Lt (A) Russell Adams, RNZNVR

Photo: NZ Weekly News

On 5th April Russell was posted to Lee-on-Solent on attachment to 14 EFTS run by the RAF, here he would fly Tiger Moths and be assessed as a pilot prior to going overseas to Canada.

Embarking for Canada in June, on arrival he was sent to 31 SFTS at Kingston, Ontario, where he would fly the more powerful Harvard, qualify as a pilot and gain his wings and commission to a Sub/Lt on 23rd October 1942.

On arrival back in the UK in November Russell was posted to 9 (P) AFU at Lee-on-Solent, then on to Yeovilton for a three month fighter course prior to joining 771 Squadron on 11th May 43.

Transferring to 824 Squadron to fly Hurricanes, he eventually arrived at Machrihanish, where sadly he lost his life in the collision on 1st September.

Russell is commemorated on the New Zealand Naval Memorial, Panel 8, located at North Shore, Devonport, Auckland, New Zealand.

With regards to NF701 Pilot Sub-Lieutenant J.W. Hayes, RNVR. No personal details were found on this pilot but we do know he attended a fighter course at RNAS Henstridge (*Dipper*) near Shaftsbury, Dorset, on 15th September 1942, and a year later was with 824 Squadron flying Sea Hurricanes.

In August 1943 Sub/Lt Hayes was one of six Sea Hurricane pilots to join HMS *Striker* for convoy escort duties covering the North Atlantic and Gibraltar routes and on one occasion he managed to encounter the enemy.

On 9th January 1944, at approx. 13:00, Sub/Lt Hayes in Sea Hurricane NF670 'Q' was providing cover for inbound SL 144 when he spotted a large 4-engine Ju-290 shadowing the convoy, however, just as he was planning his attack, his aircraft started to vibrate badly as a detached fuselage panel had come loose, so he was forced to return to the ship.

Continuing to serve with 824 Squadron, in May his ship was involved in Operation *Potluck* which involved strikes against enemy shipping off the Norwegian coast, returning to join the Home Fleet at Scapa Flow on the 15th May, when aircraft were flown ashore

An array of Seafires on HMS Indefatigable in 1945

to Hatston and Grimsetter, here the squadron busied itself with flying training and anti-submarine sweeps, during which, on June 2nd Sub/Lt Hayes was involved in a minor prang when Sea Hurricane JS222 'Q' bounced on landing and drifted into the barrier.

By November 1944 he was serving with 887 Squadron and now flying the Seafire F.III from HMS *Indefatigable* (R10) as part of the British Pacific Fleet, he continued here until February 1945.

During the Operation *Meridian II* attacks against the Japanese on 29th January 1945, Sub/Lt Hayes in Seafire NN210 of 887 squadron shared the shooting down of a Japanese Mitsubishi Ki21 (Sally) but unfortunately his own engine was hit by return fire and he was forced to ditch. He was picked up by the destroyer HMS *Undine* (R42) after spending 1½ hrs in the sea in a punctured Mae West.

Another posting came in March, when on the 15th, and by now the rank of full Lieutenant, Hayes switched to flying Avengers with 849 Squadron from HMS *Victorious* and was involved in a series of strikes on shore targets in the Sakishima Islands in the East China Seas and Formosa.

The ship sailed for Australia at the end of May and though the war in Europe had ended, for Lt Hayes it would continue for a further three months as the squadron carried out raids on the Japanese mainland until VJ Day.

Eventually returning home Lt Hayes decided to remain in the Royal Navy and served at various shore stations.

On 14th July 1957 he was awarded the Volunteer Reserve Decoration and transferred to a Specialist Branch of the navy where he was promoted to Temp Lt/Cdr thence Lt/Cdr. with seniority on 16th August 1963.

A GRIM DISCOVERY - ANSON EF820

Formed at RAF Penrhos, Gwynedd on 1st May 1942, 9 (Observers) Advanced Flying Unit operated in the 25 Group arena with a vast array of aircraft types including: The Bristol Blenheim Mk 1 & IV, Boulton Paul Defiant, Armstrong Whitworth Whitley, Miles Martinet, Tiger Moth and Lysander, but perhaps most commonly used here in late 1943, was the Avro Anson Mk 1 twin-engine trainer used for cross-country navigation exercises with new aircrew.

The Anson usually carried a crew of four or five, the latter being the case on the morning of Sunday 10th October 1943, when EF820 took off with nine aircraft at intervals, to fly a Navex to Scotland and back with one U/T navigator and one U/T wireless operator on board.

The aircraft, operating from the satellite base at Llandwrog, near Caernarfon, North Wales, had taken off at 08:12 with a crew that consisted: Pilot P/O Richard Blewett, RAF, 1st Navigator F/Lt Dennis H. Brewer, RAF, Pupil Nav. Sgt George C. McKenzie, RCAF, Staff W/Op Sgt Kenneth Ellis and Pupil W/Op Sgt Peter Jackson.

Their task that day was to fly north to Cara Isle just south of Gigha, with Sanda Island south of Kintyre as an alternative turning point if weather turned poor, they would then fly a SE heading for Pladda Island off the south coast of the Isle of Arran, before returning to base.

Weather conditions reported at the time were cloudy at 1600ft with 5/10 lowering to 600ft in precipitation. Visibility was estimated as 6-10 miles down to 2-4 miles in drizzle with a southerly wind of 10-15 mph at base.

At the pre-flight briefing the crew were reminded, as per Air Staff Signals Instructions, that `messages to base are to be sent at intervals of not less than 30 minutes`. The Anson`s last message by W/T was at 08:51 and a QDM (Magnetic bearing) was obtained from base at 08:57 which showed the aircraft to be on track just to the NW of the Isle of Man. However, weather had deteriorated and the wind speed had now increased with cloud base down to 1000 feet asl, visibility was also very poor and at this point it was stated the crew should have returned to base.

Avro Anson Mk1

It was estimated that the aircraft would have reached the Mull of Kintyre at 09:29, but after the QDM no further contact was made.

Of the other nine aircraft on the same exercise, all but one failed to complete the Navex after conditions became unfavourable in the north. The pilot who completed the exercise said he had climbed to 4,000ft when the cloud base lowered to 1000ft just west of the Isle of Man, he was then able to continue and pinpoint Sanda Island, then as visibility improved, he completed the exercise to Pladda before returning to base.

Eventually, with no further word from EF820 and the endurance for the fuel aboard having expired, all hopes of the aircraft returning to base were lost and it was officially recorded as missing.

Search and rescue services were notified and at first it was thought the Anson had crashed or ditched in the sea where an extensive search got underway, but alas nothing would be found for almost two weeks.

The aircraft had crashed in a peat bog near A'Cruach, about a mile west of an old croft named Strone on the Mull of Kintyre. A local crofter had made the grim discovery on the 22nd October, though only the tail section was visible.

The initial Court of Inquiry into what caused this tragedy was opened on 13th October by W/Cdr Faulkner of 25 Group HQ, though at this point the Anson was still missing and the inquiry was based on it having been forced down in the sea by bad weather.

The board came to the conclusion that the general cause of the accident was unknown, and aside from the thoughts on being forced down by bad weather, it was stated that *"...engine or airframe trouble may have developed, causing the pilot to force land in the sea, in such a manner that the dinghy could not be launched"*

Eleven days later when the aircraft was found, the investigation was re-opened, though the outcome was basically the same *"Cause of accident unknown"*.

Remarks added to the report were: *"It was presumed that the aircraft came down to less than safety height and struck high ground causing it to sink in a peat bog which trapped the crew.*

The period of 32 minutes elapsing since the last message may have been due to wireless failure, but if so, pilot should have returned to base or landed at the nearest aerodrome"

There were no witnesses to the accident, though a local Police Sergeant A. MacGeachey (Spelt MacBeachey in the report) from Argyll Constabulary was at the board of investigation, it is understood his involvement was due to the aircraft being reported to the police by the crofter who found it.

Only small pieces of the Anson remain on the surface today

Photo: Steven Spink

Pilot. Pilot Officer Richard Blewett, RAF, born in 1919 at Bedwellty, 8 miles south of Tredegar, Monmouthshire, South Wales, was son of Alfred and Mary E. Blewett (née Davies) of Penybryn, Hengoed, Caerphilly. He had two sisters Beryl and Margaret and one older brother, George.

Richard was a very experienced pilot and a skilled navigator. After basic training he was sent overseas where flying training was conducted at 25 Elementary Flying Training School at Belvedere, Salisbury, Rhodesia. He then went on to 20 Service Flying Training School at Cranborne and also Salisbury, earning an `Average` rating at both schools.

A Maritime Reconnaissance Course followed at No. 61 Air School (SAAF) at George, Cape Province in South Africa. Here flying was concentrated on sea navigation using dead reckoning and astro-navigation, ship and aircraft recognition, intended for future work with RAF Coastal Command.

Richard and other pupils at 61 A.S. flew in Avro Ansons as navigators, equipped with wireless operators and pigeons in case of trouble and the main operational area was between Cape Town and Port Elizabeth. All shipping that rounded the Cape was logged and photographed and a look-out kept for U-boats heading for the Indian Ocean.

At the end of the latter course the instructors remarks of Richard were: *"An above the average navigator who should develop into a good G.R. pilot"*. At the time of the accident Richard had logged a total of 526 solo flying hours, 250 of which were on the Avro Anson.

P/O Richard Blewett's grave in Kilkerran Cemetery, Campbeltown.

Photo: Author's Collection

Richard was interred with full military honours in Campbeltown (Kilkerran) Cemetery, Division 4. Grave 632 with the epitaph: `God came admiring flowers—The one he picked was ours` He is also commemorated on the war memorial in Gelligaer Parish Church, Hengoed.

1st Navigator Flight Lieutenant Dennis Henry Brewer was born in 1909 in Plymouth, Hampshire. He was the youngest son of the late Lieut. Frank Brewer. R.M. and Mrs. Brewer of Southsea and Copnor, and also husband of Marie Brewer.

Dennis had two older sisters Margaret Edith and Joan Elizabeth. He grew up in Portsmouth and in the spring of 1938 married Miss Marie R. Pullen in Lewisham, Kent.

He was commissioned as a Flying Officer on 1st August 1941, then a Flight Lieutenant on 1st August 1942.

Dennis was interred on 25th October alongside his comrades with military honours in Campbeltown (Kilkerran) Cemetery, Kintyre. Div.4. Grave 631.

2nd Navigator Sergeant George Charles McKenzie. RCAF. Born 13th July 1923 in Fort Fraser, British Columbia, Canada, was the son of George Charles and Margaret McKenzie (née Cameron) of Fort Fraser, BC.

Sgt George Charles McKenzie. RCAF

Photo: Library & Archives Canada

Educated locally, George attended Willovale Public School from 1928-36, then Fort Fraser High School until 1940. He was a keen sportsman and enjoyed playing Softball, Hockey and Baseball.

After leaving school George was employed for a little over a year at Pinchi Lake Mine and Binchi Lake. BC as an assistant diamond driller, but left to join the RCAF on 18th May 1942 at No1 Recruitment Centre, Ontario.

As an AC2 he became a pupil navigator and trained in Canada with 7 AOS at Portage la Prairie, Manitoba. He graduated as a navigator on 25th June 1943 and was promoted to Temporary Sergeant.

F/Lt Dennis Brewer's grave, Kilkerran

Photo: Author's Collection

After leaving the navigation school George was given leave prior to embarkation for the UK on 16th July. He arrived in England on the 22nd and following assessment he was assigned a course at 9 (O) AFU at Llandwrog in September, but sadly lost his life just six weeks later.

George was interred in Campbeltown (Kilkerran) Cemetery, Kintyre on 25th October in Division 4. Grave 628.

A service was conducted by the Reverend. T.S. McPhearson, Church of Scotland and Reverend R. Redfern, Scottish Episcopal Church.

Sgt Jackson's grave in Kilkerran,

Photo: Author's Collection

Staff Wireless Operator / Air Gunner Sergeant Kenneth Ellis. RAFVR, born 1923, was son of William George and Frances Eva Ellis (née Bancroft) of Leicester. Leicestershire. Kenneth was interred in Campbeltown (Kilkerran) Cemetery. Division 4 Grave 630

Pupil Wireless Operator / Air Gunner Sergeant Peter Jackson. RAFVR, born 1923, was the son of Arthur and Jessie Marion Jackson of Woodville, Derbyshire. Peter was interred in Campbeltown (Kilkerran) Cemetery. Division 4 Grave 629.

Sgt Ellis's Grave in Kilkerran

Photos: Author's Collection

BEINN BHREAC BEAUFIGHTER LZ455

Having been Formed on 1st December 1942 from No`s 3 and 4 Flights of the Overseas Aircraft Preparation Unit at Filton, near Bristol, Gloucestershire (now Avon), 2 OAFU was established as part of 44 Group Transport Command in order to carry out various modifications on aircraft assigned to units and squadrons abroad.

In the main, No 2 OAFU dealt with Blenheim, Beaufighter, Beaufort, Albermarle, Anson and Mosquito types, which when complete would be ferried to designated squadrons ready for overseas delivery, or to a Ferry Training Unit where crews would spend two weeks training on navigation and fuel consumption tests in preparation for the long overseas flights.

One such aircraft, assigned to 304 FTU which had formed at Port Ellen (Glenedgedale) on Islay in the Western Isles in February 1943, was Beaufighter LZ455 a Mk. T.F.X, built by the Bristol aircraft factory at Weston Super Mare from a production batch of 480.

Detailed to ferry this aircraft to Islay on Saturday 30th October 1943, was Pilot F/O Kenneth John Nixon RAFVR and his Navigator Sgt Angelo Bonito Solari. RAFVR.

Taking off from Filton at 13:50, their route would have taken them out to the west and over the Bristol Channel, then northwards up the Welsh coast towards the Isle of Man then a on a NW heading for Stranraer and Kintyre.

Throughout the flight there was no communication with the aircraft and the accident record states that the crew had been *"Incorrectly briefed and were thus unable to make R/T contact"* with any station along the route, and as a result, on nearing Sanda Island, they appear to have been a few miles north of their intended track.

Close to the spot where the Hudson crashed at Feorlan, the Beaufighter appears to have followed the Glen up past Torr Dubh heading NW then impacted with the SW side of Beinn Bhreac at a height of around 1,250ft asl.

Bristol Beaufighter

The aircraft broke up on impact, but there was no evidence of a fire, nevertheless, the crash resulted in the loss of both airmen. An air and sea search was made when the Beaufighter became overdue, but due to poor weather with hill fog it was 6th November before the wreckage was located.

At the crash site today is a fair amount of aluminium scattered about close to a depression and boundary fence running SE to NW. Some of the heavier parts such as the undercarriage and engine mounting frame lies buried close by.

Pilot. Flying Officer Kenneth John Nixon. RAFVR, born in Tamworth, Staffordshire in 1921, was the only son of Walter and Dora Nixon (née Hibbs) later of Edlington, Doncaster, Yorkshire.

Ken, an only child of the Nixon`s, was educated at Doncaster and Maltby Grammar schools before winning a scholarship for Leeds Training College, where as a successful student he left with qualifications to become a teacher and had been granted a post under Sheffield Education Committee, which he would have taken was it not for the war.

On joining the RAF and after basic training Ken was selected as a pilot and attended a Flying Training School in England prior to going overseas to Canada under the Empire Training Scheme.

Having graduated and returned to the UK at the end of 1942, Ken was commissioned a P/O on probation on 12th December, and promoted to F/O on probation six months later on 18th June.

Wreckage of Beaufighter LZ455 on Beinn Bhreac, Mull of Kintyre

Both photos: Geoff Bland

He was described as a keen sportsman, a brilliant scholar and a skilful pilot who had logged 196 hours flying time including 40 hours on the Beaufighter.

The funeral took place with a service conducted by Rev. J. L. Brown at the Holy Trinity Church at Wilnecote, near Tamworth on 11th November 1943. In attendance where his parents, many family members and P/O A. Neilson a friend and representative from his station. Among the floral tributes was one from his fiancée Jean whom he had met in Canada. He was interred at Wilncote New Cemetery. Grave 2557.

Ken Nixon was also commemorated on the Old Boys of the school Honour Roll at Maltby Grammar School, Yorkshire.

F/O Kenneth John Nixon. RAFVR

Photo: Author's Collection

Navigator Sergeant Antonio Benito Solari RAFVR, was born in 1923 at Eastry in Kent and was the only son of Angelo and Elizabeth Ann Solari (née Thomas) of Kent.

His parents had married in Brighton, Sussex, in the spring of 1919, but sadly his father passed away in 1933 and Antonio and his mother moved to Merthyr Tydfil, Glamorganshire where his mother re-married David Ewan Edwards at the end of 1934 and the family lived on Gellyfaelog Road, Penydarren.

Angelo joined the RAF in 1942 and trained as a Navigator both in the UK and Canada. After the accident he was accorded a military funeral at Merthyr Tydfil (Pant) Cemetery and interred in Row. F4. Grave 47.

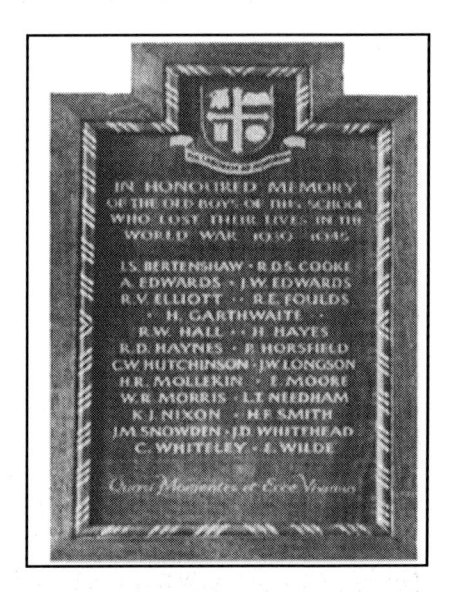

F/O Kenneth Nixon on the Old Boys of the School Honour Roll

175

MAN OVERBOARD - BARRACUDA P9737

Like any squadron during wartime, accidents and incidents became a regular occurrence, and 810 Squadron would see its fare share. One in particular occurred on 9th November 1943, when Barracuda Mk. II P9737 'Z' took off from *Landrail* and almost immediately suffered an engine failure over Machrihanish Bay

No stranger to the difficulties of ditching an aircraft, Fleet Air Arm pilot, Sub/Lt Geoff Bourke, having completed the task he was trained for made a text book landing and along with his crew Sub/Lt Peter Stocks and P.O. Fred Artlett, he clambered into the dinghy, not realizing at the time that the wind was against them as they began to drift out to sea and the inflatable would be their refuge for the next 27 hours.

A Mayday signal had been picked up and soon an air and sea search was underway. 281 Squadron, normally based at Drem, had been operating with a detachment at Ayr with Ansons flying coastal reconnaissance exercises when they were called to assist.

Rescue of ditched aircrew from an ice cold sea

Alpine 15 with F/Sgt Soules was scrambled to take part in the search, soon followed by *Alpine 11* with W.O. Haw which was diverted from practice flying, however, both aircraft were recalled after hearing a RN ship was reported to have found the dinghy.

Though the ship rescued the crew the following day, Petty Officer Artlett, according to a former representative of the Telegraphist Air Gunners association, was lost overboard between Northern Ireland and Islay during the recovery, and unfortunately he either drowned or died of exposure.

P9737 had a relatively short life, having been built as a Mk. II by the Fairey factory at Heaton Chapel, Stockport, from a production batch of 250 1s & IIs, it was delivered to 810 Squadron in April 43.

Pilot. Sub-Lieutenant (A) Geoffrey Patrick Bourke, RNVR & RNZNVR, born 16th March 1918, was the son of Michael Francis and Cecilia Bourke (née O'Connor) of Napier, Hawkes Bay, North Island, New Zealand.

Brought up in the picturesque coastal city of Napier, Geoff came from a large family of six brothers: Raymund Peter, James Michael, Hubert Joseph, Vincent Michael, Maurice Francis and John Baptist and three sisters Kathleen Mary, Eileen Mary and Moya.

Commissioned on 27th March 1941 as a Temp Sub/Lt (A) Geoff initially sailed to the UK and joined the RN as a Volunteer Reserve, and after training he joined 774 Squadron on 7th November where he flew Albacores. Here he appears to have suffered one minor accident at St.Merryn on 19th November 1941 in Albacore N4188 coded `S6A` though damage was minimal, the aircraft quickly repaired and fortunately he suffered no injury.

On 5th May 1942 Sub/Lt Bourke, serving with 810 Squadron, flying an 829 Squadron Swordfish V4712 `3L' accompanied by Sub/Lt R.T. White '3Q' and Sub/Lt A.G. McWilliams `3G' attacked and damaged the 1,379 ton Vichy French submarine *Bevezieres* at Diego Suarez, Madagascar.

The submarine was given the coup de gras by an 810 Squadron Swordfish flown by Sub/Lt W.H. Newnham. On the way back to HMS *Illustrious* V4712 suffered engine failure and Sub/Lt Bourke was forced to ditch the aircraft in the sea, fortunately he and his crew were rescued.

Geoff, still serving with 810 Squadron aboard *Illustrious*, was promoted to the rank of Temp Lieutenant on 16th March 1943 and the following month he began flying the new Barracudas and bore quite well, save for one minor carrier landing on 6th July in DP865 when he drifted into a barrier.

On 26th January 1944, Geoff travelled from Newcastle-Upon-Tyne to Glasgow, then on 29th February sailed aboard the SS *Umtata* (Master J.W. Miles) for New York and arrived 16th March. The passenger manifest describes him as being 6ft with blue/green eyes and states that he was in transit for New Zealand.

Geoff ended the war as a Lieutenant and after returning home, married his fiancée Vera in Paekakariki on the

An old postcard of the Merchant ship the SS Umtata owned by Bullard King & Co. Ltd. But formally of the Natal Line - South Africa and Portuguese East Africa

22nd June 1948 and settled in Egmont, Taranaki, where the couple raised five children. Geoff passed away in New Plymouth, Taranaki, North Island, on 22nd January 2000, having outlived all his brothers and sisters.

Observer. Sub-Lieutenant (A) Peter George Stocks, RNVR, born 6th August 1923, was the son of George and Hilda Stocks of Doncaster, West Riding, Yorkshire.

Peter was educated in Doncaster and the family lived in Wolsey Avenue. He left school to become an apprentice railway engineer in 1939, but joined the RN Fleet Air Arm as a U/T Observer at the end of 1941.

He is listed as serving with 810 Squadron on 31st May 1943 as an Acting Temporary Sub/Lt, with a promotion to Acting Sub/Lt on 6th August that same year.

Like Sub/Lt Bourke, Peter would have had a period of survivors leave in the run up to Christmas, and in the New Year was posted to 811 Squadron at RNAS Ford (*Peregrine*) West, Sussex, arriving on 6th February 1944 to fly in Swordfish.

The squadron using both Wildcats and Swordfish had detachments at Eglinton, Northern Ireland and on board HMS *Vindix*, the latter of which was used to escort North Russian convoys between September and December, with a compliment of 12 Swordfish and 4 Wildcats operating until the 9th December when the squadron disbanded.

Peter remained in the RN after the war and is listed as a Temp Lieutenant in the Navy Lists of 6th February 1946. He had married Miss Mary Woodward in late December 1945 and was living in Doncaster at the end of 1947, but died in Warwickshire in January 2007.

Telegraphist Air Gunner. Petty Officer Frederick John Artlett. RN, born 23rd August 1912, at East Preston, Sussex, was the son of Frederick William and Minnie Artlett (née Slaughter) of Littlehampton, Sussex. He had one sister Vera M. and was husband of Ada Caroline Artlett.

Fred was recovered from the sea and accorded a military funeral followed by interment in Oban (Pennyfuir) Cemetery, Scotland. Sec.1. Grave. 303.

P.O. Fred J. Artlett's grave

A VALIANT EFFORT - SWORDFISH HS448

Having earned the nickname 'Fearless Freddie' from his daring exploits off Norway while flying Skuas on escort and patrol duties with 803 Squadron, Lt (A) Philip Noel Charlton. DFC. DSC. RN had arrived at Machrihanish in August 1942 as a rest from operations. Here he joined a gunnery team and his duty would be to assess the hits by training aircraft on targets at the various gunnery range observation posts on the east and west coast of Kintyre.

A far cry from dodging flak off the Norwegian coast, getting hit, being rescued by ship, then the ship itself being sunk, or from flying Hurricanes in the Middle East where he managed to shoot down three Ju.87s and a fourth probable, before being shot down again by friendly fire from a Tomahawk, but life at the range would certainly have its moments.

On the eve of Thursday 18th November 1943, Lt Charlton was on duty in the observation tower at Crossaig bombing range, near Skipness on the east coast.

Targets had been set up for attacks by three Fairey Swordfish from 836 Squadron at Maydown, Northern Ireland. The aircraft would fly in, drop their bombs then pull out sharply, though on this occasion the exercise went horribly wrong. As HS448 piloted by Sub/Lt Ian Geoffrey Cuthbert, RNVR, with Observer Sub/Lt Redge Denis Hoskin, RNZNVR and TAG L/A Stanley Alfred Paige, RN, attacked the target, soon after releasing their bombs they turned towards the land but failed to gain height.

Closely observed by Lt Charlton in the company of his 24 year old driver Wren Elizabeth 'Beth' Booth, a former Red Cross ambulance driver, the pair watched helplessly as the aircraft, almost in slow motion, crashed down on the beach a burst into flames.

Without hesitation they jumped in the little RN utility van and drove at speed along rough tracks towards the crash, where they were greeted with a scene of utter devastation.

The flames from the fire were intense and there was a chance fuel tanks would explode. *"Better wait here with the truck in case it goes up"* said Charlton, but on the high hopes there could still be someone alive, Beth hastened to the blazing wreck.

As they got closer the heat was almost unbearable, but shielding their faces they edged towards one of the crew who was hanging half way out of the crumpled fuselage, with great effort they dragged him clear of the wreck but his flying suit was on fire and the Wren without a second thought proceeded to beat the flames out with her hands, getting burnt herself in the process, then in desperation she tore off his flying suit down to his

Lt (A) Philip Noel Charlton. DFC. DSC

Wren Elizabeth Booth with her RN Austin 10 van prior to her B.E.M award and accounts of her bravery appearing in national press. Photo: Via Fran Ralli

Elizabeth 'Beth' Booth. BEM in her Red Cross uniform

They carefully placed the injured airman in the passenger seat of the little Austin 'Tilly' van, and Beth Booth began her 9 mile tortuous journey in the darkness along a tough winding road.

Trying to avoid potholes and ditches, the young M/T driver did her best to make the journey for her injured passenger as comfortable as possible, but winced with every bump in the road.

After traveling for almost 7 miles, she noticed the airman was breathing more spasmodically and he had apparently lapsed into a coma. Trying to keep a close eye on the road knowing she still had a couple of miles to go, she glanced back at the young airman and noticed he was now slumped in an awkward position, and at that moment, she realised he had died.

Navy uniform and he was eventually clear of the fire. Although the man, who happened to be the New Zealand Observer, was still breathing and semi-conscious she hoped he would still make it.

Meanwhile, Lt Chorlton had gone back to the burning aircraft to try and free one of the others, he managed to extricate the gunner but like the pilot, he appeared to have already perished instantly in the crash. The heat and choking fumes were terrible, and several explosions rang out sending sheets of flame and burning debris into the air.

Realising nothing could be done for the others, Lt Chorlton returned to the Observer and it was decided that he stood a better chance of survival if he was taken to the nearest doctor, rather than make a two-way trip to bring the doctor to the site.

Eventually arriving at the doctor's house, he opened the door to find the young girl in a state of shock, with a smoke-blackened face, scorched uniform and blistered hands, she did her best to explain what had happened.

The doctor examined the airman in the van, but sadly could only confirm that he had passed away. Beth then drove the doctor back to the crashed aircraft, at Crossaig, but the scene was in darkness and now deserted. So realising any casualties and the Lieutenant must have gone back to base, she then drove 33 miles to the airfield at Machrihanish.

For her heroic efforts in trying to save the crew Wren Beth Booth was invited to Buckingham Palace where she proudly accepted the award of the British Empire Medal from the King. Lt Philip Charlton. DFC.DSO also received the Kings Commendation for bravery.

Soon after leaving school Ian was enrolled in the Royal Naval College, either at Greenwich or Dartmouth to become a Naval Officer, then having passed through college he signed on for the Fleet Air Arm and began his primary training as a U/T pilot at Lee-on-Solent, Hampshire.

The family don't think he went to Canada for flying training, so he likely did some of his flying training at Crail and Ayr. He was awarded his pilot wings on 3rd July 1943, promoted to Temporary Sub-Lieutenant and served with 836 Squadron at RNAS Maydown in Northern Ireland.

Sub/Lt (A) Ian G. Cuthbert. RNVR

Photo: Joan Ward

Pilot. Sub-Lieutenant (A) Ian Geoffrey Cuthbert, RNVR, born 12th January 1923 in Carlisle, Cumbria, was the only son of Hugh and Margaret 'Peggy' Cuthbert (née Bulman) of Heysham, Lancashire.

The family was originally from Carlisle, Cumbria, and Ian's grandparents Mr & Mrs J. Bulman remained there at Beaconsfield Street after his parents moved to Morecambe & Heysham.

Ian lived with his parents on Wilson Grove, Heysham, near Morecambe, Lancashire, and attended primary school there before going on to Lancaster Royal Grammar School.

Sub/Lt (A) Ian Geoffrey Cuthbert. RNVR

Photo: Joan Ward

Sub/Lt (A) Ian Geoffrey Cuthbert. RNVR.   Photo: Joan Ward via Ian Thomson

Sub/Lt Cuthbert's grave and his parents grave in Upperby Cemetery, Carlisle. His Commonwealth War Grave headstone lies to the left of the private stone.

Photo: Author's Collection

Sub/Lt (A) Cuthbert's CWG headstone

Photo: Author's Collection

After the accident Ian was interred in Carlisle (Upperby) Cemetery, with full military honours. Ward 10. Sec F. Grave 21. He is also commemorated on Morecambe War Memorial.

Observer. Sub-Lieutenant (A) Redge Dennis Hoskin, RNZNVR, born 29th June 1918 in Tariki, Auckland, New Zealand, was the only son of Reginald Dennis Thomas and Ella Vera Hoskin (née Dennis). He was also husband of Mary Patricia Hoskin (née Mulholland) of Epsom, Auckland. NZ. Redge was educated at the Te Kuiti and Ongaru Primary Schools and the Taumarunui District High School (1st XV Athletic Team). He also attended Victoria University College, Wellington, where he studied engineering, before employment with the NZ Railway in Wangerui as an engineering draughtsman.

Sub/Lt Hoskin's grave in Kilkerran

Photo: Author's Collection

After serving for eight months in the NZ Army Territorial Force, Redge joined the NZNF (redesignated RNZN on 1.1.41) with intentions of training as a pilot and embarked for the UK on 22nd July 1941, arriving at Gosport in England on the 2nd September, where he was attached on loan to the RN/FAA as U/T aircrew.

A posting to Lee-on-Solent came next on 1st December, then following assessment he was attached to 24 EFTS at Sydenham, Belfast, Northern Ireland as a U/T pilot with the RAF on Tiger Moths. However, his grades were not up to standard for being a pilot and his training ceased on 17th March 1942.

Returning to Lee-on-Solent, then Gosport on 3rd May to train as an Observer, Redge was posted first to either Eastleigh or Christchurch on 5th July, then Town Hill Camp (*Waxwing*) a Fleet Air Arm transit camp in Dunfermline, Fife, before leaving for Trinidad (*Goshawk / Piarco*) on 6th October for an Air Observers coarse.

On 15th May 1943 Redge was awarded his Observers badge and he later sailed for the UK arriving on 2nd August back at Lee. He was then posted to 836 Squadron at Crail where he flew in Swordfish from 11th October until the time of the accident just five weeks later. Redge was interred in Campbeltown (Kilkerran) Cemetery, with a full guard of honour. Division 4. Grave. 633.

Telegraphist Air Gunner 3rd Class. Leading Airman John Charles Archer Bensted, RN, born in Wandsworth, London on 22nd December 1923, was the son of Edward John and Margaret Bensted (née Huggins) of Balham, London.

John was an old boy of St.Mary's Church of England Primary School, Balham, Wandsworth. He was the youngest of two sons and joined the RN FAA in 1942. His elder brother Edward F. Bensted, born 1916, was also in the forces, but was captured by the Germans in May 1940 and spent the rest of the war in a Prisoner of War camp.

Following a service in his hometown of Balham, John was cremated at the South London Crematorium, Mitcham. He is commemorated on Panel 21 of the memorial there.

LOST IN THE CLOUDS - WELLINGTON LB137

When word came through at 16:30 that a Wellington had failed to return the C.O. and Chief Instructor W/Cdr. Ingle were immediately notified and at 17:45 (The estimated end of the aircraft's endurance) and a full scale search involving over twenty aircraft from surrounding stations was initiated.

The aircraft, LB137 '4' of 6 OTU at RAF Silloth, had taken off around noon on 2nd December 1943, for a routine navigation exercise off the Isle of Islay on the west coast of Scotland.

The crew that day, quite a mixed bunch of multinationals consisted:

Captain & Pilot F/O Harry Oxley Dransfield, RAFVR, Co-Pilot Sgt Jeffrey Alfred Duddridge, RAFVR, Navigator Charles Clifton Cooper, RAAF, and three Wireless Op/Air Gunners: F/Sgt Reginald Francis Canavan, RAAF, F/Sgt Robert John Wardrop RNZAF and F/Sgt Victor Francis Suttor RAAF.

Three other aircraft had also taken off that day on a similar exercise and it is reported that cloud was as low as 500ft with heavy rain showers and visibility down to less that a mile at times.

At 14:32 the aircraft obtained an M.F. D/F fix from the radio station at Cambar, which put it 10 miles north of its intended track, then at 14:48, what was described as a corrupt message from LB137 in its correct position, was received at Cambar and passed on to Silloth, but no further signals were heard from the aircraft.

Shortly after the Wellington became overdue, information was received that it was tracked by radar soon after the D/F fix and had been plotted on a true heading of 120 degrees, but the plot had faded a few miles short of reaching the coast of Islay, but it was later seen to pass over Port Ellen, apparently flying in a normal manner.

At 16:10 a radar plot appeared off Davaar Island, near Campbeltown and this was identified as a Wellington by the local R.O.C command post. The aircraft was flying west at around a 1,000 feet and began circling before

Vickers Wellington

heading west again at 2,000 feet in the prevailing darkness, after which no further plots were obtained. From the evidence presented there is no doubt that this was LB137 because all the other aircraft on the exercise had returned safely to Silloth.

After a long and laborious air and sea search, the shattered remains of the twin-engine bomber missing from its training base on the banks of the Solway Firth, were finally spotted the following day at a height of around 1,275ft asl on a hill known as Beinn na Lice, on the Mull of Kintyre.

In view of the other three aircraft making it back to base, and the fact that this one didn't and no one survived to say what really happened, as is customary with unexplained aircraft accidents, the Board of Inquiry suggested that some responsibility for the loss must be down to the crew, namely the pilot and navigator.

The Inquiry stated:

"This aircraft appears to have developed a sudden wireless defect sometime after 14:48 hrs. Unfortunately there is no means of establishing the nature of this failure".

The report goes on to mention that there were two factors that `probably` caused the crew to become completely lost:

"It is considered that this accident `may have` been due primarily to the failure of the navigator to plot immediately the M.F. D/F fix, because he happened to be occupied in writing out the position signal (sent at 14:48) at the time".

The investigation then turns its attention to the pilot and says:

"The secondary cause was `probably` the failure on the part of the Captain to take the correct distress action as soon as he became lost. i.e.

(1) Climb to 4,000 feet and (2) Use G.E. or wireless to home. Or (3) Fly the usual triangular courses to indicate distress".

You will be aware that the words `Probably` and `May have` are underlined here to emphasise that strictly speaking, the true cause of this accident and so many others in this area is obscure, and that these are only speculations of what might be the cause.

Even if the crew had been lost, could the accident not just as easily have been caused by the weather? Low cloud, heavy rain squalls, and/or perhaps even a downdraught? Or even Instrument or mechanical failure? Whatever happened that fateful day, we should never forget that these men were fighting for our freedom and they had made the ultimate sacrifice with their lives.

SILLOTH 10/9/43 31 COURSE `L` SQUADRON WO / AG`S

Top: Toppin, Wilding, Pike, Hitchcock, Duffey, Lawrence, **Wardrop and Suttor**

Centre: Davis, McCabe, Mailman, Ashdown, Ferrare, Keegan, Leigh and Duffield

Front: Gill, Smith, Robins, Bexall, **Canavan** and Martin

Photo: Geoff Bland

Captain & Pilot. Flying Officer Harry Oxley Dransfield, RAFVR, born 1922 in Rotherham, was the only son of Fred and Hilda Mary Dransfield (née Oxley) of Sheffield, South Yorkshire.

Harry's father was a fitter for the local Water Dept and an ARP warden when war broke out. The family lived on Charlotte Road and Harry attended Schools in Sheffield. Pre-war he was also Scoutmaster for the 218th Millhouses Methodist Scouts.

Harry joined the RAF in 1941 and having worked his way up through the ranks, he trained and qualified as a pilot in Spring 1942 and was promoted to Sergeant. He later applied for a commission which was granted on 23rd October 1942 when he became a P/O on probation.

Very little is known about Harry's service prior to joining 6 OTU, but he was promoted to F/O on 23rd April 1943 and at the time of the accident in December, he had notched up a total of 239 Solo flying hours, with 41 on the Wellington.

Harry was taken back home for burial and now rests in a private family grave with his parents at Sheffield (Abbey Lane) Cemetery, Section O. Gen Grave 7905. Though sadly the grave is in a very poor state today.

Harry is also commemorated on the Sheffield War Memorial and on the Scouts Roll of Honour in the Rover Room at the Sheffield Scouts HQ.

Co-Pilot. Sergeant Jeffrey Alfred Duddridge, RAFVR, born in 1917 at Bridgewater, was the eldest son of Bertie Alfred and Ellen Duddridge (née Higgins) of Bridgewater, Somerset. He had a sister Bridget and two brothers Ronald and Basil.

F/O Harry Dransfield in a family grave in Abbey Lane Cemetery. Photo: Findagrave

The grave of Sgt Jeffrey Duddridge in St.Martin's Churchyard, Somerset

Photo: Author's Collection

Jeff's parents had been married in Bridgewater in 1916. His father was a Police Constable for Somerset Constabulary and the family lived at Bayford in police accommodation on the eastern fringes of Wincanton, Somerset, the children having all attended early school in Wincanton.

Jeff joined the RAF early 1941 and after basic training was selected for aircrew, promoted to LAC and trained as a pilot. Having gained his wings in 1942, and a promotion to Sergeant, in spring that year he also married Miss Joan Reynolds at Wincanton.

Following the crash he was returned home for interment in West Coker (St.Martin) Churchyard, Somerset. in New Ground, South of the Church.

Navigator Flying Officer Charles Clifton Cooper, RAAF, born in Randwick, SE of Sydney on 15th May 1918, was the son of Charles and Helen Julia Cooper of Penshurst, New South Wales, Australia. He had one Brother Frank and a sister Frances.

Charlie had lived on Kurocki Street, Penshurst and graduated from college to become a draughtsman. He enlisted in the RAAF on 8th April 1941 at Penshurst and after basic training in Australia he arrived at No2 Recruiting Centre, Richmond, Sydney on 18th September 1941 to await overseas embarkation for further training as a navigator on attachment to the RAF in the UK.

191

On arrival and following assessment Charlie was selected for aircrew and as an LAC was sent to Observer School followed by an Air Gunners course where having achieved high marks he was appointed for a commission which was granted on 9th November 1942 when he became Acting P/O on probation. Having been confirmed in the rank of P/O a further promotion to F/O came on 9th May 1943.

Following the accident, at 14:00 on 10th December 1943, Charlie, along with Canavan, Suttor and Wardrop, was interred with full military honours in Campbeltown (Kilkerran) Cemetery. Division 4. Grave 635.

F/O Cooper's grave in Kilkerran
Photo: Author's Collection

Padre conducts the service for F/O Charles Cooper in Kilkerran Cemetery
Photo: AWM

192

F/Sgt Robert John Wardrop. RAAF

Photo: Geoff Bland

Wireless Operator & Air Gunner Flight Sergeant Robert John Wardrop, RAAF, born in 1923, was the son of son of John and Ellen Gertrude Wardrop of Herbert, Otago, New Zealand.

Bob, as he was known, was a former pupil at Gore High School and later worked as a farm assistant for Alan Speden at Gore, South Island.NZ.

He enlisted in the RNZAF at Rotorua ITW as Wireless Operator/Air Gunner U/T on 23rd March 1942, then embarked for Canada on 27 April and arrived on 14th May. He was posted to No2 Wireless School at Calgary on the 23rd.

Bombing & Gunnery School came next on 5th December and having completed awarded his Air Gunners wings and promoted to Sergeant on 11th January 1943. Along with other successful pupils he was then given leave prior to being posted to 31 OTU at Debert, Nova Scotia on the 23rd. Here he flew reconnaissance exercises in the Lockheed Hudson.

He arrived at No 1 'Y' Depot in Halifax, Nova Scotia on 2nd May, in preparation for embarkation to the UK, but was suddenly taken ill and from 15 –23rd hospitalized. Once recovered he was attached to the RAF and left for the UK on 23rd June, finally arriving at 12 Personnel Dispatch & Reception Centre in Brighton, on 2nd July.

Bob arrived at Silloth to join 6 OTU on 14th September 1943, and sadly just short of 11 weeks later he lost his life on Kintyre. He was interred in Campbeltown (Kilkerran) Cemetery, Division 4. Grave. 638.

Wireless Operator & Air Gunner Flight Sergeant Reginald Francis Canavan, RAAF, born 31st March 1921, at Cloncurry, Queensland, was the son of Herbert Reginald and Annie Florence Canavan (née Hill) of Ashfield, New South Wales, Australia. He had three brothers: Gerald Joseph and Thomas David and Colin, and a sister Betty.

Reginald became known to all as Rex and in 1922 the family travelled over a thousand miles to Brisbane, but by the early 1930s they had moved to Sydney where his father had been

Wireless Op / Air Gunner F/Sgt Reginald `Rex` Canavan
Photo: Geoff Bland

offered a post as bank manager at the National Australia Bank HQ on the corner Pitt & Hunter Streets. In 1933 they were living on Bland Street, Ashfield, Parkes where Rex and his siblings attended local schools.

Rex inevitably must have had good grades at school and college, for later he was employed with the Commonwealth Scientific and Industrial Research Organisation (CSIRO) in Sydney, in the agriculture department, working to improve crops.

When war broke out, although in his line of work he would have been exempt from service, he volunteered for the RAAF and arrived at No2 Recruiting Centre, (2 RC) Richmond, Sydney on 25th April 1942. After a medical and short exam he was deemed fit and ready for basic training.

It would appear that while at Richmond he met and courted a young Aircraftwoman by the name of Elizabeth Cecilia McMillan and the couple later became engaged, though sadly with his postings to various training units, the couple would see less and less of each other, except when he was home on leave.

Rex was later selected for aircrew as a U/T Wireless Operator Air Gunner and promoted to Leading Aircraftman. He continued to train in Australia at wireless and gunnery schools throughout 1942 and into the new year, but inevitably he was destined to leave for Blighty on attachment to the RAF, so he arrived at the embarkation depot on the 6th March 1943, and along with

F/Sgt Rex Canavan (left) on leave with an RAF Observer Pal

Photo: Geoff Bland

8,325 other servicemen and 874 ships crew, Rex boarded the troopship *Queen Mary* in Sydney on the 22nd, bound for Gourock, Scotland, via Freemantle, Cape Town and Freetown.

On arrival in the UK he was posted to the PRC then an OTU prior to joining a squadron, and allegedly, according to a photo at the Australia National Archives, he was with 158 Squadron, but the airmen in the squadron photo all have tropics uniforms, and this squadron never served abroad, so either the squadron number on the photo is wrong, or it was just taken during training in Australia?

195

F/Sgt Rex Canavan is described as being among this group in August 1943
Photo: National Archives of Australia

Rex was interred in Campbeltown (Killkerran) Cemetery with full military honours at 14:00 hrs on 10th December. Division 4. Grave. 599.

Wireless Operator & Air Gunner Flight Sergeant Victor Francis Suttor, RAAF, born 3rd November 1918 in Mudgee, NSW, was the son of Charles Raymond and Eva Violet Suttor, of Mudgee, New South Wales, Australia and husband of Dorothy Joyce `Joy` Suttor (née Prescott) of Coogee, New South Wales.

Vic, as he was known, attended school in Mudgee and like his father worked as a grazier before enlistment. Like Rex Canavan, Vic joined the RAAF at No2 Recruiting Centre, Richmond, Sydney, but much earlier on 20th July 1941, and his basic training, wireless and gunnery

F/Sgt Victor Francis Suttor, RAAF.
Photo: Geoff Bland

courses were conducted in Australia though prior to arrival for embarkation to the UK, he married Miss Dorothy Joyce `Joy` Prescott, his 20 year old fiancée in the City of Randwick, a suburb south-east Sydney, NSW, however, a short while later he was detailed for attachment to the RAF and after reporting to No2 Recruiting Centre on 28th March, he left for the UK on 6th April 1942 aboard the *Queen Mary* troop ship. On arrival in the UK a few weeks later, like other fellow airmen he would begin training again to acclimatise.

Following the accident Vic was interred with three of his crew in Campbeltown (Kilkerran) Cemetery with a full guard of honour. Division 4. Grave 639. His epitaph: `Cherished Memories`.

RN Bugler sounds off Last Post
Photo: AWM

The funeral procession for Rex Canavan, Rob Wardrop, Vic Suttor and Charlie Cooper in Kilkerran Cemetery, Campbeltown. 10/12/1943. Photo: AWM

View of the general crash area of LB137 in 2003   Photo: Geoff Bland

In 2003 Geoff Bland, a friend of the W/AG F/Sgt Rex Canavan, along with Kintyre man the late Duncan McArthur, went in search of the Wellington and after several hours finally located the crash site among the heather west of Beinn na Lice. A few small pieces were recovered for posterity and posted to F/Sgt Canavan's brother in Australia.

Left: Duncan McArthur at the crash site. Right: Some relics sent to the family of Sgt Rex Canavan in Australia.   All photos: Geoff Bland

Geoff Bland with remains of Wellington LB137 in which family friend Rex Canavan lost his life in 1943. Photo: Geoff Bland

DEATH DIVE AT BELLOCHANTUY
SWORDFISH HS454

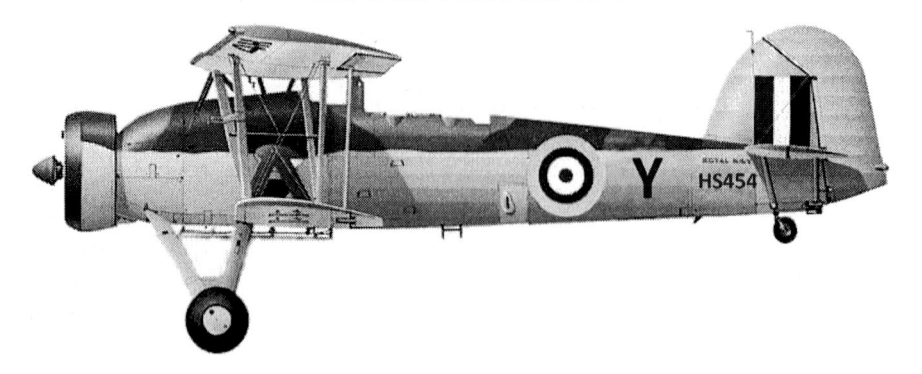

The Fairey Swordfish II, affectionately nicknamed `Stringbag` was described by its pilots as being a very manoeuvrable aircraft, easy to operate and quite a stable platform for bomb and torpedo naval operations against enemy shipping and submarines.

Well proven in these duties and effectively demonstrated against the Italian Navy at Taranto in Apulia, Southern Italy on the night of 11th and 12th November 1940, where heavy damage was achieved against the Italian Battleships *Conte di Cavour*, *Caio Duilio* and *Littorio* and shore installations. A raid which allegedly influenced the Japanese attack against Pearl Harbour a little over a year later on 7th December 1941.

On 6th December 1943, what should have been a fairly straightforward bombing exercise for the crew of Swordfish HS454 of 836 Squadron, Maydown, Northern Ireland, would end in disaster, for having arrived over the target range known as Ballure just off Bellochantuy on the west coast of Kintyre, the aircraft from the 18th Naval Merchant Aircraft carrier (MAC-Ship) Wing, was observed by the watch tower to go into a steep uncontrollable dive and the pilot apparently unable to pull up, crashed straight into the sea with the loss of all three crew members: Pilot Sub/Lt (A) William Henry Hagar Small, RNZNVR, Observer Midshipman Allan Angus Douglas-Matheson RNVR and TAG Leading Airman Stanley Paige RNVR.

In view of the flying characteristics previously outlined, various questions were asked as to what went wrong: Could it be that pilot may have blacked out in the dive? Or was he just too low and in effect still falling as he tried level out? Could it have been a mechanical or structural failure?

Following an investigation and due to the fact very little in the way of aircraft remains could be recovered from the sea, no one could determine precisely what caused this accident which occurred at approximately 15:15 hours. During a widespread search only the bodies of the two crew were found,

Fairey Swordfish in a diving manoeuvre, but seen here with a torpedo

there was no sign of the pilot. But there can be no doubt that he died instantly when the Swordfish hit the water and that he went down with the aircraft when it sank.

The area where the Swordfish crashed is not far from where the Sea Hurricane NF867 crashed just a few months earlier with the loss of New Zealand pilot Sub/Lt Russell Adams.

As a point of interest on 26th September 1939 the village of Bellochantuy, adjacent to the firing range, was sprayed by machine gun fire from the air which damaged the Argyll Arms Hotel, Proprietor Mr Dan Smith and several others said in a news interview: "*The sound of* an *aircraft overhead was noted but could not be seen even though the day was bright and clear. Later the aircraft returned and three distinct bursts of fire were heard and a shower of bullets rattled on the corrugated roof of a garage and several nickel cased bullets were located nearby*".

The hotel only suffered light damage to the premises receiving a broken skylight window, but visitors were shaken by the event. Following an inquiry the aircraft, now known to have been allied, was never positively identified but thought to have been just test-firing its machine guns prior to a patrol or exercise.

Pilot. Sub-Lieutenant William Henry Hagar Small, RNZNVR, born 13th April 1920, was the son of Douglas Arthur and Ivy Small (née Wright) of Kurow, North Otago, New Zealand.

William was educated locally and attended Kurow District High School, North Otago, where he is noted as having been (Capt. 1st IV). Kurow was known as a 'hydro town', which gradually expanded as workers who were employed in the building the Waitaki dam and a hydroelectric power station moved there during the late 1920s and early 30s. The school was built for the children of the workers. William's father however, owned a motor repair business here and on leaving school William became a mechanics assistant at the garage.

Joining the NZNF as Aircrew u/t on 28th August 1941, William embarked for the UK two days later and arrived here on 18th October. He was then transported to Lee-on-Solent for assessment.

On 22nd April 1942 he was posted to No.24 EFTS at RAF Sealand, Flintshire, as a U/T pilot flying Tiger Moths, after which on 27th June, he embarked for Canada for further pilot training with 31 SFTS in the North American Harvard at Kingston, Ontario, eventually earning his wings and a commission to Acting Sub/Lt on 6th November.

Having left Canada on 28th December, on arrival back at Lee-on-Solent in the UK he was posted on attachment to 9 (P) AFU for advanced flying training with the RAF at Hullavington, near Chippenham, Wiltshire.

Temp. Sub/Lt (A) William H.H. Small RNZNVR

Photo: *NZ Weekly News*

Next came HMS *Jackdaw*, alias Crail in Fife, where he joined a five week Torpedo Bomber Reconnaissance course on 8th February 1943, prior to being assigned to a Fleet Air Arm squadron.

On 12th April William was posted to 753 Squadron flying Swordfish from Arbroath, but on 6th June transferred to 747 Squadron who moved to Inskip a few days later.

It was here he had a close call in Swordfish DK675, when on the 22nd June while coming into land, he ran off the runway onto the grass, hit a dip and the aircraft tipped up on its nose.

His final posting on 12th August 1943 was to 836 Squadron at Maydown, until the time of his loss on 6th December.

William is remembered with honour on the New Zealand Naval Memorial at Devonport, North Shore City, Auckland, New Zealand. Panel 9.

Observer Midshipman (A) Alan Angus Douglas-Matheson, RNVR, was born in Poole, Dorset in 1924. He was the only son of Lt/Col Neil Douglas-Matheson DSO, MC, RE and Violet Matheson (née Hodson) MBE of Delphi, Parkstone, Dorset.

Midn. (A) Alan A. Douglas-Matheson's grave in Kilkerran Cemetery

Photo: Author's Collection

A prominent figure in Dorset, Alan's father had served in the First World War with distinction, having earned the Military Cross and Distinguished Service Order with the Royal Engineers.

Alan attended Winchester College, Kingsgate House in September 1937, this was a boarding school for boys and right from his early days there it was his ambition was to join the Royal Navy. 2455 members of the Winchester College community served in the Forces during World War II, among them Air Chief Marshal Lord Dowding, who was head of Fighter Command during the Battle of Britain.

He became a House Prefect for his last term and after leaving Winchester, he spent some weeks teaching before joining the Fleet Air Arm in 1942 to train as an Observer, though only managed to serve for a little over a year before tragedy struck. He was interred in Campbeltown (Kilkerran) Cemetery, Division 4. Grave 634.

Telegraphist Air Gunner 3rd Class, Leading Airman Stanley Alfred Paige, RN, was born on 21st November 1922, he was the son of William George and Elsie Lavina Alice Paige (née Steptoe) of Croydon, Surrey. Stanley had one younger brother George Edward and a younger sister Doris.

The family had lived on Dennett Road, Croydon, and Stanley had attended the local school there prior to joining the Royal Navy in 1940. He was interred in Croydon (Mitcham Rd, Cemetery) Plot Q.Q. Grave.37336.

TRAWLER RESCUE - AVRO ANSON N4988

A much travelled aircraft, N4988, an Avro Anson Mk1 had served with three RAF Squadrons: No's 44, 76, and 7 before transferring for training duties. Initially with 16 OTU, followed by 6 and 12 Service Flying Training Schools, No3 Air Observer and Navigator School (later 3 Air Observers School) and finally No1 (Observers) Advanced Flying Unit based at RAF Wigtown, Baldoon, Dumfries and Galloway.

On Thursday 9th December 1943, P/O Frederick Charles Gurr, an RAF Staff Pilot with No1 (O) AFU at Wigtown was engaged in a cross country navigation exercise with Anson N4988, when on nearing final leg of the exercise back to base from the Isle of Tiree, the aircraft began to indicate problems of fuel starvation, even though the gauges indicated that there was still sufficient left to return home.

He had decided not to chance making it home, the Anson was still over the sea but he hoped to find a suitable spot on land. Just a short while later the engines started to splutter and eventually cut out, leaving the pilot little option but to ditch in sea in the teeth of a strong easterly gale off Rubha nan Sgarbh, Kintyre, an area just off the east coast between Greenhill and Whitestone, south of Carradale, a procedure which he undertook with skill and determination. As the Anson began to settle he took charge of the dinghy drill with all his crew managing to exit safely before the stricken machine sank. He was later praised for his swift actions at the Court of Inquiry into the loss of the aircraft.

Fortunately assistance was soon at hand in the form of Skipper Donald McAnsh and his 44 foot Torrisdale Trawler "*Betty,*" (CN260) and all the crew were recovered safely. The RAF Groves and Gutteridge 60 foot General Service Pinnace 1214 arrived soon after requesting transfer of the survivors, but Mr McAnsh flatly declined.

This was in relation to an earlier incident when 1214 (with another crew) had refused to enter the bombing range south of Skipness at Grogport near Kilbrannan Sound, to rescue airmen from a sinking Swordfish due to the range being active.

Donald and his son John immediately sailed to their rescue and undoubtedly saved the lives of the three men, then transferred them to 1214 which took them to the Old Quay in Campbeltown.

An Avro Anson in a similar predicament to that of N4988 off Whitestone

Photo: AWM

P/O Gurr and his trainees were also delivered to Campbeltown, then later transferred to Machrihanish and provided with a hot meal and dry clothes before being returned to Wigtown by aircraft.

For the daring rescue of the both the Swordfish and Anson crews, the Skipper Donald McAnsh was awarded the British Empire Medal, accompanied by a reward of £50 which he generously donated to the local lifeboat fund.

His medal was presented by King George VI himself at Holyrood Palace in Edinburgh.

Right: P/O Fred Gurr pictured during No23 Course at RAF Cark

Pilot. Pilot Officer Frederick Charles Gurr, RAFVR, born 11th June 1923 in Edmonton, was the son of Frederick J and Ellen E. Gurr (née Taylor) of Edmonton, Middlesex. He had four younger sisters: Kathleen J, Beryl J, Doreen A and Joan M.

Fred joined the RAF at Euston, London in August 1940 as an Aircraftman and was sent for four weeks basic training, after which he was selected for aircrew and began pilot training.

A promotion to LAC came in 1942 and having progressed through training Fred graduated as a pilot and was awarded his wings. On 11th June 1943 he was given an emergency commission to P/O on probation and posted to the Service Pilots Training Unit (SPTU) at RAF Cark in Cartmell, Lancashire.

Fred completed his training at the SPTU on No 23 Course. The purpose of this unit was to give newly qualified pilots some training in basic dead reckoning navigation, by way of using prominent landmarks as turning points, in order to assist them when flying with less experienced aircrew on future navigation training flights.

Next came 6 (Pilots) Advanced Flying Unit at Little Rissington, Gloucestershire where on the 9th September 1943, Fred was involved in an incident with Airspeed Oxford LW743 over Radnorshire.

Having taken off on a night cross country exercise, when the weather deteriorated he became disorientated, and was unable to gain a fix from the homing beacon in area to get him on track for landing safely, he baled out at 23:40 and came down in Gwenffythern Wood, near Clyro, Hay on Wye.

The Oxford flew on a short while before crashing near Maesllwch Castle and disintegrating. (Note: Some sources state a crew of two was on this aircraft?).

An Airspeed AS.10 Oxford of 6 (P) AFU

In December Fred was with No.1 (Observers) AFU at Wigtown, where as we know he had another close call in the Anson off Kintyre, but just two days later on the 11th he was promoted to F/O on probation, confirmed with seniority on 11th June 1944.

The new year also brought with it a new wife, for Fred married his fiancée, Miss Doris Jean Bertani, an Edmonton girl who was an accomplished athlete. She was a sprinter for the Hercules Athletic Club, Captain of the Netball team and a member of the Amateur Athletics Association.

Fred remained in the RAF when the war ended and a further promotion to F/Lt came on 11th June 1945. He and his wife had a house in Wood Green, Islington and here their son Ian was born in 1949.

In 1953, Fred relinquished his commission in the RAF on appointment to join the RNZAF and emigrate to New Zealand. He arrived at the RNZAF HQ at Adelphi House, WC.2 in early June and arrangements were made for him to travel to Glasgow with 26 other airmen where they boarded the liner SS *Captain Hobson* (Skipper Capt. A. Rowlands of the Shaw & Saville line) and sailed for New Zealand on the 23rd arriving on 7th August. His wife and young son joined him later.

He served in the RNZAF from the time of his arrival to the mid-1960s and lived in air force married quarters at Marine Parade, Avon, Canterbury.

In 1969 the family were still in Avon, but he had now left the RNZAF to become a Poultry Farmer and was living in Tovey Street. Sadly, `Dot` his wife of 29 years passed away suddenly on 11th April 1973. He continued in the poultry business for a while, but then gave it up to become a clerk until retirement in 1981. Frank died on 26th June 1983. He rests alongside his wife in Woodlawn Memorial Garden, Christchurch, Canterbury, New Zealand.

The Dumbarton built SS Captain Hobson

ANOTHER DITCHING - SWORDFISH LS426

Built by the Fairey engineering factory at Blackburn, Lancashire, Swordfish LS426 was delivered to 836 Squadron at Maydown (*Shrike*) Northern Ireland on 2nd October 1943.

The squadron, under command of Lt/Cdr. Ransford Slater, was at this time heavily involved in training exercises and the Swordfish carried various arms: Dummy torpedoes, bombs and RP`s (Rocket Projectiles) the latter being fitted to pylons underneath the wings.

On 15th December 1943 Sub/Lt (A) J.L.Nichols, RNZN and crew took off with other aircraft from Maydown for an exercise at one of the ranges off Kintyre, but during the attack run the aircraft was damaged by debris from one of the rockets, though records don`t say whether the debris came from his own rocket or one of the other aircraft.

Fortunately he and his crew made it back to base and after a Cat. X2 damage assessment, the aircraft was repaired and put back into service.

A Fairey Swordfish with underwing RPs

Fairey Swordfish releasing a practice bomb

A few months later, but still with 836 Squadron, the Swordfish had been allocated for a night bombing exercise, again off Kintyre, but this time it wasn't so fortunate and failed to return.

On this occasion LS426, with Lt (A) Eric L. Heath and his Telegraphist Air Gunner L/A Arthur C. Martin, had taken off from Machrihanish early evening on 7th January 1944, but for reasons not known (possibly engine failure?) Lt Heath was forced to ditch in the sea and in doing so, his TAG either injured or unconscious, failed to get out and went down with the aircraft.

Lt Heath spent only a short time in the dinghy before being rescued by a naval vessel and brought ashore, suffering mainly from shock and exposure.

Records appear to only give a location for this accident as being off the Mull of Kintyre, which doesn't really help since the whole peninsula is often referred to in this way, however, a shipmate of the TAG said he witnessed the crash. So either he was in another Swordfish on the same exercise and it crashed near one of the ranges at Skipness or Ballure, or he was ashore at the airfield and it came down near Machrihanish Bay? Owing to this uncertainly, it is only marked by an Asterisk* on our location maps.

Pilot Lieutenant (A) Eric Lawrence Heath, born 4th July 1919 in Bromley, London, was the son of Mr & Mrs Bernard Heath. He had one older brother Bernard and was the husband of Pamela Heath (née Cosgrove) of London. The couple had two children.

Eric and his brother Bernard were former pupils at St.Alban's School, Bromley, Bernard until 1934 and Eric 1936. Both joined the services at the beginning of the war. Bernard having served abroad with the Royal Armoured Corps Tank Regiment spending much of his time in Sicily and Italy.

Having trained as a pilot with the RN Fleet Air Arm, Eric graduated at Worthy Down in August 1940 and was awarded his wings. While on leave on the 18th he married Miss Pamela Cosgrove at Westminster, but the happy couple only spent a short time together before he received a posting to join a FAA Squadron.

By July 1941 Eric, now a Sub/Lt was flying Swordfish with 812 Squadron operating from HMS *Furious,* and he is recorded as having flown Swordfish with L/A G.E.Cowsill for an attack on Petsamo, Finland, on 30 July 1941. (More info can be found on this mission in the account on N4330 on p.114).

It is understood that Eric was still serving with the 812 Squadron aboard HMS *Ark Royal* when she was hit by a torpedo from U-81 (Kptlt. Friedrich Guggenberger)on 13th November 1941, having only recently arrived in the Mediterranean and learned that the British Force H was passing through on its way to Gibraltar, Guggenberger managed to intercept and fire from close range to sink the carrier, but luckily Eric survived.

Eric's movements in 1942 are vague, but he was posted to 755 Squadron, a training unit at Worthy Down (*Kestrel*) on 3rd March 1943, flying as a pilot and instructor on the Percival Proctor.

HMS Ark Royal after the attack by U-81

He is also noted as serving as a Lieutenant at RNAS Burscough (*Ringtail*) near Ormskirk, Lancashire on 7th April 1945 until the end of the war, but his movements thereafter are unknown.

Telegraphist Air Gunner Leading Airman Arthur Charles Martin, RN, born 20th February 1924 in Walsall, Staffordshire, was the eldest son of Arthur Herbert and Rose Martin (née Noakes) of Walsall. He had one younger brother Alan Geoffrey

The family lived on Weston Street and his father Arthur Snr had served in WW1 as a medic with the R.A.M.C, first at a clearing station in England, but for much of the time in an operating theatre in France.

Both Arthur and his younger brother Alan, born in 1931, were educated locally and attended Palfrey School in Walsall.

On leaving school in 1939, Arthur worked in the transport office of Walsall Corporation Bus Company for three and a half years, and had just become a conductor when he received his call up papers for the Royal Navy in November 1942.

Following basic training at Portsmouth, he was assessed and sent on a gunnery course, thereafter a wireless school to become a Telegraphist Air Gunner in the RN Fleet Air Arm, finally graduating with his Air Gunners wings and eventually joining 836 Squadron at Machrihanish.

After the tragedy, a shipmate of Arthurs who witnessed the crash, wrote to his parents and was of the opinion that he had been knocked unconscious when the Swordfish hit the sea, and this being the reason he was unable to get out before the aircraft sank.

Sadly, despite an intensive search in the prevailing darkness, Arthur was never found and he is commemorated on the Lee-on-Solent Memorial. Bay 5. Panel 2.

L/A Arthur Charles Martin. RN

Photo: Author's Collection

The Fleet Air Arm Memorial at Lee-on-Solent   Photo: Author's Collection

NO MORE HAPPY RETURNS - SEAFIRE MB145

Construction of Supermarine Seafire MB145 was completed under contract No. B19713/3 from a production batch of 200 Mk. L.IIC's at the former RFC airfield Chattis Hill, Hampshire. The company had moved here after the bombing of their works at Hazel Road, Woolston, Southampton in September 1940.

First flown on 12th September 1942, the aircraft was delivered the following day to 15 MU at Wroughton in Wiltshire, then transferred to the Fleet Air Arm at Yeovilton on 12th April 1943 before joining 748 Squadron at St Merryn (*Curlew*) in Cornwall.

The Seafire stayed at here until May when it transferred to 885 Squadron aboard the 23,000 ton Illustrious-class aircraft carrier HMS *Formidable*, where at that time it carried the code `Ø6K`.

In November 1943 MB145 joined 809 Squadron and was reallocated to the 14,400 ton Attacker class escort carrier HMS *Stalker*.

The ship had arrived in the port of Liverpool in September for a refit after taking part in Operation *Avalanche*, the allied landings at Salerno, Italy, in September

HMS Stalker

A Seafire L.IIc from the same production batch as MB145 and at that time the same unit 885 Squadron, seen here aboard HMS Formidable

Joining 809 Squadron on 7th June 1943 having previously served aboard the carrier HMS *Unicorn*, a Royal New Zealand Navy pilot Sub/Lt (A) Stewart Ross Cameron embarked with the squadron aboard HMS *Stalker* on 29th December 1943.

Having been nominated for conversion for use as an Assault Carrier, the ship had undergone a major refit and following completion sailed from Liverpool to the Clyde for deployment in the NW Approaches, where she would begin work-up and flying exercises with Seafires of 809 and 897 Squadrons, which for a short period in January 1944 would use the airfield at Machrihanish as their temporary landing ground during exercises.

On Saturday 29th January, his 22nd birthday, Sub/Lt Stewart Cameron was airborne from the ship in Seafire MB145 and flying over Kintyre to the west of Campbeltown. He was heading towards the airfield at Machrihanish in rapidly fading light when his aircraft was observed to commence a roll at a height of around 500ft, during which it quickly entered a spin.

In an uncontrollable spiral decent with insufficient height to recover, at 15:55 hours the Seafire crashed on Aros Moss close to Aros Farm, south west of the airfield boundary and adjacent to the east/west runway. Farmers rushed to the scene but alas there was nothing that could be done for the young pilot.

213

The 809 Squadron badge portrays a Phoenix rising from the ashes with the enthusiastic motto: `Immortal` Sadly its pilots weren't. Though memories of this young flyer would doubtless be immortalised in the hearts of his family and friends.

Like the elders that farmed the land back then, all traces of the aircraft, save for a few tiny fragments have long since gone and the land is once again green pasture, leaving only this tale and the name of the pilot, posthumously etched on a headstone and war memorial as testament to the tragic passing of a brave young aviator who had died on his birthday.

Pilot Sub-Lieutenant (A) Stewart Ross Cameron, RNZNVR, born at Masterton New Zealand on 29th January 1922, was the son of Ernest Percival Stewart and Donalda Ross Cameron (née Sutherland) of Pahaua, Hinakura, Wellington, New Zealand, where he attended Wanganui Collegiate School.

Sub/Lt (A) Stewart Ross Cameron
RNZNVR

Photo: The NZ Weekly News

The family ran a farm in Pahaua and Stewart worked with his father as a shepherd as well as serving in the NZ Territorial Army Military Reserve. Then in February 1940 he joined the New Zealand Naval Force (Re-designated RNZN on 1/10/41) and was eventually posted to HMS *Phillomel* the Devonport Naval Base in North Shore City, Auckland, on loan to the Fleet Air Arm for aircrew under training.

Sailing to the UK on 18th June 1941 and arriving on 13th July, Stewart was sent to Lee-on-Solent before being posted to 14 EFTS at RAF Elmdon, Birmingham on 2nd November for specialist navy pilot training.

On 31st January 1942, along with other selectees, he embarked for Canada to join 31 SFTS at Kingston, Ontario, this unit was equipped with the Fairey Battle and North American Harvard aircraft, where after five months of rigorous training he graduated on 19th June and received his pilot's wings and a commission to Temporary Sub-Lieutenant.

Stewart returned to the UK for further training at 9 (P) AFU RAF Errol, Tayside on 10th August, followed by a fighter course at Yeovilton before joining 772 Squadron at Machrihanish on 7th December.

On 24th March 1943, Stewart was earmarked for flying the Sea Hurricane Mk IIC with 891 Squadron, but the unit was disbanded on 5th April after the squadron's Escort carrier HMS *Dasher* (D37) was destroyed by an internal explosion off the Isle of Arran in the Firth of Clyde and sank on 27th March with very heavy loss of life.

Following the loss of *Dasher*, on 24th April Stewart returned 772 Squadron at Machrihanish under command of Lt/Cdr. A.C. Mills, prior to his final posting to 809 Sqn on 7th June 1943.

Sub/Lt Stewart Ross Cameron was interred with respect and honour in Campbeltown, (Kilkerran) Cemetery. Division 4. Grave 637. His name is also recorded on the New Zealand Naval Memorial, Devonport, Auckland, and the 1939-1945 Roll of Honour at Wanganui Collegiate School where he was a pupil in the 1920s and 1930s..

Sub/Lt (A) Stewart Cameron's grave in Kilkerran Cemetery.
Photo: Author's Collection

A LUCKY ESCAPE - WILDCAT JV494

Under command of Lt/Cdr. (A) T.W. Harrington RN, 1832 Fleet Air Arm squadron had been formed at Eglinton on 15th August 1943. This was a single seat fighter aircraft squadron equipped with 10 Grumman FM-1 Wildcat Vs which moved to Stretton precisely one month later to form fighter flights of four aircraft per flight with two spare. Later they became attached to Torpedo Bomber Reconnaissance squadrons and served with escort carriers under Lt/Cdr. M. Hodern RN, until squadron disbandment on 1st June 1944.

Carrier borne Grumman Wildcat Vs   Photo: *Marion Titmuss*

Lt Eric Benson Gray in a Wildcat fighter. Photo: Marion Titmuss

A seasoned pilot, having flown many hours in Martlet IIs and IIIs with 795 Squadron from HMS *Kilele* Royal Naval Air Station, Tanga, Tanganyika and Kilindini, Kenya, Lt (A) Eric Benson Gray, RNVR, had arrived back in the UK to join 1832 Squadron in December 1943.

On Sunday 30th January 1944, Wildcat JV494, (USAAF serial 15645) was being ferried by Lt Gray from Stretton near Warrington, Cheshire to form 'C' Flight at Machrihanish, Kintyre.

Having taken off from Stretton around mid-morning, Lt Gray, accompanied by other aircraft in 'C' Flight, made his way along the northwest coast, picking up landmarks of Blackpool, Barrow and Ayr prior to crossing the Firth of Clyde to Kintyre.

In fine weather for that time of year, the flight went as planned, but on coming in to land, the aircraft's undercarriage collapsed and the robust fighter crashed to the ground sending sparks flying as it hurtled down the runway.

Eventually grinding to a halt, Lt Gray slid back the canopy, quickly unbuckled his harness, leapt down onto the wing and was away just moments before the stricken fighter burst into flames.

Crash crews rushed to the scene, but despite their best efforts, the fire was too fierce and eventually the aircraft burnt itself out, though with the efficiency of the Royal Navy it would not be long before a replacement aircraft arrived at the station, but until then the squadron would use one of the spares.

217

Lieutenant (A) Eric Benson Gray. RNVR

Photo: Marion Titmuss

Eric volunteered for the Royal Navy early in the war and trained as a pilot. He became a Temporary Midshipman (A) on 14th February 1942.

On 30th May he was posted to HMS *Afrikander,* a RN Fleet Air Arm base in Simons Town, South Africa, during which time he graduated as a pilot and became an Acting Sub/Lt (A) on 14th August and served at this station until 13th October when he was posted to RNAS Tanga (*Kilele*) in Tanganyika, East Africa, to join 795 Squadron, where he remained until the end of November 1943.

On 6th December 1944 he was posted to 1832 Squadron at Stretton and from 30th January at Machrihanish. Eric remained with 1832 until 6th April 1944, when he was posted overseas to RNAS

Lt (A) Eric Benson Gray. RNVR

Photo: Marion Titmuss

Lieutenant (A) Eric Benson Gray, RNVR, born in Ashton-Under-Lyne, Lancashire (now Tameside) on 30th August 1922, was the son of Arthur Sidney and Marion Gray (née Benson). He had two sisters Margaret and Dorenda, a younger brother Duncan and was husband of Thelma.

Eric's father was from Burnley, Lancashire where he ran a clothing business, but his mother was from Ashton-Under-Lyne. The couple had been married in St. James' Christ Church in Ashton on 20th August 1921 and Eric was the eldest of their four children.

In 1933 the family were living in Ripon, Yorkshire, but later moved to Sheffield. Derbyshire where Eric attended Ecclesall School.

Eric and Thelma on their wedding day
Photo: Marion Titmuss.

Puttalham (*Rajaliya*) in Ceylon (Sri Lanka) where he joined 890 Squadron, again flying Wildcats until August 1943 when the squadron disbanded.

The following month Eric, still at Puttalam, joined 757 Squadron and was under command of Lt/Cdr. G.W. Parrish, DSC. This was a Fighter Pool Squadron used for operational training and Eric switched from flying Wildcats to Seafire L.II's and IIIs in June 1944. The squadron also operated with Corsairs and Hellcats.

On 21st January 1945, Eric was posted to HMS *Golden Hind* for demob. This was a RN transit camp or manning depot which was situated at Warwick Farm on a former racecourse, but was commandeered by the Admiralty for the Pacific Fleet in Sydney, Australia.

Lt (A) Eric Benson Gray. RNVR

Seafire pilots of 757 Sqn Lt (A) Eric Benson Gray 3rd right standing at the back

Photo: Marion Titmuss

*Members of a RN Seafire squadron and RAAF airmen at a RN FAA base at Lorengau, Manus Island. Admiralty Islands. 25.08.1945
L to R: Lt Eric B. Gray RNVR, F/O R.G. Hambley, RAAF, Lt P.F. Dickson, RNVR, F/O J.D.Brocklehurst, RAAF and Lt/Cdr. J.H. Botiler, RN.*

Photo: AWM OG3295.

Eric's son believes his father attended the Empire Test Pilot School at Farnborough, and that towards the end of the war after returning to the UK, he had flown as a test pilot prior to demob as a Lieutenant on 14th February 1946.

Returning to civilian life Eric went to work with his father in the clothing business in Burnley, Lancashire, but always had a taste for something a little more adventurous. He was living at Redgates, Hope in Derbyshire in 1949 with his wife Thelma and son Howard, when he decided to emigrate to South Africa.

The family boarded the ship *Kenya* in London bound for Der-Es-Salaam, Tanzania, where Eric had hoped to fly as a crop duster for a firm there, but on arrival, after waiting several weeks, they still had no aircraft. Fortunately he managed to get a job with the Rhodesian Customs Office, and later became a colonial Police Officer eventually reaching the rank of Superintendent in the Tanganyaka Police.

In the late 1950s the family returned to the UK and Eric was given a post with MI6. His niece Marion recalls the family used to receive a Christmas card every year from the Queen, which she says took pride and place on the mantlepiece, but she always thought it was due to his job as a Police Officer in Africa.

Marion has fond memories of her uncle, an extraordinary man who lived life to the full.

"He always did everything with style, like wearing a cravat and smoking roll ups. As a child he used to take me out in one of his Jaguars and when I was older he gave me one of them, an old Mark IV.

He also gave me a huge leopard skin which he claimed he shot whilst out on safari, but apparently he had fallen asleep at the foot of a tree and it was above him, he was always upset at this as he loved the animals there and was a Park Ranger, however, it was him or the Leopard!

We spent every Christmas and summer staying at Gidcott Mill. He used to fly me about in his little private plane in Devon when he wanted to show me something or collect the milk".

When Eric returned to England and was living at Gidcott Mill, Shebbear, Holsworthy, Devon, he became a craft master at Shebbear College, a post he held until retirement, but it was always a far cry from the thrill and excitement of flying Wildcats and Seafires, which during the war earned him the 1939-45 star, Atlantic Star, Africa Star, Italian Star & Pacific Clasp, Defence Medal and War Medal.

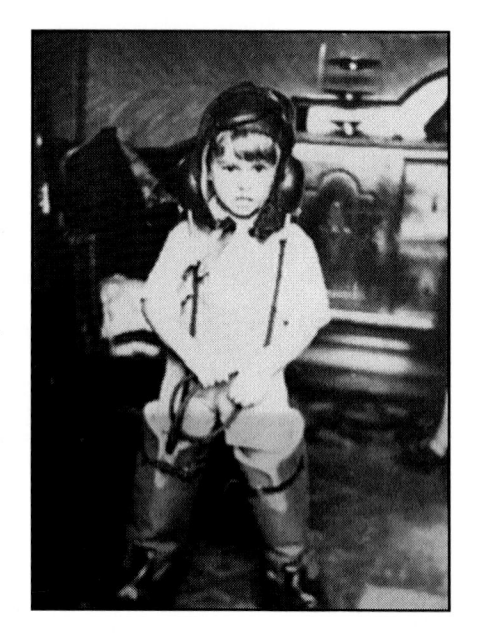

Eric's little brother Duncan tries big bro's flying helmet and boots for size

Photo: Marion Titmuss

Eventually ill health caught up with Eric, mainly from smoking and he lost a leg due to a thrombosis, but was often still out and about and loved travelling to nearby air shows in Devon and Cornwall.

On 17th May 1990, Eric was with family on a planned trip to an air display in Cornwall when it is understood he suffered a heart attack, a Royal Navy Sea King helicopter from St. Mawgan arrived to take him to hospital, but sadly he lost his life, either enroute or soon after reaching the hospital. His death was registered at St. Austell, Cornwall. A sad end for a fine gentleman and a great pilot.

NO TURNING BACK - BARRACUDA LS582

An unusually warm early spring day presented itself on Wednesday 29th March 1944, as First Officer Edward Gordon Masson Palmer, an Air Transport Auxiliary (ATA) pilot from 16 Ferry Pilots Pool at Kirkbride, Cumberland, arrived at Machrihanish to collect a Barracuda Mk.II LS582 for delivery across the Clyde to a new unit in Scotland.

Easing the five ton torpedo bomber into the air, F.O. Palmer had just begun to climb away from the airfield into a light north-easterly breeze when suddenly without warning, all power on the Merlin 32 engine cut out, the aircraft instantly lost flying speed and began to stall and with the words of warning `Never, never turn back, land straight ahead whatever the terrain!` etched firmly in his memory from his training days, he scoured the fields below for a safe place to land.

Having spotted a suitable field but with insufficient time to raise the undercarriage or lower the flaps, he crash landed wheels down close to Glencraig's Farm, off the A831 Campbeltown to Bellochantuy road, but the Barracuda, still travelling at speed was unable to stop and hit either a ditch or fence, at which point F.O. Palmer was flung forward and sustained minor injuries requiring hospital treatment. LS582 was later examined by a salvage team and discovered to be damaged beyond economical repair.

Some information on the Barracuda revealed that it had been manufactured by The Fairey Aviation Company Ltd, Heaton Chapel, Stockport, and was available for delivery on the 22nd January 1944, just prior to its arrival at HMS *Landrail*.

The aircraft's remains were removed from the field and originally thought to have been scrapped, but eight years later in March 1952, they were noted as being among numerous dismantled ex-Fleet Air Arm aircraft on the McDonnell Aircraft of Milnathort dump at RAF Baladoo Bridge, Kinross.

When making inquiries about this accident at Glencraig, it was established that at least three aircraft came down in the area, one hit a fence, (believed to have been LS582) another crashed on a hill above Kilmicheal and another Barracuda crashed in a field near Kilmaho Farm.

Fairey Barracuda II

Arial view of the general area of the crash of LS582 at Glencraigs off the A83

Photo: Author's Collection

First Officer Edward Gordon Masson Palmer, ATA, born 16th August 1899 in Wimbledon, southwest London, was the son of Edward and Isabella Palmer of Chertsey, Surrey, and elder brother of Dudley Seaman Palmer.

Edward's father was born in Kensington, but his mother was originally from Leith, Edinburgh. His father was the manager of a wholesale costume factory so the family were quite comfortably off. They lived at Alwyne Cottage, Horsell, Woking and the two boys attended schools in Surrey.

Gordon as he was known, had originally joined the military when it was still the Royal Flying Corps on 19th September 1917. The Corps became the Royal Air Force in April 1918 and he qualified as a pilot on 16th Sept 1918.

With the war over in November, he was demobbed as a Sergeant pilot, and went back to civilian life, but hoped to continue flying socially. While residing at Alwyn Cottage, Horsell, Woking, he joined the Royal Aero Club and began flying light aircraft and ex-military machines at the weekends.

During the early 1920s Gordon had been living and working as an engineer and motor mechanic in Canada, but returned to England via New Brunswick on board the Canadian–Pacific liner the SS *Montcalm* (Master Alexander Rennie) on 2nd February 1924, calling first at Glasgow on the 10th and finally arriving in Liverpool on the 16th.

F.O. Edward Gordon Masson Palmer Pictured in the Royal Flying Corps

In March 1933 he married Miss Katherine Kendall in Kingston, Surrey and the couple were later blessed with two sons Graham and Stephen.

When the Second World War broke out in Sept 1939, Gordon hoped to join the RAF as a pilot, but at 40 was considered too old, but when the civilian organisation ATA was formed at White Waltham, Maidenhead on 15th February 1940, in order to ferry both new and overhauled aircraft for the RAF and Fleet Air Arm, WW1 veterans and interwar civilian pilots of all nationalities were required, so Gordon jumped at the chance to join them and before long was ferrying aircraft of all shapes and sizes up and down the country.

Gordon behind the wheel of the family convertible, with his father Edward in the front passenger seat and his brother Dudley behind the driver.

Photo: Stuart Roberts

Ferrying aircraft could be a very hazardous job and despite being a very good pilot, not all went according to plan as he knew only too well.

Gordon was with 6 Ferry Pilot Pool based at Kirkbride and on one such occasion he had been ferrying a Tiger Moth T7241, up to Prestwick when he ran into trouble. It was nearing 13:00 on 1st March 1942, when just as he was about to land, he was hit by a cross-wind and forced to climb in order to go around again, but as he did, his engine failed and on losing height he hit the pole of a wind sock, but was luck to escape with only minor repairable damage and no injury to himself.

Another minor incident occurred on 31st August the same year when ferrying a twin engine Airspeed Oxford, apparently a short circuit in the charging switch had caused a small fire and he was forced to make an emergency landing on an unused part of an airfield in the Midlands.

Little damage was caused to the aircraft and like the Tiger Moth, it was swiftly repaired and put back into service.

Gordon survived the war and eventually returned to `civvy street`. He was a resident in Imber Grove, Esher, Surrey when he passed away on 15th September 1976 at the age of 77.

DOWN OFF CARRADALE - AVENGER FN878

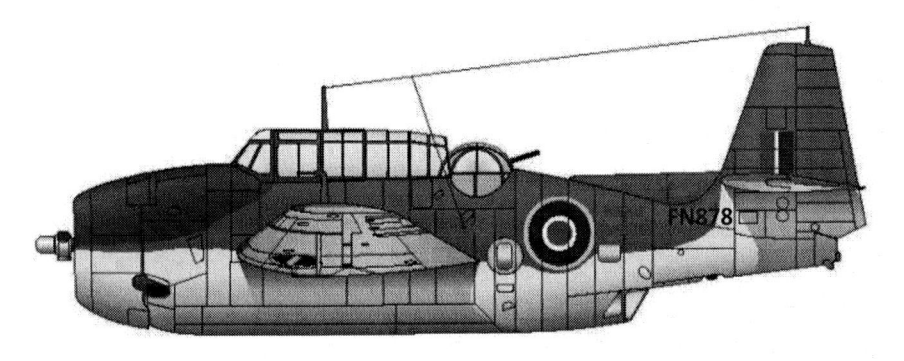

Grumman TBF-1C Avenger 1 FN878 was initially taken on charge by 849 Squadron at Squantum near Quincy, Norfolk County, Massachusetts, on the 1st August 1943, but unfortunately at the end of the month the aircraft was involved in a minor accident when Sub/Lt R.E. Swain, upon landing, failed to ensure the tailwheel was fully locked. The damage luckily was only minor and after being repaired locally the Avenger quickly returned to service.

On 1st November 1943 the Squadron was transferred on board the 16,620 ton Ruler Class Escort Carrier HMS *Khedive* (D62) and after arriving in Liverpool on the 16th the aircraft disembarked to nearby Speke airfield the following day.

Throughout the winter months of 1943/44, 849 Squadron transferred to several Royal Naval Air Stations within the UK, including: Grimsetter (*Robin*) near Kirkwall, Orkney, Maydown and Eglinton, both in Northern Ireland, and Machrihanish on Kintyre.

On 25th March 1944, FN878 was reallocated to 848 Squadron, though it remained at *Landrail*, under command of Lt/Cdr. A.P Boddam-Whetham. DSC. RN.

On Tuesday 11th April, Fleet Air Arm Pilot Sub/Lt Malcolm Sidney Beard accompanied by his Observer Sub/Lt Anthony Angel Temple and Telegraphist Air Gunner L/A John Reed, were airborne in the Avenger over the east coast of Kintyre when they ran into trouble, (possibly engine failure?) and were unable to reach land.

The pilot had no alternative but to ditch the aircraft in a cold grey sea north-east of Carradale Point, but regrettably all didn`t go according to plan, the aircraft hit hard and was soon submerged, taking with it the three crew, although

227

Grumman Avenger 1 of 848 Squadron in 1944. Photo: Crown Copyright.

the body of one, Sub/Lt Temple, was later found and returned home for burial.

There is at least one source (Landrail Death Register) which suggests a fourth man was on the aircraft, Sick Berth Attendant Albert John Brier, RN. Aged 24 from Spen Valley, West Riding, Yorkshire. The entry says that this man died on the same day at Carradale Point in a flying accident, yet oddly he is not mentioned in Ray Sturtivant's RN FAA Aircraft book of losses.

Only sparse details have been found on this crew, with virtually nothing apart from the odd death notice appearing in newspapers. Royal Navy lists and the London Gazette did contain some information on promotions and units, but these details are few and far between. Information found is as follows:

Pilot. Sub-Lieutenant (A) Malcolm Sidney Beard, RN, born 1923, was the son of Roy Glendenning and Winifred Terry Beard (née Jackson) of Kilburn, Middlesex. He had one sister Joan.

Malcolm's parents were married at St.Peter's Church in Ealing in on 9th December 1919. His father, a former Stage actor had taken over the family business as an estate agent and property surveyor, and his mother was a former telephonist. The family lived at Buckingham Mansions in London.

Malcolm joined the RN Fleet Air Arm early 1943 and as a Midshipman, then Acting Sub/Lt from 1st September 1943, he conducted part of his flying training at East Haven HMS (*Peewit*) near Carnoustie on the east coast of Scotland.

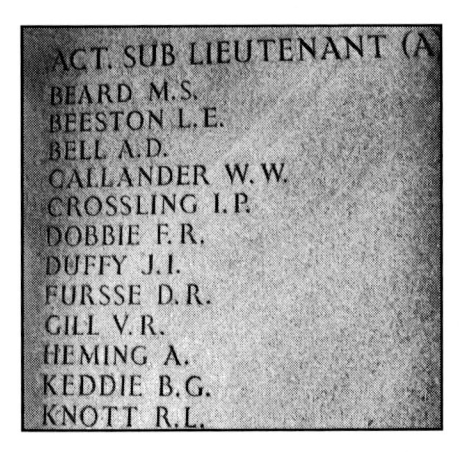

ACT. SUB LIEUTENANT (A
BEARD M.S.
BEESTON L.E.
BELL A.D.
CALLANDER W.W.
CROSSLING I.P.
DOBBIE F.R.
DUFFY J.I.
FURSSE D.R.
GILL V.R.
HEMING A.
KEDDIE B.G.
KNOTT R.L.

Sub/Lt Beard on Lee-on-Solent Panel 7

Photo: CWGC

On 8th February 1944 he was serving with 767 Squadron on board the aircraft carrier HMS *Activity* (D94) on convoy escort duties, but then transferred to 848 Squadron on 1st March at Maydown and Eglinton, Northern Ireland, and also the detachment at Machrihanish as a full Sub-Lieutenant.

Having not been found, services were held for Malcolm in his home town of Kilburn and his name is commemorated on the Lee-on-Solent Memorial to the Missing in Hampshire. Bay 5. Panel 7.

Observer Sub-Lieutenant (A) Anthony Angel Temple, RNVR, born 1922, was the son of John and Raie (Rachel) Temple (née Shaen) of Neasden, London. He had one brother Leslie and two sisters Joyce and Sylvia.

Anthony's parents were Jewish and had been married in Croydon, Surrey in 1913. Their four children all attended Jewish schools in the borough and in London.

Anthony joined the Royal Navy in 1942 and trained as an Observer, graduating on 14th August 1943 when he was awarded his brevet and promoted to Acting Sub-Lieutenant. He was interred in Willesden Jewish Cemetery, London. Section R. Row 3. Grave 12.

Telegraphist Air Gunner Leading Airman John Reed, RN, born 4th July 1923 in Sunderland, County Durham, was the son of Ernest and Mary Elizabeth Reed (née Grieff) of Sunderland. Brother of Edward and Nora and Husband of Evelyn Reed (née Wilkinson) of Surrey. John having no grave is commemorated on the Lee-on-Solent Memorial. Bay 5. Panel 3.

Sub/Lt Temple's grave in Willesden

DEAD ENGINE DILEMMA - WHITLEY BD393

Forming part of 6 Group RAF Bomber Command, 19 Operational Training Unit moved to Kinloss, near Forres on 27th May 1940, where it was equipped with twin engine Whitley and Anson aircraft for the training of aircrew for night bombing sorties.

At the end of July, emphasising the importance of these training units, the OTU was informed that in the event of an invasion in the north, it was to attack all troop-carrying surface craft and on receipt of the codeword `Julius Caesar` all training was to cease, and all available Whitley and Anson crews should be prepared for operations.

On 11th May 1942, 6 Group became 91 Group and the earlier Whitley IIIs with the rather underpowered 920hp Armstrong Siddley Tiger VIII radial engines, had already been replaced with the Whitley Mk. IV and Mk. V with V12 inline Rolls-Royce Merlin`s boasting 1,030hp and 1,145hp.

By 1944, despite the model having greatly improved with the various modifications, engine failures were still a problem and if one or both powerplants happened to fail while over the sea, not many lived to tell the tale.

Briefed for a cross country navigation exercise on Tuesday 11th April 1944, Sergeant Cyril A. White and his five crew took off from Kinloss at 09:10 bound for the west coast of Scotland.

Sgt White was new to the unit and had only flown 19hrs 45min on the type, so this daytime exercise could be considered a warm up for future night flights in order to familiarise him with the aircraft.

All had gone according to plan on the first part of the exercise and Whitley BD393 was on its return leg heading eastwards, when on nearing the coast at a height of 15,000 feet, the port engine suddenly failed and all attempts to restart it proved fruitless. The crew was now faced with a dilemma, either ditch in the sea, risk suffering from exposure and chance being found, or find the nearest landing ground. Choosing the latter the navigator gave a course to steer for the nearest available airfield, and the W/Op sent out a distress call.

It was soon discovered Machrihanish was the nearest base, and in fact quite close and dead ahead, but although the aircraft appeared to be losing height quite quickly, Sgt White, on approach and with clearance to land, saw he was

ZV-M of 19 OTU though not BD393. This is N1503 which after damage in a landing accident with 10 OTU in April 1941 was used as an instructional airframe 3073M

coming in too high (around 2,000ft) to effect a safe landing on the runway, and so after overshooting and with wheels up, at approximately 11:25 he made a perfect crash landing in a field to the east in the area of West Backs.

Fortunately with the aircraft pretty much still intact and with no fire, all the crew escaped uninjured. Rescue services were soon at the scene and the airmen taken to Machrihanish pending return to Kinloss.

Examination of the airframe later revealed structural damage and it was deemed a Cat. E write-off and Struck Off Charge on 21st April. The failed engine was removed and once stripped down it was discovered that after oil stoppage, the crankshaft overheated, a cod rod broke and the bearings seized.

No blame was placed on the pilot for the loss of the aircraft, and he was in fact praised for coping under an immensely stressful situation.

A Whitley V in a similar predicament to how BD393 ended up on Kintyre

Whitley BD393 was one of 157 Mk.Vs built and delivered between 26th April and 15th May 1942, by the Armstrong Whitworth Aviation factory at Baginton, Warwickshire.

Pilot Sergeant Cyril Arthur White, RAFVR, born 29th April 1921 in Wantage, Berks, was the son of Arthur Edward and Gladys White (née Goddard) of Ashford, Middlesex.

Arthur's parents were married in the summer of 1914 in Wantage, but after the WW1 ended the couple moved to Feltham in the London borough of Hounslow. Arthur was educated at Hampton Grammar School in London and was later employed as a clerk in Hounslow Post Office from 1937-1942.

He joined the RAF in February 1942 and after basic training as an LAC he was selected for pilot training in Canada, embarking in September that year and returning to the UK having gained his pilots wings and promotion to sergeant in May 1943.

The next 8-10 months was spent training in the UK, flying cross country navigation and bombing exercises in the Anson and Whitley, prior to spending some time at a Heavy Conversion Unit for 4 engine bombers, and a posting to 640 Squadron flying Halifax bombers from Leconfield, East Riding, Yorkshire.

After flying 10 dangerous operations over enemy occupied Europe, on the night of 25th August 1944, Arthur's aircraft Halifax NA578, having taken off at 18:30 hours, failed to return its Yorkshire base.

Sgt Cyril Arthur White. RAFVR

The Halifax had been on a bombing raid to Nazi occupied Watten, France, when likely hit by flak it crashed killing all the crew consisting: P/O C.A. White, Sgt H. Ward, F/Sgt S.Jenkins, F/Sgt J.D.Duffin RCAF, Sgt G. Warren, Sgt A.J.Aiden and Sgt R.A.J.Bosworth, all of whom now rest in a collective grave in Longuenesse (St.Omer) Souvenir Cemetery, Pas de Calais, France, Plot 6. Row C. Grave 2.

Arthur had been commissioned Pilot Officer on 16th May 1944, just prior to him going on to fly the Halifax.

A memorial plaque has been placed at Eperleques by a local French history group, at a spot which is thought to be close to where the aircraft crashed.

FALLEN FULMAR X8751

Having been stationed at RNAS Machrihanish since 15th June 1942, with their Vought Chesapeake, Boulton Paul Defiant and Blackburn Roc aircraft, 772 RN Fleet Air Arm squadron was, by Spring 1944, operating with the Bristol Blenheim, Hawker Hurricane and the Fairey Fulmar 1 & II, under the command of Lt/Cdr. P.J. Connolly since his arrival in August 1943.

The Fulmar II had been updated from the Mk.1 and instead of being powered by a 1030hp Rolls-Royce Merlin VIII, it now boasted a 1,300 hp (970 kw) Merlin XXX with a new propeller and the addition of tropical equipment. The Mk.II was also armed with eight 0.303 or four 0.50 calibre Browning machine guns.

The role of the squadron since its arrival on Kintyre was mainly to train aircrew for coastal defence, with activities here consisting of height finding exercises, target towing duties for gunnery practice, radar calibration and photography, the latter being the role of a Fulmar II crew on the afternoon of Thursday 27th April 1944.

On the day in question, FAA Pilot Sub/Lt (A) David Maddock and a RN Photographer (A) Stanley Whale, had been flying a routine photographic sortie off the west coast of Scotland in X8751 when they ran into bad weather. Unable to continue with the exercise due to low cloud, they were instructed to return base at Machrihanish.

Flying in and out of the overcast the crew apparently struggled to get their bearings and at approximately 14:30, the aircraft crashed into a hill near Black Loch, some two miles south of Campbeltown. The machine was totally wrecked and sadly there were no survivors.

Nobody saw the actual crash, but witnesses who later saw the wreckage recalled that the impact point was close to the western peak of Beinn Ghullean and that wreckage was scattered over a wide area. Mr Dugald McKendrick a farmer at No3 Tomaig, recalled that the engine lay around 200 yards from the main wreckage.

Fairey Fulmar II

Though a guard was placed at the crash site and the bodies of the two unfortunate airmen had been recovered, a group of local boys managed to retrieve one of the machine guns and belts of ammunition as souvenirs, but the authorities were quick to recover the items and gave the boys a severe reprimand.

Another man local to that area, Jock Hamilton of 4 Killeonan, was involved in the recovery operation and used his horse to drag the larger pieces of the aircraft down to his uncles house at 4 Tomaig, where his uncle William Hamilton loaded it onto a lorry for removal.

Over the years some of the smaller parts no doubt found their way into sheds and barns in the area. The aircraft's tail wheel is reputed to have been improvised on a wheel barrow, and little hose clamps used for tractor repairs.

One more sinister tale however, was that of a young man who in later years had purchased a pair of old flying goggles for use in riding his motorcycle, but was most displeased to learn later that they had belonged to one of the crew and had been found at the crash site in 1944.

X8751 had been delivered to RNAS Ford (*Peregrine*) Sussex on 8th Oct 1941, from a consignment of 200 built under contract by the Fairey aviation factory at Heaton Chapel, Stockport.

The aircraft had served originally with 768 Squadron at Arbroath (*Condor*) where it was actively involved in Deck Landing Trials, during which Sub/Lt G.R.A.Darling while landing on HMS *Argus,* overshot the wire and went into nets over the side of the deck causing Cat. Y damage on 22nd July 1942.

Having been repaired at a shore station, the Fulmar was taken on charge with 772 Squadron in December 1943, only to be written off five months later on Kintyre. On 6th July 1944 the squadron moved Ayr and began operating as a Fleet Requirements Unit with the Miles Martinet TT.1 for target towing.

Pilot Sub-Lieutenant (A) David Llwellyn Maddock RNVR, aged 20, was the son of W.E. Maddock and Mary Gertrude Maddock of West Kensington, London.

David was born in Wales and attended schools in Llandovery, a pleasant little market town in Carmarthenshire, situated on the banks of the River Tywi, but the family later moved to Kensington.

Having trained as a pilot with the Fleet Air Arm, David eventually graduated and was awarded his wings in 1943. He is mentioned in the RN Lists as having been promoted from Temporary Sub/Lt to a full Sub/Lt with seniority on 11th August 1943.

David was posted to Machrihanish soon after being promoted and served both here and at Ballykelly in Northern Ireland on detachment with 772 Squadron flying Fulmars.

Shortly after the accident he was returned home for burial and following a service in his local church, he was accorded a full military funeral with interment in West Drayton Cemetery, Uxbridge. His grave lies in Block A. Row F. Grave 27.

Photographer (A) Stanley William Whale. RN. Aged 21, was born in Edmonton, Middlesex in 1922. He was the son of Frederick George and Ellen Whale (née Davies) of Forty Hill, Enfield, Middlesex.

After basic training in the RN Stanley applied for the Fleet Air Arm, he was a keen photographer and so attended various courses to train in this trade. On graduation he was awarded his Photographer badge, which was equivalent to the rank

Photographer Stanley Whale's grave

of an Able Seaman. The insignia was a blue bellows camera which would have been worn on his sleeve. (See below).

RN Photographer's insignia

Stanley was returned home for interment in Enfield (Lavender Hill) Cemetery, Middlesex. Sec. C. Gen. Old Part. Grave 1746.

235

George McSporran with pieces of alloy from Fairey Fulmar X8751
Photo: Angus Martin

AVENGER ON DEER HILL FN867

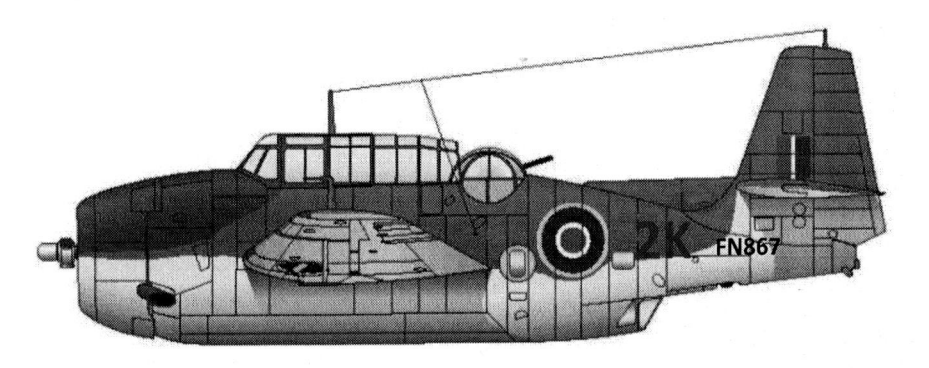

Formed at Naval Air Station Squantum, Quincy, Massachusetts, on 1st November 1943, 852 Royal Navy Fleet Air Arm squadron used this American base for advanced training with TBF Avengers in a torpedo bomber reconnaissance role.

On 19th March 1943, HMS *Nabob*, a 15,400 ton Ruler Class Escort Carrier, obtained by the RN under a Lend/Lease agreement, arrived in New York and secured alongside pier No13 at Staten Island, where she took aboard 12 Avenger Mk.1s and a number of P-51 Mustangs for transit to the UK, where they would take part in exercises in a build up to minelaying operations off the Norwegian coast. On 23rd March the carrier joined the US military troopship convoy UT10 and embarked for

HMS Nabob (D77)

Gladstone Dock, Liverpool and finally Greenock, Scotland with the Avengers stored below and the Mustangs securely lashed to the upper deck. She braved the North Atlantic in a convoy of 26 ships under escort of 12 destroyers led by the American Cruiser USS *Cincinnati* and in company of the escort oiler USS *Chemig*.

Fortunately no U-boats were detected during the crossing, but foul weather with gale force winds on two of the days did cause the convoy to alter course a couple of times, however, *Nabob* eventually arrived in Liverpool on 5th April, and after a couple of unsuccessful attempts to dock due to fog, she was finally escorted in with tugs.

Once the American P-51s had been unloaded, the following day *Nabob* embarked for Greenock and during the passage seven of the Avengers took off for Machrihanish, with the remainder being catapulted off once she was at anchor in Tail of the Bank at Greenock.

With the carrier later returning to Liverpool for refit and mods, 852 Squadron would remain at Machrihanish under command of Lt/Cdr. R.E. Bradshaw until 26th June, then operate with a small detachment at Maydown in Londonderry, Northern Ireland.

Inevitably, due to the unpredictable weather often accorded by the location of Machrihanish, minor accidents were not uncommon, but the following month tragedy struck when FN867 failed to return from an exercise.

On the morning of Sunday 28th May 1944, with low cloud and mist covering much of the Kintyre peninsula, Avenger FN867 '2K' piloted by Sub/Lt (A) Reginald Eric Lord, RNVR and his three crew consisting: Obs. Sub/Lt (A) Ronald Thomas Thwaites, RNVR. TAG L/A Alan Glenister Winder, RN and Mech AM(L)1 Edgar William Gallant, RN

Grumman Avenger 1 of the RN Fleet Air Arm

was returning from a routine bombing exercise at the Skipness range when it ran into trouble due to bad weather.

The crew must have been desperately trying to locate their position in relation to the high ground to the east of the airfield when without warning, at approximately 11:00 the Avenger impacted with a cloud shrouded hill at Cnoc nan Gabhar (Hill of Deer) high above Auchnasavil farm, two miles northwest of Carradale on the east coast of Kintyre.

It was not until the cloud lifted that the full extent of the accident scene was revealed. All the crew had perished in the crash and torn and twisted wreckage lay scattered over some distance.

Once the unfortunate crew had been removed for burial, a recovery team soon arrived and were billeted at the farm, taking almost until the end of June to recover major parts of the airframe and engine by vehicle, and leaving lorry tracks still visible on the hill for decades.

Information found on the aircraft revealed it was a TBF-1 Model G-40, Constructed by Grumman Aircraft Engineering Corporation of Bethpage, New York from a batch of 200 and given the US serial number 24153.

It was delivered and allocated to the Royal Navy under the Lend Lease Scheme agreement between the United Kingdom and the United States of America, upon which it was given the serial FN867 and taken on charge by 768 Squadron at Lewiston, Maine. It stayed with this pilot training unit for only a short while before transferring to 852 Squadron at Squantum, Massachusetts.

Pilot Sub-Lieutenant Reginald Eric Lord, RNVR, born 1917 in Ormskirk, was the only son of Walter and Sally Lord (née Hartley) of Ormskirk, Lancashire. The family moved to Southport in the 1920s where Reg attended King George V School. He was a keen sportsman and played Association football for the Southport Schoolboys team, taking part in several Lancashire county matches.

Subsequently, he also played cricket for Holy Trinity in the Southport and District League and Birkdale Cricket Club, but his real passion was rugby and in the 1930s he played for Southport Rugby Union Football Club and is understood to have been on the 1937/38 First XV team. In civilian life Reg was a Police Officer and served with Liverpool City Police and the Metropolitan Police.

Sub/Lt Reginald Eric Lord. RNVR
Photo: Southport Library

239

He joined the Royal Navy Fleet Air Arm in 1942 and after qualifying as a flying cadet he was posted overseas to America for further training as a pilot. He graduated on 27th March 1943 when he was awarded his pilots wings and promoted to Acting Sub-Lieutenant

Arriving back in the UK at Easter, Reg eventually joined 852 Squadron at Machrihanish for torpedo dive bombing exercises with the Avenger. Just prior to this on 27th September he had been promoted to the rank of full Sub-Lieutenant.

Following the tragedy on Kintyre, Sub-Lieutenant (A) Reg Lord, was accorded a full military funeral at Duke Street Cemetery, Southport, attended by family and many friends from his school and sports teams. He was interred in section 11, grave 254. His name is also inscribed on Southport War Memorial, Lord Street.

Observer Sub-Lieutenant (A) Ronald Thomas John Thwaites, RNVR, was born in Medway, Kent in 1922. He was the eldest son of Frank O and Winifred E. Thwaites (née Moore) of Gillingham and husband of Audrey Kathleen Thwaites (née Stroud) of Rochester. He had one brother Derek.

Ronald hailed from a nautical background, his grandfather John was a Shipwright, his great uncle Edward a naval engineer and his father Frank served in the RN as an Engine Room Artificer 3rd Class (ERA3) in the First World War and was awarded the 1915 Star, British War Medal and Victory medal.

On 1st February 1929, for reasons unknown, Ronald aged six, and his brother Derek who was just 6 months old, sailed with their mother Winifred to Malta aboard the 11,518 GRT passenger liner the RMS *Keiser-i-Hind*.

The two boys were educated in Chatham, and given his background it seemed inevitable Ronald would follow in his father and grandfather's footsteps and this began at Chatham Dockyard School as a Shipwright Apprentice, when he scored 221 from a possible 400 in exams at the end of his first term in August 1939. However, with the outbreak of war arriving a month later, Ronald's career would be cut short and like his father, he joined the navy.

After basic training he applied for and was accepted as aircrew with the Fleet Air Arm and began training as an observer, finally graduating and being awarded his observers badge and promotion to Temp Sub/Lt on 2nd July 1943.

His first posting was to 791 Squadron at RNAS Arbroath (*Condor*) just south of Montrose on the east coast of Scotland. Here he would fly Swordfish and act as observer for crews on target towing exercises, under the command of Lt/Cdr. (A) C.A. Crighton. RNVR.

Following the accident Ronald was interred in Gillingham (Woodlands) Cemetery, Kent, with a full guard of honour. Section A. Grave 989.

Telegraphist Air Gunner Leading Airman 3rd Class, Alan Glenister Winder, RN, was born in Hammersmith on 23rd December 1922. He was the son of Dr. Wilfred M. Winder and Mrs F.A. Winder of Chiswick, Middlesex.

Above: TAG L/A Alan Winder pictured here while training at Yarmouth in Canada on TAG's Course 46A in 1943. Photo: TAG's Assn Via Ken Sims

Alan, known as 'Ray' to other TAGs for some reason or other, joined the Royal Navy Fleet Air Arm in 1942 and following basic training in Plymouth, was sent overseas to Canada, where at Yarmouth he joined TAGs Course 46A and graduated as a Telegraphist Air Gunner in February 1943.

Alan was cremated at Mortlake Crematorium at Kew, Meadowpath, Richmond-Upon-Thames. He is now commemorated on the Cemetery War Dead Memorial Panel 13.

Air Mechanic 1st Class. Edgar William Gallant, RN, was born 23rd July 1923 in Ipswich. He was son of Edgar William and Elizabeth Gllant (née Cowan) of Ipswich Town, Suffolk.

Edgar's father hailed from Ipswich but his mother was born in St.Anthony's, Newcastle-Upon-Tyne. Following the accident he was returned home for interment in a family plot in Ipswich Old Cemetery. Grave Ref: X.H.6. 117.

Grave of AM1c Edgar W. Gallant

LOST CONTACT - FIREFLY Z1891

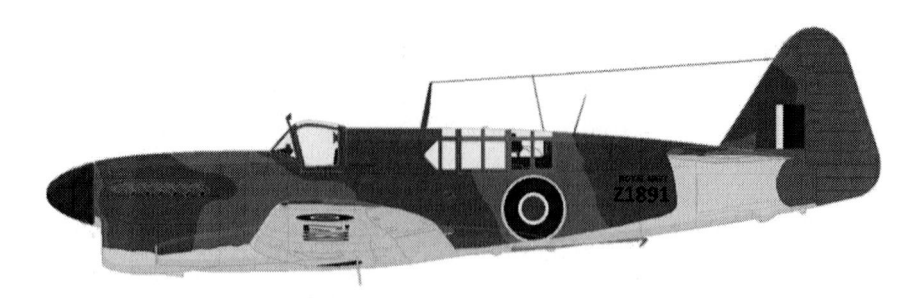

Taking off from Machrihanish airfield on the morning of Saturday 24th June 1944, Pilot Lt (A) Henry Alexander MacKay accompanied by Observer Sub/Lt Harry Kenneth Slater, eased the Fairey Firefly Z1891 'D' into the air at 09:10 and flew and climbed skyward for the days task.

Orders were to proceed to their squadron carrier HMS *Indefatigable,* an Implacable-class aircraft carrier, built by John Brown & Company, Clydebank, which was enroute to the rendezvous position situated 120 degrees and 3 miles from the island of Ailsa Craig. Then, at 09:33, they would fly a course direct to the ship which would be a distance of 20 miles.

At 09:33 they received a radio message stating that due to deteriorating weather conditions, a landing on the carrier's deck was unsuitable and a return to Machrihanish was advisable.

Sadly, Z1891 was never seen again and the only contact was a faint radio transmission from Lt Mackay at 10:25 hours before all contact was lost.

It was not until Wednesday 5th July that the sea finally released Lt Mackay`s body which was found off Southend at the foot of the Kintyre peninsula. Unfortunately, the Observer Harry Slater, despite an intensive search by Air Sea Rescue and RN vessels, was never found.

Fairey Firefly 1

Pilot Lieutenant (A) Henry Alexander Mackay. Royal New Zealand Naval Volunteer Reserve, born in Napier, NZ on 22nd September 1913, was the son of Norman and Beatrice MacKay (née Murrow) of Hawkes Bay, Napier, New Zealand. He had one brother Norman.

Henry, prior to entering the NZNF (Later RNZAF) at Napier, was employed with Napier BHS as an assistant bacteriologist with Hawkes Bay Hospital Board.

Having joined the NZNF in Spring 1941, he signed up for under training aircrew on 13th July and shortly after on the 22nd, embarked with other trainees for the UK on attachment to the RN/FAA at Gosport (*St.Vincent*) in September.

Next came Lee-on-Solent where he was assessed and got his first taste of flying in DH82A Tiger Moths belonging to the 24 EFTS, becoming a U/T pilot here on 21st December. It would be here that the grades of cadets would decide if they were good enough for pilot training in Canada.

Luckily Henry passed with flying colours and he and other successful candidates were sent to the RAF Aircrew Dispatch Centre for embarkation to Canada on 15th May 1942, where pupils would be attached to 31 SFTS under the British Commonwealth Training Plan for further classroom work and flying training on Yale and Harvard aircraft.

After graduation, pilots wings and promotion to Temp Sub/Lt, on 25th September Henry returned to the UK and was again attached to an RAF unit, 9 (P) AFU at Yeovilton for fighter training on the Seafire.

On completion of the course and following a spot of leave, he received orders to join 899 Squadron on 3rd May 1943 on board the fleet carrier HMS *Indomitable*.

Lt (A) Henry Alexander MacKay RNZNVR. Photo: NZ Weekly News

The ship sailed for the Mediterranean in June and the following month the squadron helped provide fighter cover for the Sicily landings, but alas the carrier was damaged by a torpedo and the aircraft had to disembark for Gibraltar (*Cormorant*) then transfer to HMS *Hunter*.

Henry was a spare pilot with the squadron, so on 1st July he was posted to the UK where he eventually joined 1770 Squadron on 10th September and flew Firefly aircraft.

Operating from HMS *Indefatigable,* the shore stations were often used when the ship was in port or if a landing couldn't be made on the deck due to bad weather, hence the reason for Z1891 being at Machrihanish.

Fairey Firefly 1 of 1770 Squadron aboard HMS Indefatigable
Photo: The Aviation Photo Company

Lt Henry MacKay's grave in Kilkerran
Photo: Author's Collection

After he was found at Southend, (map key 31 denotes where his body was found—The aircraft having not been located) arrangements were made for the funeral and following a service at Machrihanish, his interment in Campbeltown (Kilkerran) Cemetery was carried out with a full guard of honour. Henry now rests in Div. 4. Grave 597 overlooking Campbeltown Loch.

Observer Sub-Lieutenant (A) Harry Kenneth Slater, RNVR, born 1923 in Chorlton, Lancashire, was the son of James Henry and Gertrude Sybil Slater (née Phillips) of Monton, Eccles, Lancs.

Harry attended Eccles Grammar School (which closed in 1973) and he is commemorated on a memorial plaque in St Paul's Church Egerton Road, Monton. The church also has the Grammar school plaque. He is also remembered on the Lee-on-Solent Memorial. Bay 5, Panel 6.

THE CALLIBURN AVENGER FN772

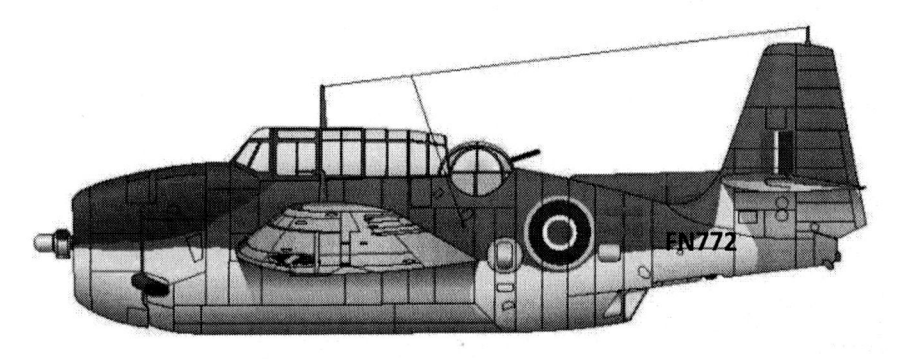

Glen Lussa, approximately 3.5 miles North East of Campbeltown and just to the west of Peninver is today overlooked by extensive forest covered hills, a tranquil place that is popular with walkers of all ages, but way up above the water of the glen one summer's evening in 1944, a very different scene would have greeted the visitor.

For appearing through the mist on the eve of Tuesday 4th July was a mass of smouldering wreckage, accompanied by the sound of exploding ammunition from the remains of yet another aircraft that had come to grief in Kintyre's hills.

Earlier in the afternoon Lt (A) Victor Selwyn Curd, RNZNVR, had taken off from RNAS Machrihanish in Avenger FN772 in order to ferry a fellow pilot, Lt (A) John Harrington Jefford RN, across to RNAS Abbotsinch in Glasgow.

Weather that day could be described as marginal, with a south-westerly wind, drizzle and low cloud hanging over the hills as the aircraft belonging to 768 Squadron, began to make its ascent through the overcast at approximately 18:45 it flew into a hillside above Calliburn Farm near Black Loch, with the loss of both airmen in an instant.

On discovery of the wreckage the following day, the bodies of the two men were recovered and conveyed to Campbeltown for formal identification, next of kin was notified and funeral arrangements were made for the New Zealand pilot at 15:00 hrs on Friday 7th July at Campbeltown (Kilkerran) Cemetery, with full military honours, and Lt Jefford transported to Glasgow for cremation a day or so later.

Partial remains of the Avenger and an impact crater in the peaty soil were said to be still visible during the late 1980's and early 1990's. These included a damaged propeller and a tail wheel, but it seems likely other smaller fragments will still remain on the hill.

Information on the aircraft revealed that it had been constructed by Grumman Aircraft under contract No. LL91367 receiving USA factory serial 06388 and was delivered 21st February 1943 to 845 FAA Squadron under command of

A Royal Navy FAA Grumman TBM Avenger

Photo: U.S. Navy National Museum of Naval Aviation photo No. 1996.253.1739

Lt/Cdr. W.H. Crawford RN, based at Quonset Point, North Kingstown, Rhode Island in Washington County, United States.

845 Squadron with its Avengers embarked for Liverpool on 23rd June 1943 on board the Attacker-class escort carrier HMS *Chaser* (D32). It formed part of the west bound convoy HX245 and undertaking anti-submarine reconnaissance enroute, it eventually arrived on the River Clyde on 6th July.

FN772 remained with this squadron for almost a year before transferring to 768 Squadron under command of Lt/Cdr. J. S. Bailey in June 1944, but served here only a short while before being Struck Off Charge following the fatal accident on 4th July.

Pilot. Lt (A) Victor Selwyn Curd, RNZNVR, born 10th August 1917, was the son of Henry and Clara Elizabeth Curd (née Johns) of Pukekohe, Auckland, New Zealand.

Following education at Pukekohe Tech High School, Vic worked for his father as a motor mechanic in their garage Cooper & Curd Ltd, Pukekohe. He also served in the NZ Army Territorial Force in the 3rd Auckland Regiment 1935-37.

Vic was a finalist in the New Zealand Herald Aviation Scholarship and was granted associate membership of the Auckland Aero Club in May 1936, where he later gained his `A` Class Pilots licence on 4th January 1938.

Lt (A) Victor Selwyn Curd. RNZNVR

Photo: *NZ Weekly News*

Noted as having logged a little over 42 flying hours prior to joining up, Vic enlisted as aircrew in NZ for the RN/FAA on 16th January 1941, he sailed for the UK on the 18th and arrived on 28th February on attachment to the RN at Gosport for basic training and classroom work.

Vic's first posting to Lee-on-Solent on 2nd October was followed by 24 EFTS at Sydenham, where as a U/T pilot he learned to fly in Magisters and Tiger Moths. He was later posted to 1 SFTS at Cark where he finally graduated, received his wings and a commission on 9th February 1942.

As a Sub/Lt Vic joined his first squadron 756 based at Crail, for a Torpedo Bomber Reconnaissance course on 19th September, he then went on to Arbroath on 16th November for Deck Landing Trials followed on 28th December by a two week course at the RN College Greenwich, to learn Officers etiquette.

On 20th January 1943 he joined 781 Squadron back at Lee-on-Solent, where in the main he would fly the Fairey Albacore and practice aerial reconnaissance, before going on to fly Swordfish with 818 Squadron on board the carrier HMS *Unicorn* and her detachments at HMS (*Caroline*) Belfast and Machrihanish between April and April 1944.

Vic arrived at Stretton, HMS (*Blackcap*) near Warrington on 15th May, possibly to ferry an Avenger up to Abbotsinch where he was to take up residence with 768 Squadron.

His final flight as we know was with this unit at the time of his death. He rests in Campbeltown (Kilkerran) Cemetery, Division 4. Grave 593.

His elder brother Lieutenant Ivan H. Curd was also in the RNZNVR and served actively overseas, but was more fortunate to have survived the war.

For years after the accident Vic's family placed remembrance notices in the personal columns of local newspapers. He was also remembered on a plaque in the Pukekohe Memorial Hall There is also a unique roll of honour on display in the RSA (Royal New Zealand Returned Services Association) club behind the town hall. Labelled the 'C and C Roll of Honour', this lists the names of 22 former staff members of the local firm Cooper & Curd Motors Ltd, who served in the armed forces during the Second World War, including Lieutenant (A) V.S. Curd and Private R. J. Adams, who were both killed on active service.

Passenger (FAA Pilot) Lieutenant John Harrington Jefford, RN, born 15th May 1921, was the son of Francis Robert and Irene Rosa Jennie Jefford (née Taunt) of Cheltenham, Gloucestershire. He had two brothers Peter and William and was husband of Selina Jefford.

Lt (A) John Harrington Jefford. RN

Photo: Cheltenham Chronicle

John's father Robert had served in the Army in France during the First World War with the Gloucester Regiment and had finished as a Captain with the 8th Tank Battery. His parents had married in Willesden, Middlesex in the summer of 1919.

John was educated in Cheltenham and became interested in flying at an early age. He entered service at the RN College in 1939 and on 13th March became a Midshipman. He commenced his early pilot training at Gravesend, Kent on the 26th June, where he flew the DH82 Tiger Moth with the RAF at 20 E&RFTS.

Lt (A) Victor Selwyn Curd's grave in Campbeltown (Kilkerran) Cemetery

Photo: Author's Collection

Next came No1 Service Flying Training School at Netheravon, Wiltshire, where he flew the North American Harvard, first with an instructor and then solo for his wings. It was here on 11th September 1939 that he almost lost his life. He described in great detail the events of that day in a letter to his brother, who in turn decided to share his dramatic tale with readers of the *Gloucestershire Echo* two weeks later:

`Mid. (A) John H. Jefford, R.N. Son of Mr. F. R. Jefford, the Borough Sanitary Officer for Cheltenham, and Chief Food Control Officer, has qualified to join the select membership of the Caterpillar Club. Membership is only open to airmen who have saved their lives by making a parachute jump. Mr. Jefford, who is attached to the Fleet Air Arm, was receiving instruction at Netheravon when the 'plane was put into a spin at about 9,000 feet. It remained in the spin, and at about 4,000 feet he bailed out and made a safe landing`.

Unfortunately the instructor remained in the machine and lost his life. Midshipman Jefford said:

— *"I went up with my instructor, a F/O, to go spinning. We climbed up to 8,000 feet and he did one to the left. We shot round, but came out quite O.K. Back again we went to 9,000. Straight away he shot her into a right-hander and down we went. We went on spinning, 8,000 —7,000 (some spin this, still I suppose he knows what doing?) 6,000 something is wrong whip the stick backwards and forwards still spinning— jump! I FOUND I WAS STUCK! So I slid back the hood, tore off the Sutton harness, I couldn't see the machine and harness and stood up, but thought I might fall into the prop—so turned around, leant half-way out, and found I was still stuck.*

The pack had caught on the cover and I could feel the stick wrapping' my leg and thought I would never get clear. Things were getting desperate when I fell and was flung right out—hung for a few seconds, kicked out, hit the wing and shot into space head first....

North American Harvard

drifted down towards a hill, I juggled with the cords to steer away from a small wood, then swung like mad—I remember it was like jumping off a 15ft. wall—and crump! Did that dirty bit of wet meadow feel comfortable! You bet!

I gathered up the 'chute, and up walked a dame and a car in which she took me to the nearest house, where I tried to find out if anyone had seen my Instructor come down, but of course, nobody had. I telephoned the 'drome, and beat it to look for the rest of the outfit. About a mile away on a hill we came across the crash. Poor old Genders, (F/O Douglas Genders) there was nothing we could do for him.

249

It's just the luck of the game...and I was lucky, very lucky".

According to the newspapers, the "*dame*" he mentioned was probably Stephanie Hurd (wife of Sir Anthony Hurd) and mother of Douglas Hurd (who became well known as a Cabinet Minister in the UK Government from 1979 to 1995).

On 26th May 1940, with Britain now at war with Germany, John, having gained his pilots wings was promoted to Sub/Lt was given a weeks leave, after which he was posted to 826 Squadron flying Albacores from Bircham Newton, near Kings Lynn, Norfolk.

HMS Victorious (R38)

Photo: Lt R.G.G. Coote. RN

Further postings came throughout the year and in 1941 he was serving 829 Sqn aboard HMS *Formidable*. In February the carrier was deployed with the East Indies Fleet in support of military operations in Somaliland and on the 13th John and his crew: Obs. Sub/Lt G.P. Simpson and TAG L/A F.H. Shiel, were carrying out a night attack on Massawa in Albacore L7168, when they suffered damage and had to force-land 20 miles north of the town.

John and his crew were captured and taken POW but fortunately were released when Massawa was taken by the allies on 11th April 1941.

On 15th March 1942 he joined 832 Squadron at Hatston, Orkney, and also served on board HMS *Victorious* with the Home Fleet in Scapa Flow flying ops off the Norwegian coast. John was promoted to Temp Lt on 25th March.

For reasons unclear on 13th January 1943, John was serving with HMS *Sussex,* this ship was a Heavy Cruiser that had just re-joined the 1st Cruiser Squadron at Scapa Flow for convoy defence and interception duties in the Atlantic, mainly due to the continuing threat by German capital ships.

In February he was back on board *Victorious* with 832 Squadron, and was now flying the new TBF-1 Avengers which were on loan from the USN. On the 8th he had a minor prang in 06053 when the arrester hook pulled out on landing and he crashed into the barrier causing Cat.Y. damage, which basically meant it had to be sent away for repairs once the ship docked. A similar accident occurred again on 22nd May that year when John, now a Lieutenant, was landing in 06098, the hook came out, he applied the brakes and the Avenger nosed over causing Cat.X. damage. It was repaired and put back into service within a couple of weeks. Again, he was uninjured, save for a little pride.

After the Kintyre accident John was cremated at Glasgow Crematorium. A sad end to a gallant naval aviator.

NO PLACE FOR A PEER - BEECH TRAVELLER FT529

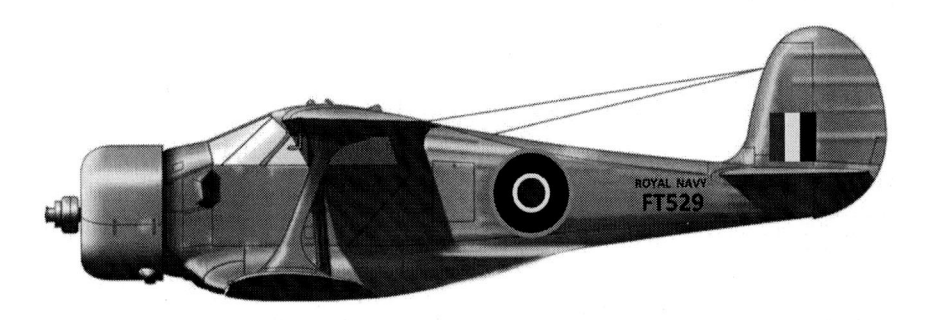

Lieutenant Commander The Honourable John Michael Southwell, RN, of 725 Squadron, eased his Fleet Air Arm Beech GB-2 Traveller FT529 off the main runway at Royal Naval Air Station Eglinton, HMS (*Gannet*) Northern Ireland and soon disappeared into the dense overcast sky as he circled the airfield to set a course for RNAS Machrihanish enroute to heading home for Christmas.

Normally just a short hop and an easy flight in good weather, but on this occasion Friday 22nd December 1944, it was a day of low cloud, sea fog and rain squalls over much of Northern Ireland and the Kintyre peninsula.

Lt/Cdr. Southwell, a very experienced pilot having commenced his flying career in 1924, had successfully navigated across the bleak Irish Sea and despite the conditions, made it to Kintyre in good time. However, on nearing the airfield at Machrihanish and still in poor visibility, the aircraft was heard by witnesses on the ground to veer in a north-easterly direction and moments later at approximately 11:55 it struck a hill north of Kilkenzie village.

A coastal fog still shrouded the hills but the aircraft had burst into flames on impact and the glow and crackle of the flames soon led farmers to the scene, where it was soon discovered that Lt/Cdr. Southwell had died instantly.

Police at Campbeltown were quickly notified and arrived to take charge. The body of the airman was recovered and taken into custody by the naval authorities.

Witnesses seemed to be of the opinion that the pilot had lost his bearings as he neared the airfield, but perhaps due to wind direction he just intended to come around and approach from the eastern end of the runway but was too low?

According to a wartime grid reference in the casualty file, the Traveller is understood to have crashed into rising ground NE of Tangy Lodge, east of the main A83 and close to the road junction leading to Tangy farm. It was reported in the Kintyre Aircraft Crash log that a farmer still ploughed up small pieces of the aircraft, though the area is near a plantation and enquiries made on the precise location proved fruitless.

A Royal Navy Fleet Air Arm Beech GB-2 Traveller 1 similar to FT529

A distinctive design with a negative wing stagger the Beechcraft GB-2 Traveller FT529 was a five seat communication aircraft. One of 75 constructed in the United States at the Beech Aircraft Corporation based in Wichita, Kansas for the Royal Navy FAA under the Lend-Lease Scheme.

Built under contract No. AC-31386 C 90, FT529 was shipped to Newark, New Jersey and arrived in the UK on 16th February 1944. It was eventually delivered to 725 Squadron, a Fleet Requirements Unit at former RAF Eglinton, Co. Londonderry, N. Ireland.

Pilot Lieutenant Commander The Hon. John Michael Southwell, RN, born 17th December 1901, was the youngest son of Major Arthur Robert Pyers Southwell (5th Viscount Southwell) and Dorothy Katherine Southwell (née Walrond) Brother of Cdr. Robert Arthur William Joseph Southwell. RN, and husband of Daphne Lewin Watson of Bournemouth, Hampshire.

On the 15th September 1915 John attended the Royal Naval Colleges, Osborne and Dartmouth and was promoted to Midshipman on 1st May 1918. He later served on board the 27,600 ton Battlecruiser HMS *Renown* until 1920.

John gained promotion to Sub/Lt on 15th May 1922 and was posted to the Battleship HMS *Centurian* during February 1923. A further promotion to Lieutenant came on 15th October and the following year on 12th November he attended a naval pilots course at RAF Leuchars in Fife on the east coast of Scotland, where he remained until January 1925.

It was at this station that John, now with the temporary RAF rank of Flying Officer, was involved in a flying accident on the afternoon of 12th January 1925, when his Fairey Flycatcher Fleet Fighter N9860 of 404 Flight HMS *Furious*, suffered an engine failure at 100 feet over woodland that led to a crash in a ploughed field adjacent to the airfield, owned by Mr Walker of Leuchars Castle.

Fairey Flycatcher Fleet Fighter N9928

He had suffered head and arm injuries, though on subsequent examination at Dundee Royal Infirmary his injuries, although extremely painful were deemed not to be life threatening.

A sketch of Lt/Cdr. Hon. John Michael Southwell of a photo held at the National Portrait Gallery

On 30th July 1924, John was posted to the aircraft carrier HMS *Furious* to form part of the Atlantic Fleet. He remained with this ship until May 1926 when he was transferred to HMS (*Columbine*) a naval base at Port Edgar on the Firth of Forth.

Here he undertook training for the Fleet Air Arm before leaving on 24th January 1927 to join HMS (*Tamar*), a British Royal Naval base in Hong Kong where he served as a pilot in 401 flight.

Returning to the United Kingdom in July, John eventually joined HMS *Victory* at Portsmouth on 21st January 1928 and remained here until June the following year, but also served for a brief period on loan to the Royal Air Force.

In August 1929 he attended another flying course prior to being posted on 6th February 1930, for pilot duties on board the Light Cruiser HMS *Emerald* of the 4th Cruiser Squadron which lay at anchor in the port of Trincomalee, Ceylon. The ship accommodated one Fairey Flycatcher N9670, used for reconnaissance. It was launched by catapult and fitted with floats for landing in the sea, the machine would then be winched back on board with a crane.

The ship returned to Devonport for refit on 5th January 1931 and John received orders to join 404 Flight on board HMS *Courageous,* a former Cruiser that had been converted to an aircraft carrier. A well earned promotion to the rank of Lieutenant Commander followed on 15th October 1931, and with it came a posting to the world's first purpose-designed aircraft carrier the 10,850 ton Sir W.G. Armstrong-Whitworth built HMS *Hermes*.

253

He served on board the carrier in Hong Kong during January 1932, but only for a short period of time before retiring from active service on 14th March 1932.

On 29th September John married Miss Daphne Lewin Watson, at St James's, Spanish Place, London, she was the daughter and only child of Sir Geoffrey Lewin Watson, 3rd Bt. (1879-1959) and Gertrude Margaret Mountain, of Bournemouth, Hampshire.

This high society couple were often in the limelight throughout the 1930s attending various functions, charity balls and sporting events, especially winter sports, where he and his wife frequented high alpine ski resorts in Switzerland.

Hon. John Southwell and wife Daphne in Brompton Road, on their way to the wedding reception for the daughter of the Marques and Marchioness of Bute in May 1933. Photo: The Tatler

During in the mid-30s John became an investor for several businesses and in June 1936, was the Director of the company E.H. Fuel Injection Ltd on St.Alban's Road, London.

In January 1937 John was skiing at a resort near Saint Moritz when he collided with his companion Captain Robert Cunningham-Reid during a snowstorm, John suffered a broken leg and various cuts and bruises and was detained in Samaden Hospital, Engadin, St. Moritz, his friend was later discharged after treatment for minor injuries.

Hon. John Southwell and wife Daphne at an event in December 1932

Photo: The Tatler

Having been in South Africa on business and hearing of the unrest in Europe, it led to his decision to return to the UK. John and his wife Daphne embarked aboard the liner *Winchester Castle* at Durstan and arrived in Southampton on 28th April 1939.

When war broke out in September John returned to the Navy in his previous rank of Lieutenant Commander and arrived at Lee-on-Solent on New Years Day 1940. On 28th August he was posted to Donibristle, Fife. Though his role here is uncertain as it was just described as various duties, but given his age then of 39, this was presumably more in an administrative role than flying.

John`s next posting was to Hatston (*Sparrowhawk*) Orkney, on 15th January 1941, and it would be during his time here that *Bismark* was spotted by a 771 Squadron Martin Maryland and within a week the mighty German battleship was sunk. John remained at Hatston until December.

In June 1942 he was posted to HMS (*Afrikander*) a RN Station in Simons Town, South Africa, where on the staff of Captain M. Farquar, he reported for flying duties, likely as an instructor. He served at this base for a year before returning to the UK.

There appears to be a bit of a gap in his records for 1943 but that year he was posted to Eglinton (*Gannet*) at Londonderry, Northern Ireland as a pilot with 725 Squadron, a Fleet Requirements Unit, where he remained until the accident on Kintyre in December 1944.

With the passing of his father in August, John had inherited the title 6th Viscount Southwell, but on his death the title 7th Vicount went to his brother Robert.

Lt/Cdr. Hon. John Southwell was interred with a full guard of honour in Campbeltown (Kilkerran) Cemetery. Division 4. Grave 591. He is also commemorated on the Longparish War Memorial in Hampshire.

Grave of Lt/Cdr. Hon. John Southwell in Campbeltown Kilkerran Cemetery

Photo: Author`s Collection

255

CRUEL FORCES OF NATURE - WELLINGTON LP351

Normally military aircraft are designed to withstand a great deal of punishment from flak and fighters, but at times the forces of nature can be more of a threat than the enemy and are really something not to be reckoned with.

Formed on the 5th April 1943, 105 (Transport) Operational Training Unit was based at RAF Bramcote situated 4 miles south-east of Nuneaton, Warwickshire. This unit was initially equipped with Vickers-Armstrong Wellingtons, but in March 1945 they began to receive the Douglas Dakota, though evidently both types would be used to train crews for air transport duties.

At 09:55 on Monday 5th February 1945, Wellington Mk.X. LP351 took off from Bramcote on an operational training exercise with a crew of four consisting: Pilot F/O Ronald Moxon Leeming, Staff Flight Engineer F/Sgt Leslie Thomas Magson Dowding, Navigator Sgt John Benjamin Field and Wireless Operator F/Sgt Francis Edward Morgan.

Vickers Wellington Mk. X

Vickers-Armstrong Wellington

From all accounts despite poor weather, the exercise had proceeded normally until the aircraft approached the area of North Kintyre and encountered a violent thunderstorm and unable to avoid the dark cumulonimbus clouds, LP351 was immediately subjected to a tremendous battering from wind, rain and hail.

The forces within this storm were so severe that the aircraft is reported to have been hit by lightning before control was lost. At 14:30 it dived into the sea off Kilberry Head at the south-western tip of Knapdale and sadly there were no survivors.

Following a widespread search only one airman, 22 year old Sgt John Field was recovered from the sea. He was interred with honour and respect in Botley Cemetery, Oxford. Plot H/3. Grave 173. The remainder of the crew are still classified as missing and their names are inscribed on the Runnymede Memorial to those of the Royal Air Force who have no known grave.

Pilot. Flying Officer Ronald Moxon Leeming, RAFVR, born 13th September 1921 in Kilburn, London, was the son of Arthur Moxon and Rosa Leeming (née Turner) of Ipswich, Suffolk and husband of Daphne.

Ronnie, as he was often referred, was educated first in London and later Ipswich where the family lived on Cromer Road. On leaving school he was employed by Ipswich Borough Council in the Electric Supply and Transport Department.

Having joined the Air Training Corps in the late 30s, he volunteered for the RAF and was accepted in February 1941. He then arrived at RAF Uxbridge on 26th March and having passed his medical as A1, he was selected for pilot training.

Arriving at the Aircrew Reception Centre in Regents Park, London at the end of July, and after passing his exams and finishing square bashing, on 3rd October Ronnie was promoted to LAC.

A short period of leave followed before reporting to RAF Wilmslow, Cheshire, where he was given orders to travel to Greenock, Scotland along with other successful candidates for an overseas journey to Canada, then on to the United States by train for further flight training.

Ronnie's diary of 1941, kindly shared by his nephew Brian, had the following entries:

October 14th. *"Left Wilmslow at 3am for Greenock where we embarked on H.M.T 'Louis Pasteur'. Billeted: E Deck, 6 berth. Had glorious views of the Clyde"*

16th. *"Shifted down the Clyde to mouth of the river where we lay at anchor awaiting the tide."*

17th. *"Ship left on tide at 11.15 pm."*

18th. *"Well out in the Irish Sea, very rough. Many lads Seasick."*

"Escort: Aircraft Carrier : 'Victorious' 6 Destroyers, 1 Merchant Cruiser, 1 Cargo boat which held us back"

With the dreaded U-boat threat in the North Atlantic, one can almost feel the sense of anxiety in that last entry of having to hang around for the straggler.

Thankfully the crossing went without incident and his first port of call was Halifax, Nova Scotia on the 25th. On arrival at 31 Personnel Depot, Moncton, New Brunswick, Ronnie and other selectees destined for training in the States were issued with ID cards and travel passes, before boarding a train for the 1483 mile journey to Montgomery, Alabama in America's deep south.

HM Troopship SS Louis Pasteur

His pre-flight training was conducted at Maxwell Field Recruitment Training Centre as part of a four phase training plan, then as a successful candidate at RTC he got his first taste of flying at the Primary Training School, where he took to the air in a PT-17 Stearman.

Ronnie would have also had more ground classes in navigation, meteorology, communication, engineering and the theory of flight, before soloing after 10-12 hours and completing the course after 60 hours flying time. Though during his time here he was involved in an accident which set him back and a note in his diary simply reads: *"Crashed 81 –Complete wreck."*

The accident happened on 29th January 1942 in Stearman 40-1768. Apparently he had been on his second approach to the aerodrome Reynolds Auxiliary Field, when through his own admission, a slight error of judgement had caused the wing to strike a tall tree which resulted in the aircraft flipping over on its back. Fortunately, by the time the instructors and others had arrived at the scene, though a little dazed, he had managed to free himself.

Wrecked Stearman '81' 40-1768   Photo: Brian Leeming

Ronnie had escaped the crash a little shaken up, but uninjured, save for a dent in his pride.

Next came Pilot School at Macon, Georgia in February, where he was introduced to a new monoplane type, the Vultee BT-13 Valiant, a two-seat trainer, followed in May he by advanced pilot training at the Southeast Air Corps Training Centre, Dothan, Alabama, here he flew the more powerful North American T-6 Texan (Harvard) and after having finally graduated in Class 42-F on 3rd July he received his RAF and USAAF wings before embarking for the UK on the 20th.

Once back home from late July 42 to Feb 43 he trained on twin engine aircraft, then on 14th April he began work with No.1 FS ferrying Beaufighters to airfields in the Middle East.

Right: Ronnie at home in Ipswich 1942

Photo: Brian Leeming

Sgt Ronnie Leeming with his father (middle) brother (right) and young nephew Brian

Photo: Brian Leeming

Ronnie finally gained a commission with promotion to P/O on 25th June 1943, then on 26th December was promoted to F/O. The following November he was posted to 105 OTU at Bramcote and it was on the cards for him to later join BOAC but alas the tragic accident cut short his career.

On 1st January 1945 his name appeared in the London Gazette when he was awarded the King's Commendation for valuable service in the air. At the time of the accident he had logged a total of 596 flying hrs.

Sadly, Ronnie has no grave and is commemorated on Runnymede. Panel 267.

Left: Ronnie and Daphne on their wedding day in 1943.

Photo: Brian Leeming

F/O Ronnie M. Leeming. RAFVR. Rather oddly his USAAF wings placed on the photo form almost the same shape as his shadow. Photo: Brian Leeming

Staff Flight Engineer. Flight Sergeant Leslie Thomas Magson Dowding, RAFVR, born 5th September 1915, was the son of Thomas Ewart and Florence Elizabeth Dowding (née Simkin) of St. Pancras, London. He was also husband of Megan.

Leslie's parents had married in London in October 1914, his father at that time was a hosier salesman and the couple lived in Gordon House Road, where Leslie, their only son was born the following year.

Educated in London, Leslie left school to become a salesman in the wine trade and in 1937 he married Miss Megan Davies in Hampstead. The couple lived in Alexander Road, Camden, but later moved to Adelaide Road, with neighbours the likes of Music Composer Thomas Sterndale Case Benneth, Actress Joan Bennett and Portrait Artist Carl Hemel.

His father had answered the call for King and Country in the first war and joined the RFC as an Aircraftman on 22nd August 1916, so likely following in his father's footsteps when the Second World War broke out, Leslie joined the RAF as a Volunteer Reserve and after four weeks square bashing, was selected for training as a flight engineer and passed through various training schools.

After a course at the School of Technical Training at Locking near Weston-Super-Mare, a final 16 week course was then conducted at St.Athan, near Cardiff, Glamorgan, where on completion Leslie would be awarded his Engineer's brevet.

His job from then on would be to relieve pressure on the pilot by flying as aircrew in order to monitor instruments and fuel systems. Leslie has no known grave and is commemorated on the Runnymede Memorial, Surrey, Panel 270.

Navigator. Sergeant John Benjamin Field, RAFVR, born 1922 in Wandsworth, Surrey, was the son of Frederick James and Ada Mary Field (née Pearson) of Streatham, Wandsworth. London.

John was the only crew member found and he was laid to rest in Oxford (Botley) Cemetery, Oxfordshire, with full military honours. Plot H/3. Grave 173.

Oxford (Botley) Cemetery

262

Wireless Operator. Flight Sergeant Francis Edward Morgan, RAFVR, was born 11th June 1921 in West Derby, Lancashire (Now Liverpool). He was the youngest son of Francis and Maud Mary Morgan (née Pealing) of Liverpool. He had one older sister Frances D. and an older brother Thomas J.

Ted, as he was known, was an old boy of Roscoe Primary School, Liverpool, the family lived in Townsend Avenue and his father was a motor mechanic for a local garage.

Prior to joining the RAF in 1941 Ted had been employed as a Junior Clerk for the Liverpool Central Oil Company Ltd.

Ted is today commemorated on the Runnymede Memorial, Coopers Hill Lane, Englefield Green, Surrey, Panel 272.

F/Sgt Francis Edward `Ted` Morgan
Photo: Liverpool Echo

Looking south towards the accident scene from Kilberry   *Photo: Author`s Collection*

263

MYSTERY SEAFIRE 411

The war in Europe had ended but as the conflict in the Pacific theatre continued, the Royal Navy Fleet Air Arm still busied themselves with training exercises in the UK, operating from both carriers and shore stations .

On 1st July 1945, 805 Squadron, having previously disbanded in Jan 1943 in order to provide other squadrons with more experienced pilots, had reformed at RNAS Machrihanish with twenty five Seafire Mk. L.IIIs, but these were replaced with XVs in August for operational service with the 20th Carrier Air Group until the end of the war in the Pacific in August 1945.

Commander of the squadron at that time until the end of September 1947, was Lt/Cdr. (A) Peter J. Hutton. DSC. RNVR a former pilot with 801 Squadron that had seen action during Operation *Torch* at El Alemein, flying from HMS *Eagle* and HMS *Furious* in 1942 where he even managed to bag himself 3.5 confirmed kills, with 2 probable's and another damaged.

On Wednesday 1st August 1945, one of the new pilots Petty Officer (A) James Douglas Griffin, RN, took off from Machrihanish in a Seafire L.111 on a routine training flight, when suddenly just over Machrihanish Bay to the west his engine cut out.

P.O. Griffin had attempted a controlled ditching, but either the sea was too rough or he hit too hard which resulted in him being thrown from the aircraft and being killed, as the stricken fighter sank beneath the waves.

An air and sea search was made soon after the tragedy, but crews failed to find him. Then, the following afternoon, his body was washed ashore on a nearby beach and he was returned home for burial.

On 28 August 1948, 805 Squadron reformed at Eglinton as a Royal Australian Navy squadron, by this time they were equipped with Hawker Sea Furies as they embarked on board HMAS *Sydney*.

Petty Officer James Douglas Griffin, RN, was born in Gravesend, Kent on 28th December 1925. He was the youngest son of Laurence Albert and Lavinia Griffin (née Goodwin) of Gravesend.

James' parents had married in this ancient market town in the summer of 1922 and the couple had two children, James and his elder brother John M. Griffin born in 1924.

Accorded a full military funeral 19 year old James Griffin was laid to rest in Gravesend Cemetery. Plot B.12 Grave 1335.

Other than the aircraft being listed as a Mk. L.III with 805 Squadron, the serial number has thus far not been traced, though a Seafire L.III lost on this date is listed in 'Fleet Air Arm Aircraft 1939-1945 by Ray Sturtivant and Mick Burrow with the cryptic number of '411' but oddly no serial of any Seafire used by 805 Squadron bears these numbers in sequence, so the identity of this aircraft is still a bit of a mystery, though one possible explanation is that these were carrier codes for operation in the Pacific as depicted in the profile pic.

The CWGC Headstone for P.O. Griffin and private grave of his brother John in Gravesend Cemetery.

Photo: Author's Collection

LOST BENEATH THE WAVES -BARRACUDA ME121

Situated just to the north of Tayinloan on the west coast of Kintyre, the bombing range at Ballure was so named because it was within the boundaries of Ballure farm. Observation posts here were managed by Fleet Air Arm personnel, usually Wrens from Machrihanish (*Landrail*) with the targets being located on the Ballure Marches.

The main bombing target itself was a structure that had been built on top of Sgor Cainnteach, a skerry lying immediately offshore, but in 1943 a wrecked cargo steamer was also placed off Gigha to be used as a target ship.

On Wednesday 28th March 1945 the crew of a Barracuda torpedo bomber, Pilot Sub/Lt (A) Vivian H. Wake, SANF, Observer Sub/Lt (A) Leslie J. Daultrey, RNVR and TAG P.O. Peter John McGregor, had been using the range for simulated anti-submarine bombing attacks in preparation for future operations both at home and abroad.

With the exercise finished, the Wrens in the Royal Navy bombing range observation tower watched closely through their binoculars as Fairey

Barracuda ME121 a Mk.III belonging to 815 Squadron at Machrihanish, exited the area on a southerly course down through the Sound of Gigha to return to base.

By all accounts the Barracuda appeared to be flying normally until it arrived about midway between the Rhonahaorine Point, Kintyre and Ardminish Point, on

Fairey Barracuda in a dive

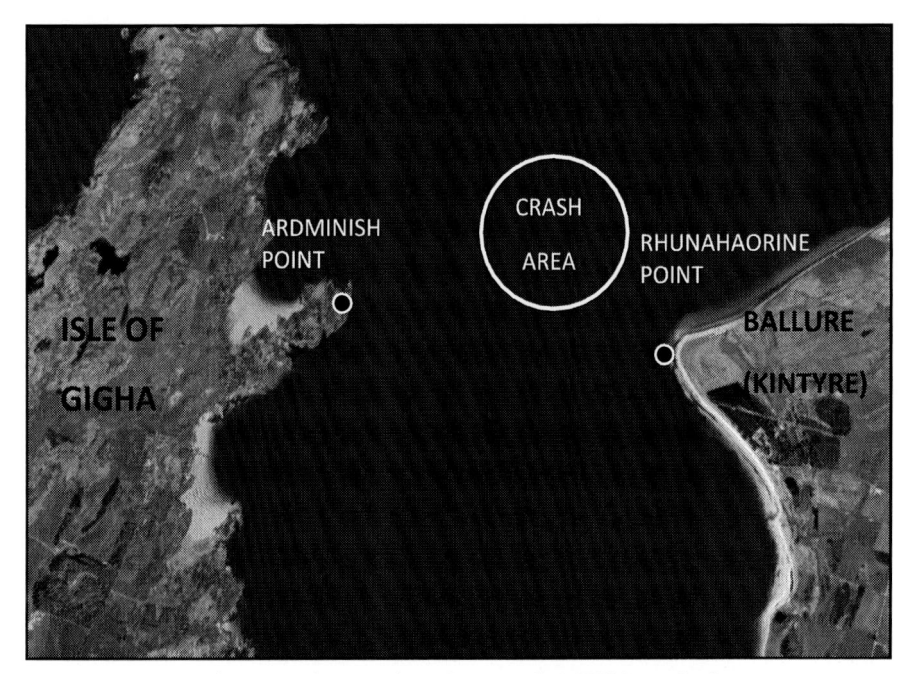

The general area where Barracuda ME121 crashed

the east coast of Isle of Gigha, when at approximately 350 degrees and 1.5 miles north east of Rhonahaorine Point, it suddenly dived into the sea, broke up and sank beneath the waves leaving only traces of oil and small pieces of wreckage on the surface.

There were no survivors and despite an intensive air and sea search, no trace of the crew was ever found. Of those on board: Pilot Sub/Lt Vivian Hereward Wake was a member of the South African Naval Forces and Sub/Lt Leslie John Daultrey as well as being the Observer was also a qualified pilot.

Due to the complete loss of the aircraft, it could not be determined what caused the accident, though it was observed to be still under power when it hit the water.

ME121, constructed by Boulton Paul Aircraft factory at Wolverhampton, was powered by a 1640 hp Rolls Royce Merlin 32. V12 liquid cooled engine, and fitted with an improved ASVX (Anti Surface Vessel) radar system housed in a radome under the rear fuselage. This system could detect a submarine at a distance of 12 miles and a ship at 40 miles within an accurate bearing of one to two degrees.

Unfortunately with the increase in overall weight of the Mk.III due to the ASVX installation and the overall performance of the RR Merlin 32, it soon became clear that despite several weight saving modifications the Barracuda could not safely carry a torpedo, therefore anti-sub operations became its prime directive.

This Barracuda Mk.III clearly shows the new ASVX radar radome

ME121 was completed and available for collection by a Ferry pilot, on 19th December 1944. It was delivered and taken on charge by 815 Squadron during the month of January 1945 at the former RAF and USAAF airfield of Mullaghmore, County Londonderry, under command of Lt/Com J.S. Bailey. OBE. RN before transferring to *Landrail* on 15th March.

Pilot Sub-Lieutenant Vivian Hereward Wake, SANF, was born in 1920 in South Africa and is believed to have hailed from Simon's Town.

Very little is known about Vivian Wake, other than he joined the South African Naval Forces around 1943, and was attached to the Royal Naval Fleet Air Arm in the UK. He became a Sub/Lt (A) on 25th August 1944 and some sources say he was a Temp Lieutenant at the time of his death, though the CWGC still lists him listed as a Sub/Lt.

Vivian was commemorated on the Plymouth naval Memorial to the missing Panel 95, Column 1 and also on the Simon's Town, Naval Memorial. Cape Town, Western Cape, South Africa.

Observer Sub-Lieutenant (A) Leslie John Daultrey, RNVR, born 1920, was the son of Alfred Arthur and Gertrude Annie Daultrey (née Mattacks) of Cowley, Oxford. He had one sister Irene Louisa. His father Alfred was a Lance Corporal in the First World War and served with the 10th London Regiment from 1913-1915 but was invalided out in April 1915. His parents were married on 16th January 1916 at St.Barnaba's church in Bethnal Green, London and Leslie is commemorated on Lee-on-Solent Memorial. Bay 6. Panel 3.

Telegraphist Air Gunner. Temp Acting Petty Officer Peter Gordon McGregor, RN, born 1st July 1925, was eldest son of Peter Gordon and Isabel Kathleen McGregor (née Crick) of Diss, Depwade, Norfolk. He had three brothers: Leslie G, Geoffrey D and Donald K. Peter is commemorated on Lee-on-Solent Memorial. Bay 6. Panel 1.

THE KILKENZIE SEAFIRE SW857

Temporary Acting Sub-Lieutenant (A) Peter Roxburgh Payn Winch, RNVR, was a member of 806 Fleet Air Arm squadron based at RNAS Machrihanish (*Landrail*) under the command of Lt A.C. Lindsay. DSC. RNVR.

The squadron, at that time equipped with the Rolls Royce Griffon powered Supermarine Seafire F.XV had been reformed here on 1st August 1945, after previously being disbanded and absorbed into 803 Squadron in East Africa in January 1943.

On Friday 14th December 1945, Sub/Lt Winch had been briefed to undertake formation flying practice. He was observed by ratings on the airfield as having accomplished a satisfactory take off from the main runway then make a steady climb to form up with members of his squadron. It was during this manoeuvre that his Seafire SW857, for reasons unknown, suddenly entered a spin and a rapid descent from which he failed to recover.

At approximately 10:15 the Seafire crashed to the ground in a field tenanted by Mr. Hector McMurchy, Blacksmith at Kilchenzie Village just to the north of the airfield. It had narrowly avoided hitting the nearby Smiddy and four cottages across the road.

The aircraft disintegrated upon impact and wreckage was scattered over a wide area. The pilot was killed and was discovered later by two of the villagers who had been repairing a fence.

Duncan Colville of Kilmaho Lodge said in an interview with local press:

"I was at my window telephoning when I heard a bump and a crackling sound and on going out of the house, I discovered that a plane had crashed in the field and that parts of the machine had broken down some of the telephone wires. I ran back into the house to notify the aerodrome by telephone but the phone was out of action, so I went over and got my car to drive to the air station where I asked one of the duty policemen to put a call through saying what had happened.

By the time I got back home, two local men (Probably the pair mentioned in the paper that had been repairing a fence nearby) *had extricated the body of the pilot from the wreckage. He had been killed instantly.*

The plane came to rest some yards from the Campbeltown to Tarbert road. Had it been ten or fifteen yards off its course, it would have crashed into the cottages on the other side of the road".

Pilot. Temp Acting Sub-Lieutenant Peter Roxburgh Payn Winch, RNVR, born in Brentford, Middlesex on 1st February 1925, was the son of Hubert Edward and Dorothy Beatrice Winch (née Mais) of Brentford. He had one younger brother Guy and a sister Mary.

Above: The Smiddy (Blacksmiths) as it looks today.

Photo: Author's Collection

The field where SW857 crashed with the Smiddy far left

Photo: Author's Collection

Peter's parents had been married in Brentford in the summer of 1919. His father was a merchant for the fruit industry and his mother was originally from Kingston, Jamaica.

The couple often travelled back and forth to Jamaica on business. Sometimes taking the children but other times leaving them with their aunt Elena Fabel, in Flackwell Heath, Buckinghamshire.

On 10th May 1927 when Peter was just two, they made the journey from Avonmouth to Kingston aboard the *Patuca*, owned by Elders & Fyffes Ltd and skippered by Master G.E. Martin. Then, having returned to England a year later, the family departed once again on 5th May 1931, this time sailing from London aboard the banana boat *Jamaica Producer*. It must have been quite an adventure for the kids, in between all the seasickness.

Peter it would appear stayed in Jamaica with the family until the beginning of August 1939, when at the age of just 14, he sailed for England and arrived back in London on the 29th to attend Rossall Boarding School near Fleetwood, Lancashire, though during the holidays and after leaving school, he went back to Flackwell Heath to stay with his aunt.

Peter had joined the Royal Navy at the age of 18 and trained as a pilot in Canada. Having gained his wings at the end of 1944, on 21st January 1945 he was promoted from a Midshipman to

Jamaica Producer owned by Jamaica Direct Fruit Line Ltd

Acting Sub-Lieutenant and posted to a training unit in the UK. On 1st August, now with the rank of Sub/Lt (A) he joined 802 Squadron at Machrihanish flying Seafires until his untimely accident in December.

Following the crash Peter was interred with full military honours in Campbeltown (Kilkerran) Cemetery, Division 4. Grave.590.

His epitaph:

"He followed where faith & duty led".

At the time of visiting the area of the crash in September 2017, permission to access the field in order to search for any remains of the aircraft could not be obtained as the owners of the land could not be contacted, therefore it is not known if anything still remains at the site, but being so near to the main road it seems unlikely that anything other than tiny fragments would be found.

Grave of Sub/Lt Peter Winch. RNVR in Campbeltown (Kilkerran) Cemetery

Photo: Author's Collection

TWELFTH TEE TRAUMA - FIREFLY VT490

Formed in April 1933 at RNAS Gosport in Hampshire, from 446 and 455 (Fleet Spotter Reconnaissance) Flights of the Royal Air Force, 821 RN/FAA squadron was equipped with the Fairey Aviation Company III-F before converting to the Fairey Seal for transfer aboard the 24,200 ton carrier HMS *Courageous* serving with the Home Fleet on 5th May 1933.

During the Second World War they served with a variety of Fleet carriers including *Courageous* and *Ark Royal*. First with Fairey Swordfish then later the Fairey Barracuda Mk II and III.

With the war over 821 Squadron eventually disbanded on 3rd February 1946. But in September 1951 the squadron reformed at Arbroath, Angus in the anti-submarine role with the Fairey Firefly AS.6. However, the following May the Admiralty required a further strike squadron and 821 was transferred to this type of operation and received the Firefly FR.5.

The FR.5 was a fighter reconnaissance version, powered by a Rolls-Royce Griffon 74 V-12 liquid cooled 2,035hp inline piston engine.

Fairy Firefly FR.5

On Thursday 8th May 1952, 821 Squadron, now based at Machrihanish, was notified of a change of Command and Lt/Cdr. J. R. N. Gardner RN was succeed by Lt/Cdr. B. H. Notley RN.

That same day Pilot Lt William Alexander Bell and his Observer Acting Sub/Lt Bertram P. Brushett, were airborne in Firefly FR.5 VT490 207/R and after an exercise were approaching from the west to land in heavy rain, but before the aircraft could reach the end of the runway, it was observed to stall and dive into the ground, hitting a bank near the airfield boundary and close to the 12th tee of Machrihanish Golf Course. Sadly both occupants lost their lives in the accident.

This was the first fatal aircraft accident since the airfield was re-commissioned by the RN Fleet Air Arm in December 1951, and since flying operations from the base began again in January.

Following a memorial service at the airfield chapel held by the resident Royal Navy Chaplin, the two Union Jack flag draped coffins were placed on board a vehicle for transportation to the airmen's respective hometowns for interment.

Information found on Firefly VT490 revealed that it had been ordered by the admiralty on 16th November 1946 and was built and delivered to the Receipt & Dispatch Unit (RDU) at Culham, Oxfordshire on 18th October 1948 where it remained until July the following year.

This aircraft saw active service with 814 Squadron from March 1950 to January 1951 before being stored at RDU Anthorne, Cumberland between July and Jan the following year. It had just joined 821 Squadron shortly before the crash.

Pilot Lieutenant William Alexander Bell. RN. Aged 23, was the eldest son of James Logie and Heather Mary Stilgoe Newman Bell of The Woll, Ashkirk, Selkirk, Scottish Borders.

William's home in the small village of Ashkirk is situated on banks of the Ale Water in the Scottish Borders area of Scotland. It is located on the A7 road, approximately midway between Selkirk to the north and Hawick to the south. William was buried in St.Mary's and St.Cuthbert's Kirkyard, Hawick.

St.Mary's & St.Cuthbert's Episcopal Church sign in Hawick

Photo: Author's Collection

274

St. Cuthbert's Church, Hawick   Photo: Walter Baxter. Under CC Licence.

Observer Acting Sub-Lieutenant Bertram Philip Brushett, RN, was born 6th October 1931 and according to press at the time of the accident his home was in Chester, Cheshire, but the BDM register and the Ancestry site, have no record of him having been born here.

The only sparse detail that was found on this airman, assuming that this is one in the same person? was in the Royal Navy List of 1951 which has a Midshipman P.B. Brushett on charge with the navy on 12th April 1950.

Sub/Lt William A. Bell in St.Mary's and St.Cuthbert's Kirkyard, Hawick

Photo: Author's Collection

MARITIME MISHAP - NEPTUNE WX545

Thirty six squadron RAF Coastal Command having been equipped with Mosquito FB.6's since October 1946, was disbanded at Thorney Island precisely one year later. The squadron was reformed on 1st July 1953 at RAF Topcliffe, North Yorkshire, under control of 19 Group but was now operating with Neptune MR.1s.

The Lockheed manufactured Neptune MR.1 (P2V-5) had entered service with the Royal Air Force in 1952, with the first delivery of 52 aircraft landing at St. Eval, Cornwall on 27th January for joint operations in support of the Avro Shackleton in the maritime reconnaissance role.

Early October 1956 Neptune WX545, accompanied by six other squadron aircraft, flew to Ballykelly, N. Ireland to undertake anti-submarine exercises with the Royal Navy at the Joint Anti-Submarine School HMS (*Sea Eagle*).

Airborne at 17:21 hours on Wednesday 10th October, WX545 was engaged on a low level anti-submarine training exercise close to the shore of the Mull of Kintyre, the crew that day consisted:

Captain and 1st Pilot F/Lt Geoffrey Finding, Co-Pilot, F/O James A. Campbell, Navigator, F/O Gilbert Rishton, F/Eng. Sgt Cyril Armstrong, W/Op. F/Sgt Raymond Fox, and four Air Signallers, F/Sgt Ronald M. Noble, Sgt Eric Honey, Sgt Bernard E. Lynn and Sgt Roy V. Smith.

As per the briefing, WX545 rendezvoused with the target and following completion of the simulated attack on a Royal Navy submarine, the navigator plotted a course to steer and the crew began to head home.

However, in the prevailing mist they had drifted slightly off track and while heading in a south-easterly direction, and at a dangerously low altitude of around 1,000 feet asl, the aircraft failed to clear high ground to the south of Balmavicar on the Mull of Kintyre.

At approximately 21:55 hours, after a flight duration of 4 hours 34 minutes, the Neptune crashed into the rugged hill known as Eagle Rock, broke up and caught fire with the loss of all nine crew.

Lockheed Neptune WX545

William Crowe, at that time a 56 year old principal keeper at the Mull of Kintyre lighthouse, is understood to have been the first to witness the crash and recounted the events to a reporter from the Campbeltown Courier the following day:

"I heard a plane going over around 10 o'clock. It sounded very low, I looked out and seconds later there came the sound of a crash and a flash from the direction of the hills behind the lighthouse. The fog was heavy at the time.

I phoned the coastguard at Southend and a search party was organised. I gave them all the information I could and my assistant keepers, Mr John Mann and Mr Malcolm McPhee, joined the searchers while I carried on at the lighthouse alone".

The Police and local ambulance services were also contacted and soon arrived from Campbeltown. A party of around 12 searchers gathered to take to the hills, led by Malcolm Bannatyne a 56 year old shepherd from Ballinamoil.

Coastguard officers from Southend, Mr Rowlands and Edward Wordsworth were among the searchers and Mr Wordsworth described the arduous trek across the hill:

"We climbed the hillside in the darkness and in thick fog. It was heavy-going through the heather, bog and peat and over great boulders, and because of the density of the fog we couldn't see a thing most of the way"

As the party drew closer to the site, an orange glow was seen through the fog and they soon spotted flickering flames from pieces of burning wreckage. It was a tragic scene with widespread wreckage everywhere, and it soon became apparent that no one on board had survived.

At 02:00 on the morning after the crash, a voice on the tannoy rang out at RAF Leuchars, near St.Andrews, Fife. *`All members of MRT to report to Mountain Rescue section immediately!`* The team quickly gathered their kit together as sparse bits of information came in about the crash. By 02:30 they were all on board the trucks and speeding along the winding roads to Campbeltown, a journey of almost 200 miles. As always, they had hopes of finding survivors.

The team arrived around 06:30 but the news was not good, the police informed them that the first search party had found only bodies, and so the job of the team now would now be recovery rather than rescue.

Arthur Helsby, ex-MRT RAF Leuchars recalled what happened next:

"After hot cups of tea provided by the wife of the police sergeant, the convoy set off along the narrow winding road which leads to the lighthouse on the Mull of Kintyre. At a point where the track starts to drop steeply down to the lighthouse, the convoy came to a halt and a forward base camp was set up. The crash site was a mile to the north of base camp on the west slope of Beinn na Lice at around 1300ft (Actually nearer 1200ft) It took the team only 20 minutes to reach the wreckage but what they saw was a scene of devastation and carnage.

The only recognisable sections of the plane were the tail unit, the partially burnt fuselage and part of the starboard wing. The plane had disintegrated on impact leaving a 300-yard trail of scorched heather and debris, starting with the tail-plane and finishing with the starboard engine.

Some airmen had been thrown clear, but others were still in the fuselage.... There was evidence that at least one member of

RAF Mountain Rescue Team at The Gap on the Mull road the following day

Photo: Campbeltown Courier

Tail section of WX545 the day after the crash in 1956 at the first point of impact

Photo: Arthur Helsby

the crew had survived the initial impact and crawled several yards before he died.

The first job was to extract those in the wreckage and to collect the others ready for evacuation to the road. Not many of the team had experienced this kind of situation before and the fact that they carried out their task in a dignified and professional manner was great credit to them, for nothing in their training had prepared them for this.

The very presence of `Doc` Rennie who supervised the gruesome task, was of tremendous support and the fact that no one member wanted to let the rest of the team down, instilled an inner discipline which saw them through that dreadful day.

The team only carried one Thomas stretcher so this had to be supplemented by standard canvas and pole stretchers supplied by the police. The casualties were then taken down to the road where they were placed on a BRS lorry and covered with a tarpaulin sheet, before being transported to Campbeltown police station where cells acted as a temporary morgue..... The team having completed their task were taken to RNAS Machrihanish, where they were provided with a hot meal and accommodation for the night. In the meantime I had arrived at the police station where `Doc` Rennie was carrying out a preliminary examination to formally identify the deceased. This task completed, both the Doc and I were taken to Machrihanish where we joined the team.

The main crash area of the Neptune in 1956 the tail can just be seen on the horizon
Photo: Arthur Helsby

Shepherd and a rescue worker at the crash site the following day
Photo: Arthur Helsby

We found our colleagues tired and in a sombre mood. It had been 20 hours since they left Leuchars and nearly 48 hours since they had a good night's sleep.

The following day, Friday, the team headed back to Leuchars, arriving at mid-day when they finally stood down, 33 hours after they had been called out.

It took the team some time to come to terms with what they had witnessed. Some members chose to talk freely about their feelings, whilst others kept their emotions to themselves. For some it had been a very distressing experience and they were left to overcome their emotions in their own individual way".

By all accounts the chapter on this aircraft should have ended here, but some new information which came to light from a former crew member of WX545, casts some doubt on the Board of Inquiry's original findings that: the Captain be held responsible *"By not taking reasonable precautions in the vicinity of high ground". Also that:*

"The Navigator may have made an error in his working or failed to have warned the Capt of high ground in the immediate vicinity. Furthermore the radar operator presumably did not report land contacts ahead, but then the radar may have been switched off or on stand-by?"

In contrast the Inquiry stated that the *"Commander in Chief was of the opinion that no court or authority can categorically state that pilot error was the cause of this accident".* But in all fairness, it was discovered years later, that all the facts had not been presented to the board for one reason or another.

36 SQUADRON RAF TOPCLIFFE 1955/56

L to R: F/Lt. Finding, F/Lt Hillman, F/O Mason, F/O Rishton, Sgt Armstrong, F/Sgt Ball, F/Sgt Jones, Sgt Kirk, F/Sgt Noble and Sgt Lynn.

From this group:
Finding, Rishton, Armstrong, Noble and Lynn were on the fatal flight

In his autobiography *The Hidden Truth*, Maurice Hamlin, a former F/Sgt Air Signaller with 36 Squadron at Topcliffe, gave a startling account of the events.

F/Sgt Hamlin had been at the pre-flight briefing on the date of the accident and should have been on the aircraft that day but for a twist of fate. He explained in in his book how the day began:

"On the 10th October we attended a detailed inter-service briefing explaining how the joint Navy/RAF anti-submarine operation was to be conducted. An Admiral was in overall command and addressed the briefing of all NATO services involved.

He made a special point to all RAF Squadron aircrews about aircraft safety. He said that despite bad weather, blanketing fog and heavy rain clouds which were giving very poor visibility, he knew that the aircrews wanted to detect and catch submarines, however, he continued, despite the fact that the subs have anti-aircraft radar detection equipment "all RAF aircrew are to use their hazard radar detection intermittently as a safety measure, even within inshore waters".

He went on to say that it was essential to do this to avoid the danger posed by the notorious mountainous crags of the Mull of Kintyre.

At the end of the briefing our Squadron Commanding Officer.....ordered all aircrew to remain seated. When only aircrew remained he countermanded the Admiral's direct order stating: "Aircrew were not to use radar within inshore waters" Apparently in a bid to catch the Navy off guard.

"I was the senior Air Signaller of F/Lt Finding's crew. Late in the evening of 10th October all the crew, including myself, went out to the Neptune MR1 (WX545) preparing for take off. As I entered the aircraft, I collapsed (apparently with flu) and was carried out and taken by ambulance to the Base Hospital. The following morning I was woken in hospital and told that my aircraft had crashed on the Mull of Kintyre and all of my friends were dead".

With regards to the investigation that followed, not only did the hearing lack F/Sgt Hamlin's testimony with regards to what was said at the pre-flight briefing, but also that of another former Neptune crewman, Air Signaller Sgt Jeff Jenks, who almost lost his life that same morning but for a strange premonition.

In later years, Mr Jenks gave a statement to Maurice Hamlin, explaining what happened on his flight earlier that day:

"I was a junior signaller on the Neptune which was the first to take off on the night of October 10th, weather conditions were very poor, and as I understand it the exercise was devised by a scientist who was working with Coastal Command. The object of the exercise was to take off with radar switched on, then gain height until we detected a submarine, which was lying submerged in the lee of the Mull, then, after making a note of its position we were to switch off the radar and maintain radio silence throughout the experiment.

The aim was to see how near we could get to an attacking position, using instruments only, before the sub detected our presence. When we were in the vicinity of the sub I had an awful premonition and surreptitiously switched on the radar and saw a large land mass ahead of us. I shouted to our pilot and he hauled back the controls taking evasive action to such an extent that he lost power in one engine. I switched off the radar again and we headed back to base observing the order to maintain radio silence.

We landed and WX545 took off to repeat our exercise without having had any information passed to them about our near miss. I was only a junior signaller, and didn't feel that I could have had any say in the events". Likely for fear he would be reprimanded by the C.O. for switching on his radar set.

Eventually the court agreed with the C in C in that the crew could not be held responsible and it concluded by stating: `Cause of crash, unknown`.

On Tuesday 16th October more than 200 servicemen, relatives and close friends, formed a procession in Topcliffe for the funeral of five of the Neptune's crew. A military truck carried the Union Jack flag draped coffins one and a half miles from the airfield to the parish church, accompanied by another lorry with a mountain of flowers and wreaths.

W/Cdr. Reverend W.V. Scott, padre of RAF Topcliffe, conducted the service after which the casks were carried by 30 members of the squadron to their

Funeral procession for five of the crew in October 1956. Photo: Pat Juby

The procession being led into Topcliffe parish church. Photo: Pat Juby

final resting place, where Rev Scott read from the scriptures, followed by a volley from a firing party and the last post played by a lone bugler.

Captain and 1st Pilot. Flight Lieutenant Geoffrey Finding, RAF, born 19th November 1923, in Glossop, Derbyshire, was the son of Wilson and Evelyn Mary Finding (née Alvey) of Sandhills Road, Barnt Green, Worcestershire. He had one brother Anthony.

Geoff's parents were both from Yorkshire, his father was born in Hull and his mother in Bradford. The couple had been married on 25th January 1923 at Dinting Vale, Glossop, Derbyshire, and had resided here for a short while before moving to the Midlands.

Having joined the RAF in 1942 and after training as a pilot, Geoff was granted a commission to P/O on 6th July 1944 followed by promotion to F/O on 6th January 1945.

Geoff flew Halifax bombers during the war and two of his former crew, Bomb Aimer Dave Thomas and Air Signaller Ken Wood attended the service for the ill-fated crew on the Mull of Kintyre when the memorial was placed on 9th July 1998.

A very experienced pilot. At the time of the accident he had amassed a total of 2,145 flying hours, with 734 solo on the Neptune. Geoff Finding was interred alongside four of his crew in Topcliffe, St. Columba's Parish Churchyard.

James was interred with full military honours in St. Columba's Churchyard, Topcliffe, Yorkshire.

Navigator Flying Officer Gilbert Rishton, RAF, born 2nd September 1928, was the son of Mr & Mrs Gilbert Rishton of Blackburn, Lancashire.

Gilbert had joined the RAF in 1951 and gained a commission to Acting Pilot Officer on probation on 2nd January 1952. His rank of P/O was confirmed on 25th August 1953 and promotion to Flying Officer came on 26th August a year later.

Following the accident Gilbert was one of the five crew interred in St.Columba's Churchyard, Topcliffe.

F/Lt Geoff Finding's grave, Topcliffe

Co-Pilot. Flying Officer James Alexander Campbell, RAF, born 16th January 1934, was the son of Mr & Mrs A. Campbell from Stanmore, Middlesex.

James joined the RAF soon after leaving school and became a Commissioned Pilot Officer flight cadet at Cranwell College on 14th December 1954, then a Flying Officer with seniority from 14th December 1955.

But for a twist of fate James wouldn't have been on the fatal flight. Originally his place would have been filled by F/Sgt John William Larkin, but a phone call stating that John's mother was seriously ill shortly before the flight saw him having to rush off to hospital.

F/O Gilbert Rishton's grave in Topcliffe

Flight Engineer Sergeant Cyril Armstrong, RAF, born 26th January 1929, was the son of William and Florence Armstrong (née Bennett) of Houghton-le-Spring, Co. Durham. But prior to leaving for Ballykelly, when serving with 36 Squadron at Topcliffe his home was in Thirsk, North Yorkshire.

Following the accident a service was held in his hometown and Cyril was cremated at Sunderland Crematorium. He his remembered, as are the other crew members on the Armed Forces Memorial at the National Arboretum, Staffordshire.

Sgt Raymond Fox

Photo: Pat Juby

Radio Operator Sergeant Raymond Fox, RAF, born 30th August 1924, was the son of Richard and Florence Mary Fox and husband of Lilian Violet Fox (née Horne) of Thanet, Kent. The couple had two children Angela and Richard.

Ray, as he was known, was originally from Sheffield, South Yorkshire, where his late father Richard was a former steel worker. Ray and his wife had moved into married quarters at Topcliffe when he joined the squadron there.

He would have undergone similar training to that of Roy Smith (see Roy's bio for details) and following the accident he was returned to his former hometown of Sheffield and interred in Abbey Lane Cemetery. Section P. Grave 1916.

Sgt Raymond Fox's grave in Sheffield

Photo: Stephen Farnell via Findagrave

286

Air Signaller Sergeant Roy Vincent Smith, RAF, born 30th November 1931, was the son of Albert and Florence May Smith. He had one brother Geoff and was husband of Queenie Maud Smith (née Juby) of Caterham, London.

Roy enlisted as a boy entrant the RAF soon after leaving School in 1947, and at his own request from the age of 18 he signed on for 12 years service and began his basic training as an Aircraftman.

One of the stations Roy trained at was No.1 Air Signallers School at RAF Swanton Morley, Norfolk, where both in the classroom and in the air in Anson Mk.22s and Proctors, he would complete a course in wireless and Morse and be awarded his Signallers badge and a promotion to Sergeant on 27th May 1953.

Sgt Roy V. Smith

Photo: Pat Juby

Sgt Roy Smith (Standing in centre top row) at RAF Swanton Morley   Photo: Pat Juby

Roy (2nd right) Sandbag filling detail during the Norfolk floods 1953. Photo: Pat Juby

It was at Swanton Morley that he met his future wife Queenie in 1952. She lived in nearby Reymerston (Former home village of legendary autogyro pilot W/Cdr. Ken Wallis) and used to cycle to dances on the base. The couple were engaged in July 1953 and wed on 4th April 1954 at St. Peter's Church, Reymerston.

In July 1953 Roy was posted to the Central Gunnery School at Leconfield, Yorkshire, where he flew in Avro Lincolns on air and sea cine-gun exercises, achieving 'Above Average' grades. A further posting to RAF St. Mawgan came in September and on the 26th he flew for the first time in an Avro Lancaster with F/O Elliot to begin a course on radar, completing the course by 2nd December.

231 OCU was next, and on 22nd January Roy arrived at Kinloss and began flying in Lockheed Neptunes on

Roy and his bride Queenie in 1954

Photo: Pat Juby

288

Mungo, Joe, Jack, Luke, Ginge and Smudge (Roy)   Photo: Jack Giblen via Pat Juby

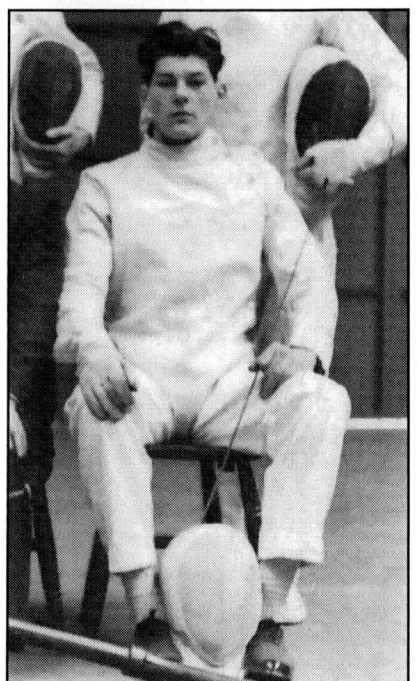

maritime patrol exercises. Like with all the military services, sport in the RAF was compulsory and encouraged and during his time at Topcliffe his chosen subjects were fencing and swimming and he excelled in both. He fenced bayonet for the RAF Royal Tournament and managed to win a medal. He also had a certificate for swimming.

He eventually arrived with 36 Sqn on 22nd April to become part of F/Lt George Burden's crew. From 1st October 1956 he flew just two sorties with F/Lt Finding prior to the accident.

Roy was interred in St.Columba's Churchyard, Topcliffe, along with four of his crew.

Left: Roy on RAF fencing team

Photo: Pat Juby

Air Signaller Sergeant Bernard Edward Lynn, RAF, born, 3rd November 1929, was the eldest son of Albert Edward and Mary Millicent Lynn (née Wisternoff) of Swansea, Glamorgan, Wales. He had two brothers Peter and Rex and was husband of Nanette.

Known as 'Taffy' to his crewmates, Bernard is understood to have joined the RAF in 1952. He was married to Miss Nanette Friel, the daughter of Mr & Mrs Patrick Friel of St.Joseph's Avenue, Londonderry, principal of Long Tower Boys School. She herself was a former teacher in Loreto Convent, Omagh, Northern Ireland.

Bernard and his wife had only been married 15 months and while he was stationed at Topcliffe, the couple had been living in Skelbank, Ripon, Yorkshire.

Having arranged a week's visit, his wife had arrived in Londonderry on Wednesday (the day of the crash) and was looking forward to meeting him on Thursday evening, but instead was greeted by the shocking news of the crash.

At the request of his wife, Bernard was returned to Northern Ireland for interment with full military honours in the City Cemetery, Londonderry, Section N, Row: Class D, Grave 2131.

Air Signaller Sergeant Ronald Mark Noble, RAF, born 4th July 1925, was the son of Mark and Isabel Jane Noble (née Heads) He had a sister Doreen and was husband of Annie (née Tweddell) of South Shields, Co. Durham and also father of Raymond.

Sgt Ron Noble

Ron, as he was referred, was married in Durham in summer 1949. He and his wife had lived on Branton Avenue, Hebburn, Tyneside, prior to moving to married quarters at RAF Topcliffe.

After the accident he was interred in Hebburn Cemetery, with full military honours.

Air Signaller Sergeant Eric Honey, RAF, born 12th September 1932, was the son of Stanley David and Gwendoline Mary Honey (née Perry) of Plympton St.Mary, Devon. He had a younger sister Ruth and was husband of Agnes and father of two children Linda and Lesley.

Eric, who resided in married quarters at Topcliffe, was interred in St.Columba's Churchyard, Topcliffe alongside four of his crew.

Graham Calder and Stuart Hamilton with one of the engines in 1995

Photo: Geoff Bland

Dave Ramsey with a sonar buoy and radio set at the site in 2000

Photo: Author's Collection.

Tail fin from WX545 in September 2017   *Photo: Author's Collection*

Neptune memorial on the Mull.   Photo: Author's Collection

GREY LADY DOWN - SHACKLETON WB833

Disbanded on 30th June 1945 after operating throughout the war years with the Short Sunderland Flying boat, 204 Squadron reformed at Kabrit, Egypt on 1st April 1947 with the Douglas Dakota C.4 but later converted to the Vickers Valetta C.1.

Renumbered as 84 Squadron in early 1953, the unit regained its original identity on 1st January 1954 at RAF Ballykelly, County Londonderry, Northern Ireland and received the Shackleton MR2 built by Avro at Woodford in Cheshire. These aircraft were later converted to the MR1A for twelve months before reverting back to MR2's during the month of May 1959.

One aircraft WB833 was withdrawn from the type MR1 production line and reconfigured to MR2 standard. First flown on the 17th June 1952 after completing several A&AEE performance trails and following two minor accidents, it was repaired and delivered to 210 Squadron on 16th December 1966 to join the Ballykelly Wing, comprising: 203, 204, and 210 Squadrons.

At 07:53 on the morning of Friday 19th April 1968, Shackleton WB833 departed Ballykelly with a 204 Squadron crew consisting of: Pilot and Captain Squadron Leader Robert Clive Leonard Haggett, Pilot. F/O David Robert Burton, Pilot. F/O Michael Creedon, Nav.1 F/Lt Roger John Duncan Denny, Nav.2 F/Lt George Craigie Fisken, Air Eng. Sgt John Richard Frank Creamer, Air Elec Off. F/Lt Rodney Hellens, Air Elec 2 F/Sgt Thomas Frederick Anglin Buttimore, Air Elec 3 Sgt Bruce Robert Dixon, Air Sig M/Sig Ronald Cecil Stratton and Air Sig Sgt Nathaniel Michael Duffy. Orders were to conduct an anti-submarine exercise with the Oberon class submarine HMS *Onyx* (S21) in Area Juliet to the south of the Mull of Kintyre.

HMS Onyx

With visual and radar contact having been established with the submarine and several home runs completed successfully, the weather began to deteriorate with low cloud and mist rolling in, though radio contact between the aircraft and submarine continued until 09:34 when all communication was lost.

Shackleton WB833 seen here with 204 Sqn in the earlier scheme of coastal white with grey upper surfaces. Photo: A. V. Roe & Co. Ltd Ref: 308-25-C

The submarine had tried to contact the Shackleton at 09:45 but to no avail, it was later established that WB833 with all engines under power and in level flight, had banked to port 20-25° and crashed in a field south west of Garvalt Cottage and Farm on the lower slopes of Glenmanuilt Hill. The cloud base at this time was down to around 200 feet and witnesses stated that this was the second time the aircraft had been heard in the area within a period of five minutes.

John Reid, a gardener at Carskey Farm to the east of the crash site recalled:

"The plane was flying very low and seemed to be lost in the thick morning mist. It circled for about 20 minutes then flew towards the hill.

The pilot must have spotted the danger at the very last minute, because the plane banked steeply before crashing into a gully.

There was a series of explosions and I ran to the spot, but there was nothing I could do. The wreckage was burning furiously. There were things exploding left, right and centre".

Witness Mr John Reid

The tail section of WB833/T was one of the few recognisable pieces of the aircraft. Photo: KMRT

Mr Reid's boss, Ewan Johnstone had also rushed up the hill to the scene and told of his findings:

"There were several airmen lying on the ground and I could see one in the plane, but there was nothing that could be done for any of them".

Once the alarm was raised, Police, Fire and Ambulance services soon arrived at the scene from RAF Machrihanish and the area was quickly cordoned off. Later that evening the RAF Kinloss Mountain Rescue Team arrived to assist in the recovery of casualties from the hill.

In the days that followed investigators arrived at the scene to try and establish the cause of the accident, meanwhile services were held in Ballykelly and the various hometowns of the airmen who died that day.

During the investigation members of the Flight Safety Board established the following:

"A reconstructed plot of the aircraft track indicated it had penetrated inland by half a mile either at the end of an outbound leg, following a homing run against the submarine, which was approximately 7 miles off the coast, or while orbiting.

The Board of Inquiry was unable to allocate responsibility for the accident, but considered that the Captain had been operating close to the prudent limit of safe airmanship in continuing the exercise in the prevailing conditions.

Members of RAF Kinloss Mountain Rescue Team with a Shackleton mainwheel

Below: The total carnage that greeted the rescue services.

Both Photos: KMRT

Looking S.E. from the crash site across Carskey Bay. Photo: Steven Spink

The CFSO was inclined to believe the radar had developed a fault and events then unfolded rapidly with a loss of situational awareness. It was thought the 1st Navigator had been manning the 'Attack Plot' position and coordinating the homing runs with the Radar Operator, while the 2nd Navigator was probably in the bomb-aiming position to practice simulated weapon releases, thereby leaving responsibility for terrain separation with the Captain and Radar operator."

All the wreckage was later removed from the site by an RAF Maintenance Unit, though small fragments still litter the scar on Glenmanuilt Hill, which lies adjacent to a poignant memorial for the crew.

In 2009 Angie Ingles, Kintyre resident and former fiancée of Sgt Duffy one of the ill-fated crew, contacted The Shackleton Association to ask if any members would be interested in raising funds for a memorial to be placed at the crash site, if of course permission could be obtained from the landowner. A visit was arranged with Tom Helme, the owner of Carskey Estate and permission was granted. Mr Helme even suggested the design and the most suitable spot on the hill in which to place it.

The memorial on Glenmanuilt Hill for the crew of Shackleton WB833

Photo: Author's Collection

Small pieces at the crash site. Below: The Plaque. Both Photo's: Author's Collection

The campaign began and requests for donations came flooding in from members of The Shackleton Association and families and friends of the crew. A local builders; McFadyen's of Campbeltown also offered to help by providing the necessary transport, building materials and labour free of charge.

Fifty years on, a stone memorial now sits proudly on the hill overlooking the bay, though for Angie Ingles, there was one more thing she had to do and that was to have a plaque made in honour of her fiancée Air Signaller Sgt Nat Duffy. This she achieved and it was placed on a wall in Keil Cemetery, Southend, Kintyre.

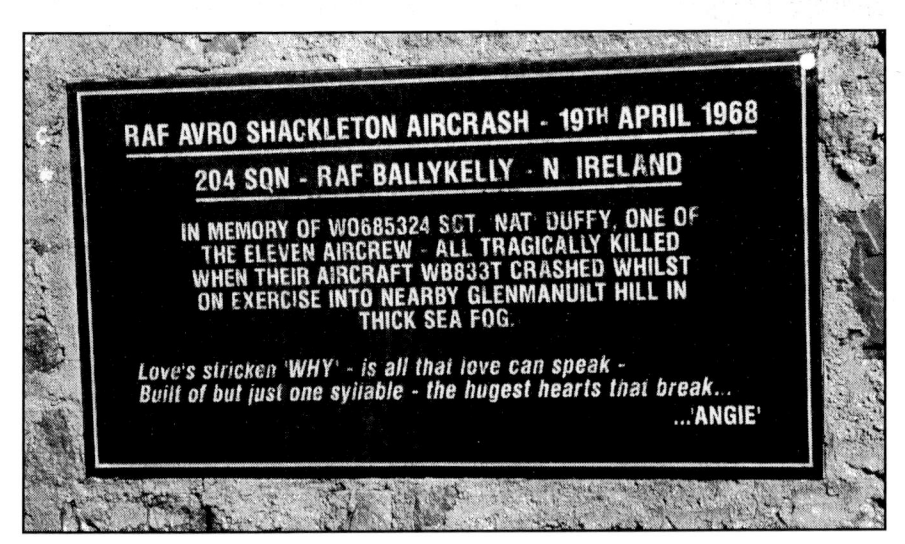

RAF AVRO SHACKLETON AIRCRASH - 19TH APRIL 1968
204 SQN - RAF BALLYKELLY - N. IRELAND

IN MEMORY OF W0685324 SGT. NAT DUFFY, ONE OF
THE ELEVEN AIRCREW - ALL TRAGICALLY KILLED
WHEN THEIR AIRCRAFT WB833T CRASHED WHILST
ON EXERCISE INTO NEARBY GLENMANUILT HILL IN
THICK SEA FOG.

Love's stricken 'WHY' - is all that love can speak -
Built of but just one syllable - the hugest hearts that break...
...'ANGIE'

Captain and Pilot. Squadron Leader Robert Clive Leonard Haggett, RAF, born 6th August 1944 in Merthyr Tydfil, Glamorganshire, was the husband of Audrey L. Haggett (née England) of Balderton, Nottinghamshire.

Clive, as he was referred, was a very experienced pilot having joined the RAF in the early 1950s. He was commissioned as a cadet pilot on 12th March 1952 and had signed on for 8 years active service with 4 years on reserve.

He conducted his basic and early flying training in the UK, but later went overseas to Rhodesia, South Africa.

On 2nd April 1953 Clive was promoted to P/O and awarded his pilots wings. Further promotions to F/O and F/Lt followed on 12th June 1954 and 5th November 1958 respectively.

During the latter period he married his fiancée Audrey England in 1957 at Holderness, East Riding, Yorkshire and a year later their son Christopher was born.

Following the accident a service was held in his hometown attended by family, friends and members of his squadron. He was interred in Newark-on-Trent Cemetery, Nottingham with the epitaph:

Treasured memories of a beloved husband & son
- Greater love hath no man`

Grave of S/Ldr. Clive Haggett. RAF in Newark Cemetery, Nottingham.
Photo: Alan Clark

Pilot. Flying Officer David Robert Burton, RAF, born 7th March 1945, was the son of Leslie David and Phyllis Edith Burton (née Carter) of Bedford, Bedfordshire.

David was granted a commission in the RAF and became a cadet pilot and P/O on probation on 29th November 1963. He graduated as a pilot the following year, was awarded his wings and promotion to full Pilot Officer with seniority on 29th November. He was subsequently promoted to F/O on this date in 1965.

A family service was held for David in his hometown of Bedford, followed by cremation at Bedford Crematorium.

Pilot. Flying Officer Michael Creedon, RAF, born 29th February 1944, was the son of Anthony Michael and Lily Creedon (née Town) of Morley, Wakefield, Yorkshire. He had two sisters Valerie and Victoria.

Mike's interest in aviation was probably inspired by his father who was an RAF aircraft designer and engineer for the Fairey Aviation Company, Heaton Chapel, Stockport, Greater Manchester.

His parents were both from Wakefield but had married in Nottingham in 1939, and due to his occupation his father travelled around quite a lot but returned home after the war.

Mike was commissioned as Acting Pilot Officer cadet pilot on 14th June 1963. He was awarded his wings on this date the following year and promoted to P/O with seniority. A further promotion to the rank of F/O came in June 1965 and in the spring of that year he married his fiancée Miss Marilyn C. Gilbert in Epping, Essex.

At the time of the accident Mike had only recently joined 204 Squadron for conversion to the Mk. II Shackleton, after having served a tour on Mk. III's with 120 Squadron.

He was interred in Tamlaught Finlagen Churchyard, Ballykelly, Londonderry, Section W. Grave 28.

Navigator 1. Flight Lieutenant Roger John Duncan Denny, RAF, born on 4th June 1936, was the son of John and Moira Denny. He had a sister Ann and was the husband of Sheila R. Denny (née Western) of Spring Hill, Tramore, County Waterford, Ireland.

Roger was commissioned as a cadet navigator P/O on 27th February 1961, promoted to F/O on 22nd May 1964 and that spring married his fiancée Sheila Western in Bristol.

On 10th February 1967, shortly before joining 204 Squadron he was promoted to F/Lt. Following the accident Roger was interred in Tamlaught Finlagen Churchyard, Ballykelly, Londonderry, Sec W. Grave 25.

Navigator 2. Flight Lieutenant George Craigie Fisken, RAF, born 2nd June 1941 in Dundee, Angus, was the son of George Craigie and Christina Fisken (née Reid) of Crieff, Perthshire. He had a brother and four sisters and was a married man with one daughter.

George grew up in Carnoustie where his father managed a farm. He had joined the RAF around 1960 as a cadet navigator and on graduating was commissioned P/O on 9th March 1963. He was promoted to F/O on 9th March 1964 and F/Lt on 9th September 1967.

George had married Judith V. Sturman, a fellow RAF Officers daughter from Heywood, Lancashire and it is believed he met her during training. The couple were wed in Cirencester in 1966.

George was interred in Tamlaught Finlagen Churchyard, Ballykelly, Londonderry, Sec W. Grave 24.

Air Electronics Officer Flight Lieutenant Rodney Hellens, RAF, born 12th April 1942, in Gainsborough, Lincs, was the son of Wilfred H. and May Hellens (née Feetham) of Berkshire. He had a brother Paul and was husband of Rosemary.

Rodney's parents were living in Yorkshire during the war and had been married in Thurn, West Riding, in October 1941, they later moved to Berkshire where they resided at Eggleton Cottages on Chavey Down Road with their two sons Rodney and Paul.

Commissioned Acting Pilot Officer in the RAF on 13th February 1960, Rodney had originally signed on as a cadet pilot, but appears later to have remustered as an AEO and was confirmed in his rank as P/O on 13th February 1961.

Rodney was promoted to F/O on 13th February 1962 and in December that year married his fiancée Miss Rosemary Hunt in Leicester, but the couple later lived in Winkfield Row, Berkshire.

Posted to 204 Squadron at Ballykelly, his final promotion to F/Lt came on 13th August 1965. Rodney was interred in Tamlaught Finlagen Churchyard, Ballykelly, Londonderry, Northern Ireland. Section W. Grave 26.

Air Engineer. Sergeant John Richard Frank Creamer, RAF, born on 23rd February 1941, was the son of Alfred Charles Frank and Marjorie Ellen Creamer (née Dixon) of Illford, Essex. He had one brother Barry and a sister Diana.

Tamlaght Finlagen Church, Ballykelly. Photo: Bob Dennis—Via Findagrave.

Air Electronics Operator 2. Flight Sergeant Thomas Frederick Anglin Buttimore, RAF, born 18th July 1934, was the only son of William and Sarah Anne Buttimore (née Anglin) of Kinsale, Co. Cork, Ireland.

Known as Freddie, his parents were married at Skibbereen, Ireland in the autumn of 1921 and lived in Kinsale on the southwest coast of Ireland. Freddie was the couple's only child, though his father, a widower, had four boys and two girls from a previous marriage. Sadly his father passed away in 1944, followed by his mother a year later.

It is believed Freddie left Ireland for England in the 1950s and that he joined the RAF in the early 60s. At the time of the accident his residence was given as Shepton Mallet in Somerset.

Freddie was interred in Tamlaught Finlagen Churchyard, Ballykelly, Londonderry, Northern Ireland. Section W Grave 27. He is also remembered on his parents grave in Templetrine Graveyard (Old) Ballinspittle, Co.Cork.

Templetrine Church, Ballinspittle, Cork

Air Electronics Operator 3. Sergeant Bruce Robert Dixon, RAF, born 2nd January 1944, was the son of John Robert and Hazel Lavina Dixon of Bexley Heath, Kent and husband of Daphne A. Dixon (née Stacey) from Dartford.

Bruce was interred along with other crew members in Tamlaught Finlagen Churchyard, Ballykelly, Londonderry, Northern Ireland. Section W. Grave 29.

Air Signaller Master Signaller Ronald Cecil Stratton, RAF, born 22nd December 1924, was the son of Mr & Mrs H.G. Stratton of Wallingford, Berkshire. He had one brother Leslie.

Ronald was a long serving RAF man who had been awarded the King's Commendation for valuable service in the air in the New Years Honours List January 1952.

He was a married man and at the time of the accident was living in Belfast, Northern Ireland. At this time it is not known by the authors where he is buried, so possibly a private family grave.

Air Signaller Sergeant Nathaniel Michael Duffy, RAF, born in Dublin on 15th June 1942, was the son of Mrs & Mrs M. Duffy (née Gologhy) of Dublin. He had two brothers.

Nat, as he was known was interred in Deans Grange Burial Ground, Black Rock, Dun Laogaire, Dublin, Ireland. Section C1. Grave 7.

All the Shackleton crews names are recorded on the Armed Forces Memorial at the National Arboretum, Staffordshire along with another monument by The Shackleton Association dedicated to honouring all the airmen that served with Shackleton units.

A STING IN ITS TAIL - WASP HC XT789

Originally designated as the Sea Scout, the Westland Wasp H.A.S.1 XT789 (C/n F.9671) was primarily designed to operate from the Royal Navy Tribal and Leander class Frigates.

Manufactured by the Fairey Division of Westland Helicopters Ltd, Hayes, Middlesex and completed on the production line at Yeovil, XT789 was one of a total of 96 Wasps to enter service with the Royal Navy Fleet Air Arm, serving with several squadrons and training units throughout their career from mid-summer 1963 until the late 1980's.

XT789 was first flown on 28th March 1967 by Mr W.R. Gellatly, Chief Test Pilot of Westland Helicopters Ltd.

It was eventually allocated to 829 Squadron and stationed on board the 2,450 ton Leander class frigate HMS *Dido* (F104) on 16th February 1970 as '473'.

On Wednesday 10th August 1970, XT789 flown by Lt/Cdr. David M. Carr and accompanied by Lt (E) Trevor Blakeley was engaged on a night flying exercise under Ground Control Approach to HMS *Dido* located off the west coast of Scotland, escorting Her Majesty's vessel the Royal Yacht *Britannia* with the Royal family aboard, the ship being on her way to Aberdeenshire.

A low lying fog covered the south of Kintyre, making flying conditions very

HMS DIDO

difficult and in the prevailing darkness and poor visibility the helicopter struck rising ground about a half mile west of Borgedalemore Point, above sea cliffs on the southern tip of the Mull of Kintyre.

Once word of the missing helicopter came through, a widespread search was conducted by *Dido* and the Campbeltown lifeboat, with shipping in the area being asked to keep a watchful eye out for the missing helicopter.

The Campbeltown lifeboat had been out for almost seven and a half hours, but nothing was found. The following day an Avro Shackleton was despatched from RAF Ballykelly, Londonderry and located the accident in a small valley on the other side of the ridge where it had first hit, close to an old settlement.

Police from Campbeltown and the Coastguard from Southend, scrambled up the hill, clambering over rocks and negotiating a path through boggy ground and heather to reach the site, where they discovered Lt Blakeley dazed and injured in a glen.

The injured man was given first aid by Surgeon-Commander John Lawrence-Owen from the Royal Yacht of whom had been flown in by helicopter. Lt Blakeley was then flown to the station SQ at RAF Ballykelly, before being transferred to Altnagelvin Hospital in Londonderry.

The pilot Lt/Cdr. Carr had received fatal injuries in the crash and had died almost instantly, but Lt Blakeley was thrown clear and though his injuries were not deemed life threatening, he was in a terrible state of shock.

Westland Wasp HAS.1 XV624 '409' Photographed here while serving with the Royal Navy 2,800 ton survey ship HMS Hecla (A133)

The wreckage of XT789 was salvaged by a Westland Sea King XV656 052/R of 824 Squadron, Culdrose and delivered by road to the Accident Investigation Unit at Lee-on-Solent for examination.

During the accident investigation it was found that: *"The helicopter hit the hill while flying under IFR (Instrument Flight Rules) conditions whilst being vectored by HMS Dido's radar and SCAT team".*

Initially it was thought that the Wasp could to be of use for Ground Instructional purposes, but the project was abandoned and the airframe subsequently scrapped. Just five days after the Wasp's recovery, Sea King XV656 was involved in an minor incident when the engine anti-icing warning system functioned during heavy rain, fortunately Canadian Armed Forces pilot Captain Myrhaug landed safely and the fault was fixed.

The Wasp being recovered by RN Sea King helicopter XV656 on 12th August 1970

Photo: Campbeltown Heritage Centre

Above: The shattered remains of Wasp XT789. Photo: Campbeltown Heritage Centre

Below: Looking down towards the area of the accident.   Photo: Author's Collection

Pilot. Lieutenant Commander David Marshall Carr, RN, born 9th May 1938, was the son of Mr & Mrs Carr of Hemel Hempstead, Hertfordshire.

David was a married man and when not at sea aboard *Dido,* his usual residence was at Redruth, Cornwall. He was a very experienced pilot having joined the Royal Naval College at Lee-on-Solent (*Daedalus*) as a cadet on 1st May 1957 and gained his pilots wings a year later.

On New Years Day 1960, David, now an Acting Sub/Lt was posted to HMS *Dryad* in Hampshire for navigation and radar courses, then in spring 1962 as a full Sub/Lt he was based at Yeovilton flying helicopters.

As a Temp Lieutenant in August 1964, David was in the headlines for receiving the Queen's Commendation `For valuable services in the air in support of ground forces in Borneo`.

It would appear that between 1962 – 1964 he was flying the Wessex HAS.1 from HMS *Albion* with 845 Squadron.

By Spring 1968 he was a full Lieutenant on attachment to HMS (*Albatross*) a Naval Air Station in New South Wales, Australia. He later returned to the UK and having been promoted to Lieutenant Commander he served with HMS *Dido* until the time of his passing.

David is commemorated on the Armed Forces Memorial at the National Arboretum in Staffordshire.

Passenger. Engineer Lieutenant (E) Trevor Blakeley, RN, CEng, FRINA, FIMarEST, FIMechE, was born in 1943 in Goole, East Riding, Yorkshire and he attended early schools in Leeds.

Trevor enrolled in the Britannia Royal Naval College, Dartmouth as a cadet engineer from 1st September 1963, then the Royal Naval Engineering College at Meadon where he earned his degree.

Promotion to Lieutenant came on 1st August 1968 and as Naval Engineering specialist he enjoyed a wide range of seagoing and shore appointments.

Trevor served at sea in minesweepers, frigates, destroyers and aircraft carriers as well as numerous shore appointments which included specialist technical teams, ship construction, training and general staff appointments in technical and personnel support.

After recovery from his ordeal on Kintyre, Trevor became a Chartered Engineer and later a Fellow of the Royal Institution of Naval Architects, the Institute of Marine Engineering, Science and Technology and the Institution of Mechanical Engineers.

He is the Chairman of the Council of the Confederation of European Maritime Technological Societies (CEMT). And is the Chief Executive of the Royal Institution of Naval Architects. Trevor now resides in Hampshire

BIRD STRIKE - F-111E 68-008

Designed in the 1960s and still operating with the RAAF until December 2010, the General Dynamics F-111 supersonic medium-range interdictor and tactical attack aircraft, was used in a variety of roles such as strategic bombing, aerial reconnaissance and electronic warfare.

Nicknamed the *Ardvark,* the F-111 pioneered several new technologies for production aircraft, including: variable-sweep wings, Pratt & Whitney afterburning turbofan engines, and automatic terrain-following radar (TFR) for low-level high-speed flight.

In order to keep crews combat ready busy training schedules had to be adhered to. These training missions were often flown over rural environments with rugged mountainous terrain, which in the UK was usually Scotland or Wales.

During the Cold War, Upper Heyford near Bicester, Oxfordshire, was one of the former RAF bases chosen to house the United States Air Force Strategic Air Command (SAC) strategic bombers on 90-day TDY deployments until 1965. From 1966 United States Air Forces In Europe (USAFE) tactical reconnaissance aircraft were here and from 1st June 1970 the 20th Tactical Fighter Wing had relocated here from RAF station Weathersfield, Essex, with their F-111 Tactical Fighter Squadrons, the 55th, 77th and 79th, with the first two F-111Es arriving on 12th September.

Joining the 77th in 1972 was Captain Andrew `Andy` J. Peloquin, a senior former RF4C Phantom pilot and a Vietnam veteran with a hundred plus reconnaissance missions under his belt.

Also at Upper Heyford was Major Ariel `Al` Alvarez, a Master Navigator and Weapons Systems Officer. He too had flown a tour in Vietnam having been in the Air Force since 1956.

At 08:55 on Tuesday 15th May 1973 Capt. Peloquin and Maj Alvarez attended a pre-flight briefing, during which the Duty Officer informed the pair that they would undertake a low level training exercise off the West Coast, consisting of a VFR flight to the bombing range followed by a navigation exercise up to Scotland, then return to base on instruments.

Their aircraft that day F-111E 68-008, had been fuelled up and configured with pivot pylons loaded with an

F-111E 68-009, Sister aircraft to the one that crashed at Glenreasdale
Photo: The Aviation Photo Company

SUU-21 dispenser on station 6 carrying six Mk.106 practice bombs, giving a gross total take-off weight of 80,000 pounds.

The scheduled take off time was 10:55, and the exercise would be just a routine affair for this experienced crew, but soon after the briefing and quite out of character, Capt. Peloquin rang his wife Eileen to tell her that he loved her, a thing he didn`t normally do before a flight, knowing she had two young children to cope with all day so he wouldn`t want to wake her.

This of course was in the days before mobile phones and the phone was on the other side of the house in the kitchen. On answering, she replied in kind and told him to have a good flight.

After boarding the truck they arrived at the aircraft and began running through the pre-flight checks, everything was normal until they came to check the IFF transponder, when it was discovered that the UHF transmitter was inoperative and so the aircraft couldn`t be identified by ground stations as being friendly, a dangerous thing during the Cold War period.

The take off was aborted whilst a maintenance crew rectified the problem and then, with the trouble located and problem fixed, the aircraft finally took off at 11:04 but due to the delay it was decided to spend less time over the range before heading up north to Scotland for the second part of the exercise.

Having circled several times off Wallasey under control of Northern radar, the F-111 now over the Irish Sea and under Ulster radar control , made its way northwards towards the entry point for low level flying south of Arran.

F-111E 68-002 from Upper Heyford. Photo: M/Sgt Patrick Nugent under CC Licence

As the jet flew over Kilbrannan Sound east of Kintyre, a large bird was spotted by Maj Alvarez and a split second later by Capt. Peloquin who quickly took evasive action by banking left and up, but it was a split-second too late and as the bird passed below the canopy to the right, a large thump was felt, followed by severe aircraft vibrations.

The bird had been sucked into the engine air intake and into to turbo fan, tearing up blades along the way which in turn severed fuel lines. The cockpit began to fill with smoke and the Master Caution Panel was alive with hazard warning lights.

The fire warning light for the right engine came on and the WSO pressed the extinguisher button, then the wheel well hot light came on, soon followed by the fuselage fire warning light, and again the extinguisher was used, but the fire warning light stayed on and after flying on for a while the nose began to drop and the aircraft started to roll to the right and the situation became critical as Capt. Peloquin wrestled with the controls to try and stay airborne.

Meanwhile on the ground, Brian Gee of Carradale, an RAF Sergeant based at Machrihanish had been out in the hills with a group of men to visit the Tacan radar site above and to the east of Clachan, when he spotted the jet in trouble near Skipness.

"We heard the sound of an aircraft approaching from the SE and immediately knew something was wrong as

the engine didn't sound healthy. The aircraft came into view and we saw flames coming from the rear".

Back in the air, Capt. Peloquin, unable to counteract the roll using stick and rudder, gave the order for the WSO to pull the ejection handle and in an 80 degree right bank the cockpit capsule was blasted from the stricken jet.

Brian recalled what happened next:

"When it was almost due east of us we saw a parachute deploy and a short while later heard the aircraft crash. I phoned ATC at Machrihanish and reported the crash and seeing a single chute. I was asked if I saw a second chute as the aircraft had a crew of two. (he said he hadn't) I was then authorised to take my men in the direction of where the parachute came down and we set off across the moorland.

I had assumed that the parachute was the size used by a person, but what neither I nor ATC knew then was that the F-111 used an ejection system where the complete cockpit capsule was detached by explosive bolts, and a very large parachute deployed. Because of the size difference, the parachute was further away than we assumed and before we could get near a helicopter had appeared at the scene".

This dramatic artwork by an unknown American artist from 1966 shows the moment the cockpit escape capsule ejects from an F-111 jet

As the capsule drifted down, the crew caught sight of their burning aircraft as it crashed to the ground at the edge of a plantation at Glenreasdale. It exploded in a ball of flame scattering pieces of burning wreckage across a field for a distance of almost quarter of a mile, but fortunately with no loss of life but several sheep were scalded by burning aviation fuel as it narrowly missed the house at Glenreasdell Maine.

Kintyre farmer Hugh Kerr of Grassfield Farm said: *"I was working my sheep on the hill when I saw the jet screaming earthwards...The pilots jumped out on the hill* (he saw the parachute) *then there was a terrific explosion"*

Another farmer Colin McNichol of Gartavaich said: *" I was just sitting down to dinner when I heard this awful bang. I didn`t like the sound of it at all"*

The cockpit escape capsule and recovery crew in May 1973.   Photo: Keith Peloquin

This crash scene photo taken in May 1973 shows Glenreasdell Maine amidst trees

Photo: Keith Peloquin

The escape capsule itself came down on rough moorland to the south of the crash, and on vacating the capsule the crew spotted a farmhouse, believed to be Escart, further down the hill.

Fortunately the occupants were home and on inviting the two American airmen into their house and they were able to use the phone. First to call their wives as they didn't want them to worry if they heard about the crash on the news, and then they rang their base.

Keith Peloquin, the pilot's son recalled that when his father phoned home he said that they were OK but they *"Took a bird"*. The wives soon after getting off the phone, dug out a map but embarrassingly mistook the cause of the crash for a location named *'Tookabird'* thinking it was one of those old English towns off the beaten track.

A short while later a RN Sea King helicopter from 819 Squadron HMS (*Gannet*) Prestwick arrived and flew the crew to Ayr, where an ambulance was waiting to take them to hospital for a check up. Keith recalls his father telling him that although the helicopter ride was uneventful, the trip in the ambulance was 'Utterly terrifying'.

The 18 year old ambulance driver according to his Dad, appeared to be full of excitement and adrenaline and tore down the road like a Formula One racing car driver, wholly insistent on getting the two crash survivors to hospital as quick as possible, but the two airmen, with arms and legs braced against the side of the ambulance to steady themselves, just hoped they would make it to hospital in one piece.

Thankfully they did make it and though Capt. Peloquin needed a neck X-ray, everything was clear and both were later discharged and deemed fit enough to travel back to Upper Heyford.

In the days that followed a team of investigators arrived at the crash scene, photographs of the site were taken, the cockpit capsule was airlifted by Chinook helicopter to Machrihanish and this along with the two engines, was returned to Upper Heyford for analysis.

Damage caused by the jet consisted of around 300 fir trees destroyed, an acre of pasture burned, 100 feet of wire and 100 feet of barbed wire fence torn down, two acres of ploughed field was littered with wreckage and a stream polluted. A couple of parts even ended up across the road but luckily missed the farmhouse.

Tail fin port side.
Photo: Keith Peloquin

The starboard side of the tail fin with serial number. Photo: Keith Peloquin

The two Pratt & Whitney TF-30-P-3 turbofan engines from 68-008 being examined in a hangar at Upper Heyford in 1973. Photo: Keith Peloquin.

At the time of the accident a cordon was quickly placed around the site, with local folk being warned to stay well clear as there was an imminent danger of radioactive contamination.

A team of maintenance men was sent to the crash site from Upper Heyford and throughout May spent time clearing the field, plantation and stream of debris, though no doubt some small pieces will still remain today.

The investigation board after examining all the data and the recovered engines, confirmed that the loss of the aircraft was due to a large bird being ingested into the starboard air intake and engine which resulted in an inflight fire at a height of 1,000 feet agl, and after climbing to safe height at a IAS of 298 knots (343 mph) the capsule separated.

No blame was placed on the aircrew and they continued flying F-111's.

Keith Peloquin says that after the investigation was over, his father was given the control column and ejection handle as souvenirs of his near miss and Keith still has these today (See photos on following page).

He also recalled that his grandparents travelled over from Minnesota the following summer and the family drove up to Scotland and Kintyre where they visited the crash site, still littered with small fragments of wreckage.

F-111 cockpit showing locations of the control column and ejector handles. Pilot's control column and ejection handle from 68-008. Photos: Keith Peloquin.

Andy J. Peloquin

Class of 58 photo

Pilot. Captain Andrew Joseph Peloquin, USAF, born 5th May 1940, was the son of Mr & Mrs George P. Peloquin, brother of George, husband of Eileen, and father of Stephanie and Keith of Duluth, Minnesota, USA.

Andy, as he was referred, graduated from Duluth High School and attended the University of Minnesota, Duluth, for his undergraduate degree and it is understood that during a visit to UMD by a recruitment officer in the Air Force Reserve Officer Training Corps, that Andy became intrigued by the idea of flying military aircraft.

Described as always being a very responsible and reliable person, doing things that had a purpose and sense of duty, it is no surprise that at School he was on the school play committee, student council, the home room president, and a reporter for the college newspaper `The Spectator`. He was also a violinist in the 7th grade orchestra.

After graduating from UMD with degrees in chemistry and mathematics, Andy joined the USAF and trained as a pilot and on completion of his undergraduate training at Laredo AFB in Texas, he was awarded his pilot wings on 19th October 1964 by the Hollywood legend, actor and former WW2 B-24 bomber pilot, Brigadier General James `Jimmy` Stewart.

After undergoing further rigorous training courses Andy eventually went on become an RF-4C Phantom pilot. At some point in between he attended

2/Lt Andy J. Peloquin. USAF soon after graduating as a pilot

Photo: Keith Peloquin

survival school (Likely Homestead AFB in Florida) and his son recalls him reminiscing about getting dropped by helicopter into the ocean off Florida and being left to float around in a tiny one man survival raft for several hours before being recovered. This, he was told, was in order to get a feel for what being alone truly felt like in the case of a bale out situation.

Andy's first assignment on RF-4Cs was in the UK at RAF Alconbury, Cambridge, Huntingdon, here he served with either the 1st or 32nd Tactical Reconnaissance Squadron of the 10th Recon Wing. It was here he met Miss Eileen Martell the Base Commanders eldest daughter, who was home from her studies at the University of Maryland, Munich, Germany, and after a brief courtship the couple were married in the summer of 1966.

However, with the war in Vietnam still raging, the happy couple had just six months together in England prior to Andy being assigned to the 432nd Recon Wing in Thailand, flying reconnaissance missions over North Vietnam from the Royal Thai Air Force Base at Udorn. Missions flown from this Thai base were extremely hazardous, the lone Phantoms armed with only cameras being constantly under threat from SA-2 SAM's (Surface to Air Missiles) and MiG Fighters. These missions were flown like clockwork as the powers that be ordered RF-4Cs to go in after each strike and photograph the damage, needless to say the enemy were expecting them and many were lost.

On one occasion on 7th November 1966, Andy, now a 1/Lt had been flying as a GIB (Guy in Back) pilot over North Korea, photographing targets in the area of Biet Tri on the banks of the Red River, when they were tracked and locked onto by a SAM. Having spotted the missile heading towards them, Andy, being the senior pilot, took control of the aircraft and whilst maintaining a steady course and altitude, at the very last minute he rolled the Phantom on its back then pulled hard to break down and away from the exploding array of shrapnel which passed just beneath the 28,000 ton jet.

An RF-4C of the 10th TRW taking off from Alconbury in 1966. Photo: USAF

Major Andy Peloquin. USAF

Photo: Keith Peloquin

They managed to level off just above the river and flew at treetop height to make sure North Vietnamese fishermen and troops were just as scared as they were.

The pair finally made it back to safety and landed at Udorn without so much as a scratch. For his actions in saving the crew and aircraft, and successfully carrying out the latter mission Andy was awarded the DFC.

Despite his award Andy always felt angry about the losses they had incurred due to bureaucracy in Washington. He described how potential military targets such as MiG airfields and SAM sites were photographed, the pictures then sent to Washington for orders, only to be delayed by months, by which time men both in ground forces and in the air had been killed by the enemy operating from those target areas, when they could have been knocked out early.

Having been accosted by the bomber guys the RF-4C pilots took it upon themselves to have a duplicate set of pictures made for in-country distribution to the strike crews. Eventually successful bombing missions were achieved resulting in a considerable reduction in losses.

Andy finally flew his 100th mission and returned home to the States in spring 1967 where he was assigned to the 67th TRW at Mountain Home AFB in Idaho. In April that year he was also promoted to the rank of Captain.

Later that year he began training on the new F-111 with the 428th Tactical Fighter Squadron at Nellies AFB, Las Vegas, Nevada. In 1972 he was posted back to the UK for assignment to the 77th TFS in the 20th TFW at Upper Heyford.

While stationed in Oxford Andy and his family rented a 200 year old manor house named Thetford Hill House, just outside Banbury, his two children loved it and attended English schools there.

In 1976, having reached the rank of Major and served as Flight Instructor on F-111s, he returned to the States to become a non-flying project development officer at Wright-Patterson AFB, Ohio, for what would become the EF-111 Raven, a more advanced unarmed electronic warfare development of the F-111A.

Jordanian Air Force Northrop F-5E   Photo: Via Keith Peloquin

Andy remained at Wright-Patterson until the summer of 1980 when he was accepted for a post he had applied for as an Air Force Attaché for the US Embassy in Amman. However, before heading out to Jordan he had to attend a language course in Springfield, Virginia to learn Arabic and also the State Dept Language School, where within a year he became proficient in both spoken and written Arabic.

In addition to learning the language in this new post he was required to fly with the Jordanian Air Force in their Northrop F-5Es, and so before leaving the US he was posted to Luke AFB in Arizona to familiarize himself with this aircraft.

The post in Jordan was a two year assignment with a third year on the cards if he liked his position there. He really did like the country and flying the F-5 which he recalled in later years was flat out, the most fun to fly and was akin to driving in an open-air MG sports car, zipping down curvy roads and having a blast. Just as light and nimble as could be, especially flying down low to the deck.

Andy really enjoyed his time in Jordan and even met and exchanged aviation talk with King Hussain, who was himself a pilot. By the end of the first year life was good and he had signed up for a third year, but sadly a little after two years there, he was diagnosed with an aggressive cancer that needed immediate treatment and chemo in Germany. Although the treatment was successful, he was later forced to retire from the military on medical grounds.

Originally Andy was told he had but 10 days to live when first diagnosed but for two years, though extremely ill from the treatment, he battled on and pulled through. Eventually living another 15 years to see his son graduate as a pilot, his daughters wedding and be a loving grandfather for two years before his passing at home in June 1999.

Major Ariel Alvarez. USAF

Weapons Systems Officer Major Ariel Alvarez, USAF, born 12th August 1933 in Ponce, Puerto Rico, was the son of Fernando Luis and Andrea Alvarez Caraballo of Puerto Rico, USA.

Al, as he was known, would have commenced his Navigator training in the TC-45 Expeditor or TB-25 Mitchell, followed by transition to the T-29 Flying Classroom. Although by the late 1950s, all aircrew training had been consolidated in the T-29 at Harlingen AFB, Texas, Ellington AFB, Texas and Mather AFB, in California. Having graduated as a Navigator on the 23rd January 1956, Al, like some of the other cadets who had qualified, went on to train as Radar Navigator/Bombardier, Electronic Warfare Officer or Radar Interception Officer.

In 1965/66, by which time he had risen to the rank of Major, Al became a member of the 'Wild Weasels' a term used to describe aircraft involved in attacking SAM (Surface to Air Missile) radar installations in North Vietnam by flying in two-seat Republic F-105 Thunderchief jets, armed with AGM-45 Shrike anti-radiation missiles.

Many of the EWOs chosen for the Weasels were taken from B-52 and EB-66 crews, although later recruited from the Air Force Electronic Warfare Schools. They then went to McConnell AFB, Kansas to qualify on the F105, practice bombing and use of on board radar systems with their pilots and listen to 'old hands' experiences on bombing techniques. Pilots and Navigators would then go to Nellis AFB for a six week course with instruction on the Shike and other weapons including hostile radar detection systems.

Al finished the Weasels course on 17th October 1965 and soon after went to North Vietnam. Here he was involved in some very dangerous operations, with Weasel flights usually consisting of four aircraft led by a single F-105F or G two-seat aircraft aided by its EWO's electronic receivers & analysers, plus three F-105Ds and sometimes two 'F's, each with a 'D' flying as wingman operating independently.

The missions would precede strike flights, sanitizing the target area of radar guided Surface-to-Air Missile SA-2 'Guideline' threats, leaving the threat area last, which sometimes would result in 3.5-hour missions before returning to the Royal Thai Air Force Bases.

This was achieved by turning towards the air defence site in a threatening manner, firing radar homing missiles at the site or visually locating the site to dive bomb it. These tactics were attempted while under attack by MiGs and anti-aircraft artillery during which many Weasels were lost.

The F-105D you see in the photo with Al is 60-0442 of the 421st TFS, 388 TFW, based at Korat. It was lost on 20th April 1966 after being shot down while flying over the annamite mountains near Don Bai Dinh, close to the border with Laos whilst flying an armed reconnaissance mission. The pilot Capt. J.B. Abernethy, survived and was rescued by a HH-3 helicopter from Nakhon Phanom.

Al went on to fly in F4 Phantoms and as we know the F-111 later on. He was rated Master Navigator on 27th January 1971 and it is believed after serving in England until the mid-1970s, he went on to instruct in the USA. He passed away in Carolina, San Juan, Puerto Rico on 26th August 2009.

Major Ariel Alvarez with an F-105D

Republic F-105 Thunderchief carrying AGM-45 Shrike anti-radiation missile.

CARSKEY BAY SEA KING XV706

Lieutenant Rodger John Cooper was a very experienced combat helicopter pilot and having served with the Royal Australian Navy as a Sub-Lieutenant, he completed a tour with the 3rd Contingent of the 135th RAN Assault Helicopter Company near Biên Hòa in Đồng Nai Province, South Vietnam, from 9th September 1969 to 8th October 1970, piloting the Bell UH-1 Iroquois better known as the 'Huey'.

Bell UH-1 Iroquois

On Monday 22nd July 1974 Rodger, now a Lieutenant attached to 819 Squadron Royal Navy, Fleet Air Arm based at Prestwick on the south west coast Ayrshire, was undertaking an exercise in Sea King HAS.1 XV706 over the sea off south Kintyre, when with little warning the tail rotor disconnect coupling failed.

He Immediately made for the shoreline as he knew the Sea King could land and float successfully on water in reasonable sea conditions, and although losing directional control he was able to successfully land the heavy helicopter, wheels retracted, in a barley field at Carskey Bay to the west of Southend on the Kintyre peninsula. Fortunately without injury to himself or his three crew Co-Pilot Lt A.E. Washbourne, Navigator /Radar Operator Sub/Lt P. Blackman and Winchman P.O. C. Larcombe.

Evidently his ability, calmness and resourcefulness achieved in the skies over South East Asia under pressure, shone through in this emergency situation. XV706 sustained Category 4 damage having severed the tail boom which could not be repaired on site. The Sea King was recovered by Chinook and transported by road to Naval Air Trial Installation Unit, RNAS Lee-on-Solent, then to the Royal Naval Air Yard Fleetlands, NE of Gosport in Hampshire.

Finally the helicopter returned to active service on 29th September 1976, but was now with 814 Squadron at RNAS Culdrose, Cornwall (*Seahawk*) where it was re-coded 267/H.

The Sea King XV706 soon after the forced landing near Carskey Bay
The full extent of the damage can be seen below.

Photos: Campbeltown Heritage Centre

325

Westland Sea King HAS.1 XV706 (C/No. WA677) was ordered on 30th November 1966 to specification HAS.261 under Contract K/191/055CB.25 (a) and constructed by Westland Helicopters at Yeovil.

It was first flown on 7th September 1971 by Mr Donald Frank Farquharson OBE, a former Barracuda, Firefly and later Sea King project pilot for Westland Helicopters. It was then allocated to 819 Squadron at Prestwick as 307/PW.

Test pilot Don F. Farquharson OBE

During the afternoon of 30th May 1973 while hovering over the sea, XV706 suffered complete failure of No1 engine causing Lt J.H. Eldridge to land in the Clyde 3 miles south of Pladda Island near Arran. After removing all surplus equipment and jettisoning fuel Lt Eldridge skilfully undertook a single engine take off and managed to return to base.

Pilot Lt Rodger John Cooper Royal Australian Navy was born 8th December 1941 in Loxton, the main town for a local farming community in South Australia.

He joined the RAN around 1967 and trained as a helicopter pilot, then after qualifying he was commissioned as a Sub-Lieutenant.

Following his tour in Vietnam from Sept 1969—Oct 1970, twenty year old Rodger Cooper, now residing in Waterloo, South Australia, was Mentioned in Dispatches on 15th December 1970 with a citation for " *his ability and calmness under fire... and being resourceful and courageous."*

Having later been promoted to Lieutenant and finally Lieutenant Commander on 21st December 1984, Rodger took over from Lt/Cdr. K.W. Eames. RAN as Commanding Officer of 817 Squadron based at NAS Nowra (HMAS *Albatross*) until 5th December 1986.

It is understood Rodger retired from the Royal Australian Navy in 1987.

Co-Pilot Lieutenant A.E.Washbourne. Royal Navy. Little is known about Lt Washbourne, but an entry in the London Gazette of 17th December 1973 stated he was to be promoted from Sub/Lt to Lt on 26th December that year. Then on 31st October 1978 he is listed as being on the RN emergency list on completion of a short career commission for a period of 4 years w/e 3rd November.

Radar Operator Sub-Lieutenant P. Blackman, RN, was subsequently promoted to Lieutenant on 14th January 1976 and continued to serve with the Royal Navy into the eighties.

Winchman Petty Officer C. Larcombe. RN had been involved in four minor incidents prior to the Sea King at Carskey. The first occurred on 15th January 1965 when he was part of the crew of a Westland Wessex HAS.1 XM870 of 815 Squadron. The port forward cabin window detached in flight and they were forced to return to base, but managed to land safely.

The next incident came while serving with 829 Squadron aboard a Westland Whirlwind HAS.7 XN380 M, when on 6th June 1966 the engine momentarily cut and a precautionary landing had to be made at Swansea airport. Again, they got down safe.

The latter helicopter can now be seen on display at The RAF Manston History Museum in Kent.

Still with 829 Squadron, on 16th May 1967, P.O. Larcombe was aboard another Wessex HU.5 XS864 when the pilot experienced a loss of stick trim during flight, he swiftly returned to base.

Finally, on 3rd November 1967, whilst serving with 737 Squadron, he was aboard Wessex HAS.1 XP116 in which a precautionary landing had to be made at Portland following an unexplained bump felt in flight.

Footnote: During the war Carskey Bay was the scene of another incident, when on 19th January 1942, the 4,000 gross ton Belgian cargo ship SS *Mobeka* ran aground in a gale while bound from Liverpool to West Africa. Thankfully all 52 souls were saved.

Looking across Carskey Bay towards the field where XV706 crash-landed
Photo: Author's Collection

A HIGH PRICE FOR PEACE - CHINOOK ZD576

The final account in this book concerns one of the most controversial flying accidents in UK military aviation history, with the cause of 'Gross Negligence' on the part of the deceased pilots causing public outcry and disgust by the families of those involved, prompting further investigations and a campaign by relatives to overturn the verdict in a court battle lasting over 17 years.

Throughout the past two decades accounts of this accident involving an RAF Special Forces Chinook HC2 helicopter ZD576 appeared in the press the world over, but despite many theories on what might have happened, based on the findings at the crash site and that of other accidents involving the Chinook, there was no concrete evidence to say that the pilots were to blame, other than no other reason for the crash could be proven.

The troubles in Northern Ireland with the IRA were still rife and a combination of 25 high ranking Police, Army and British Intelligence Officers had been selected to travel up to Fort George, near Ardersier, NE of Inverness for a security conference on Thursday 2nd June 1994.

Their transport that day would be an RAF Special Forces Chinook helicopter belonging to 7 Squadron at RAF Odiham, Hampshire, on detachment to RAF Aldergrove, Belfast. The pilots chosen for the trip were F/Lt Jonathan Tapper and F/Lt Richard Cook, accompanied by two Loadmasters M/Sgt Graham Forbes and Sgt Kevin Hardie.

Earlier that day the two pilots had test flown the Chinook, a new Mk. II version, and on return at 15:20 F/Lt Tapper informed Cpl. Dave Guest, an engineering avionics technician, that the GPS was only tracking five satellites instead of seven, but when checked by the technician, no fault could be found with the system.

An hour or so later the passengers would begin to leave their dwellings for the drive to RAF Aldergrove and Susan Phoenix, wife of RUC Detective

Fort George the intended destination for the passengers. Photo: Author's Collection

Inspector Ian Phoenix, one of those passengers, recounted later in a biography on her husband, the events of that day.

Susan had offered to drive her husband to the airport and the couple left around 16:30. On arrival at the first security gate their car was checked and they were waved through, then on to the next gate, where on passing through they spotted a man wandering around as if lost, though Ian instantly recognised him as one of the Intelligence Officers and suggested that if he she saw him on the way out, his wife should point him in the right direction for the helicopter.

On arrival at the hangar, her husband kissed her goodbye, got out of the car and she watched as he made his way in then on to the check in prior to boarding.

Susan drove by the hangar where the man had been stood, but he had now left so she presumed he must have found his way.

Meanwhile, due to the duty authorizing officer being busy with another briefing, F/Lt Tapper briefed his crew on the flight, signed the Flight Authorization Sheet and filed a copy of the flight plan with operations officer.

When discussing the route and weather conditions the previous day, it was decided that because of the de-icing limitations of the new Mk. II Chinook, and the chance of freezing temperatures at greater altitude in cloud, fog and rain, then the flight would be carried out under Visual Flight Rules (VFR) at low level.

A Boeing Chinook HC Mk II similar to the one on Kintyre. Photo: Authors Collection

The route planned was to fly three straight legs. The first being Aldergrove to the Mull of Kintyre Lighthouse, next along the west coast of the Kintyre peninsula and up Loch Linnie to Corran, then NE to Inverness, an expected flight duration of two hours.

At approximately 17:42, with its precious cargo of VIP passengers seated in two rows with their backs either side of the fuselage, the huge twin-rotor helicopter took to the air.

ZD576 callsign: `F4J40` (*Foxtrot four Juliet four zero*) flew low over the countryside towards Carnlough and Garron Point, then out over the sea to Kintyre.

The last acknowledged message from the Chinook came shortly before leaving the Irish coast when 81 Signals Unit, callsign `Architect` was contacted in order to relay a message to Aldergrove, that everything was OK and they had 29 persons including the crew on board the helicopter.

Chinook: `Foxtrot four Juliet four zero. Request relay to EGAA Ext 30370. Operations normal and we have 29 POB`

81 SU: `This is Architect. Roger. Ops normal and 29 POB. Will relay. Anything further? Over`.

Chinook: `Foxtrot four Juliet four zero. That`s no. Over`.

81 SU: `This is Architect. Roger. Listening. Out`.

As the Chinook etched its way towards the Mull light, it was spotted in level flight at around 2-400 feet asl by a yachtsman Mark Holbrook. Cloud was low on the hills but still clearly visible was the white lighthouse perimeter wall.

Still manned at that time, the Mull of Kintyre lighthouse was that day occupied by Principal Keeper Hector Lamont and his wife Esther along with assistant keeper David Murchie and his wife Margaret.

The time was approaching 18:00 and Hector and his wife having been in Campbeltown for provisions, were driving down the road in their Land Rover in thick fog when they first heard the noise of the Chinook's rotors.

Just moments after passing a bend in the road the Chinook hit the hill with a glancing blow, bounced over the road and impacted the heather-clad slopes of Beinn na Lice at a height of around 900ft asl, some 505ft from the summit.

The burning wreckage of the helicopter and its occupants was scattered over a wide area for about a square mile, and with the whole hill ablaze there was little hope of anyone having survived.

Hector and his wife didn't actually hear the crash, but he had seen an orange glow through the mirror of the Land Rover. Nearing the lighthouse he met David Murchie on his way up the road and after dropping his wife at the house Hector and David made their way back up the road, meanwhile Margaret telephoned the emergency services.

First at the scene were Russell Ellacott and Tony Bracher, they had been on holiday on Kintyre and were very lucky to have escaped being hit by the Chinook as they made their way northwards to visit an old deserted village at Balmavicar and a WW2 aircraft (See Whitley P5041 story).

The men had witnessed the carnage and were still in a state of shock as they reached the road where they met the two lighthouse keepers.

Hector and David, following the trail of burning debris began to encounter some of the Chinook's former occupants, sadly it soon became evident that all had perished.

Det Insp Ian Phoenix's wife Susan had been visiting their daughter soon after saying goodbye to him. She was on her way home when she heard the devastating news on the car radio. Apart from close friends and relatives, not many people knew about her husband's secret work. She would eventually write a book in his memory entitled: 'Phoenix –Policing the shadows.

While local emergency services made their way slowly up the road from Campbeltown, the RAF Kinloss Mountain Rescue Team was being scrambled. One fast party consisting Dave Whalley, Jim Smith and four others boarded a Sea King that had been dispatched from RAF Lossiemouth, while other team members followed on by road.

Dave Whalley MBE, BEM recalled the events of that fateful day:

"The flight, about an hour from Kinloss was so fast we just hammered across the mountains. I remember flashing by Ben Alder and heading low and fast to the Mull. The information was scant and even though it had just happened more was coming in all the time.

Members of Kinloss MRT arriving in the swirling mist on Kintyre in June 1994.
Photo: Dave Whalley. MBE. BEM

In the back of the aircraft you feel out of it, but then a scrap of paper appears and we were told it was a military helicopter, a Chinook with a lot of passengers.

As we neared the Mull of Kintyre the mist was down and the helicopter could only land at the lighthouse landing site in thick mist. It was too difficult to try to get us further up the hill. We could hear all the emergency beacons going off from our aircraft just before we landed in a swirling mist right by the lighthouse".

As the MRT arrived at the crash site they were greeted by members of the Fire, Police and Coastguard along with a local Doctor Geoffrey Horton and paramedic Calum Lawson, both of whom had tried to resuscitate one of the helicopter victims when they thought they had found a faint pulse, but alas they realised they were too late.

Dave Whalley continues:

"We arrived at the scene to find the helicopter a crumpled mess, fires and smoke made the place seem like a war zone and we split up to locate the crew. A grim job, with the aircraft still burning and banging like a scene from a movie, but this was real life.

After the initial survey around the very dangerous crash site, where we moved fast and in pairs, with all the 29 on board located we had to ensure that all the evidence at the crash site was not touched. This meant that all the casualties had to stay in place and await the Police and Air Accident Investigation Board (AAIB) to arrive.

The local Police, Fire and Ambulance were already at the scene and were glad of our experience.

A local minster (Rev. Roddie McNidder from Southend) *arrived and wanted to visit the site and say a few words. It was tricky as the casualties were still in place until the Police and AAIB investigated, this would be at first light. I took him to the scene with a group of us and the minster said a few words then left, he was visibly shaken by what he had seen".*

The Kinloss MRT had been on the hill for around five hours and for the team and other emergency services it had been a very traumatic night. All had done a splendid job under very difficult circumstances. It was now left to the investigation team to try and establish what caused this awful tragedy.

Senior Inspector and Accident Investigator Tony Cable and his team really had their work cut out with the Chinook. For it was discovered that there were no survivors or any eye witnesses who saw the actual impact. No Flight Data Recorder or Cockpit Voice Recorder, no radar or radio communications close to the time of the crash, plus fire damage.

Over the past twenty four years several books, TV documentaries and numerous newspapers, news bulletins and magazines have covered the Chinook story in great depth, so most people reading this account will already know the eventual outcome. But to those who don't, here are some basic details.

This Chinook, built by Boeing Vertol as CH-47D serial N37079 at Ridley Park, Philadelphia, Pennsylvania, USA in 1984, was delivered to the RAF as a HC1 in December of that year as ZD576. It had served with 240 OCU at Odiham and with 18 Squadron in the Persian Gulf with the BFME during the Gulf War before returning to the UK for conversion to HC2 and service with 7 Sqn.

With regards to the cause of the accident, there appears to have been far too much speculation based upon sparse findings during the investigation to say with any degree of accuracy the primary cause of this accident.

There was a whole host of administrative, technical and mechanical failures leading up to the loss of this Chinook and no doubt all were contributory factors in some way or other. One theory that was quickly ruled out was sabotage, but in view of the ever present terrorist threats at that time, one has to ask why was the government so quick to dispel this theory? How do we know that parts allegedly destroyed by fire don't lie at the bottom of the sea? Or that the parts destroyed by fire weren't tampered with or connected to the cause of the accident? And the question that has been raised so many times: Why were so many VIP passengers on the same aircraft?

The true cause of the accident to ZD576 therefore still remains a mystery.

On 13th July 2011, the 17 year campaign by the families to clear the pilots of the original verdict by two Air Marshalls in the RAF of 'Negligence to a gross degree', finally came to an end when Judge Lord Alexander Philip, after spending nine months reviewing the case and previously unheard evidence exonerated the two pilots. The Defence Secretary Dr. Liam Fox also apologised to the pilots families.

Captain and Pilot Flight Lieutenant Jonathan Paul Tapper. RAF. Born in Woolwich on 21st July 1965, was the son of Mr & Mrs Michael Tapper. He was a married man with two children who lived in Burnham Thorpe, Norfolk.

Jon attended Dulwich College, a boarding and independent day school for boys in Southeast London. The College has a well-established CCF (Combined Cadet Force) that has been running since the organisation was founded in 1859. Boys can choose between three sections: Army, Navy or RAF with most joining in year nine. Jon chose the RAF and battle craft trips, flying days at Benson and expeditions to the arctic or desert were some of the opportunities in store.

At Dulwich Jon won a scholarship for flying school and had already gained his private pilot's licence by the age of 16. He then joined Cranwell College in 1984 as an Aircraftman with appointment to a commission and was awarded his pilots wings on 8th June 1985 and gained a promotion to F/O on that date the following year.

While at Cranwell he met fellow pilot Rick Cook and the two became good friends. Both were clocking up flight hours on helicopters, Jon, by the early 1990s having already amassed over 2,000 hours.

By the time he was selected as a Special Forces pilot flying Chinooks he was a F/Lt and already experienced this type, the Gazelle, Wessex and the Huey having spent two years with the Omani Air Force.

Jon was married in October 1989 and the couple had the first of their two children in 1993. Jon arrived at Aldergrove

F/Lt Jonathan P. Tapper. RAF

for his second attachment on 22nd April 1994 where he became senior Chinook pilot. His wife was pregnant with their second child at the time of the accident in June, and so sadly he never got to see his new baby born just six weeks later.

After the accident Squadron Leader Strangroom, senior officer in charge of the Chinook crews at Aldergrove, expressed his feelings that Tapper and Cook were both very experienced and well qualified pilots who were very safety conscious. F/Lt Kingston said Jon Tapper was a very honest, friendly and likeable person and was quite certain that neither he, nor Rick Cook would have taken unnecessary risks.

F/Lt Richard D. Cook. RAF

Handling Pilot Flight Lieutenant Richard David Cook. RAF. Born 11th May 1964, was the son of John and Joy Cook. He was a married man with one daughter and hailed from Basingstoke, Hampshire.

Rick, as he was known, also attended Cranwell as an Aircraftman cadet. He was commissioned Acting Pilot Officer on 20th October 1983 and P/O a year later having been awarded his pilots wings.

Like Jonathan Tapper Rick was a very experienced pilot on the Chinook, he had served in Germany and on detachment from RAF Odiham to various parts of the world, notching up almost 3,000 hours flying time, with 2,500 hours on Chinooks.

Promotion to Flying Officer came on 20th October 1985, thence Flight Lieutenant on 20th April 1989. He had just got married around that time.

Rick was promoted to Operations Officer during the Gulf War and was due to be posted to the staff of SAS (Special Air Service) in September 1994.

Having arrived at Aldergrove on 26th May that year, like his previous attachments to the base, for a third time he was expected to take up the role of senior Chinook pilot, once Jonathan Tapper had returned to Odiham.

Master Air Loadmaster Graham William Forbes, RAF, born 10th May 1958, was the only son of Mr & Mrs Michael Annesley Atholl Forbes of Kingston Upon Thames, Surrey. Graham was interred in Troon Cemetery, Dundonald Road, Troon, South Ayrshire.

Grave of Graham Forbes in Troon

Loadmaster Sergeant Kevin Andrew Hardie, RAF, born 25th September 1963 in Oakman, Rutland (Leicestershire). Kevin was cremated at The Park Crematorium, Aldershot, Hampshire.

The V.I.P. Passengers List.

Assistant Chief Constable John Charles Brian Fitzsimons. MBE. Aged 53. Was a leading figure in the IRA Brighton bombing investigations which led to the arrest of Patrick Magee. John was husband of Anne Fitzsimons of County Down, Northern Ireland. He had a son and two daughters. A former head of RUC Special Branch in Northern Ireland, he rests in Comber Cemetery, County Down.

Detective Chief Superintendent Desmond Patrick Conroy. Aged 55. BEM. QGM. Based with Special Branch at RUC HQ was Interred in Roselawn Cemetery, Belfast, Northern Ireland.

Detective Chief Superintendent Maurice Neilly. Aged 45. Was the man in charge of the RUC Special Branch agents operating in the northern region.

Detective Superintendent Phil Davidson. Aged 45. Was described as a first rate RUC officer and was a future candidate for the head of Special Branch.

Detective Superintendent Robert Foster. Aged 41. Was a liaison officer for the RUC's elite surveillance unit. E4A.

Detective Superintendent William Rutherford `Billy` Gwilliam. Aged 50. Was a leading figure in RUC Special Branch.

Detective Superintendent: Ian Phoenix. Aged 51. RUC Special Branch was a former paratrooper in the armed forces.

Detective Chief Inspector Denis Bunting. Aged 39. Was already a senior officer in the RUC, but was due for promotion and according to Statewatch, he was the head of the E3A section within RUC Special Branch at the time of his death.

Detective Inspector Stephen Davidson. Aged 39. Was a senior officer in the RUC. He had recently been appointed Staff Officer for ACC Brian Fitzsimons.

Detective Inspector: Kevin Magee. Aged 44. RUC Special Branch had recently been assigned to work in Portadown, County Armagh.

MI5 Branch. Anne Catherine James. Aged 42. Was born in Lexontown near Glasgow. She had formally worked at GCHQ in Cheltenham for 24 years prior to taking up office in Belfast. Anne had been a former pupil at St Machan's and St Ninian's High School, Kirkintilloch.

MI5 Branch. Martin George Dalton. Aged 37. Was an agent with MI5 Intelligence Bureau. He hailed from Peterborough, Cambridgeshire.

MI5 Branch Michael Bruce Maltby. Aged 57, was considered by Intelligence writer Stephen Dorrill to have been one of the most important members of MI5. His main aim was to monitor the laundering of funds for the IRA by loyalist terror organisations.

MI5 Branch. Stephen Rickard. Aged 35. According to writer Stephen Dorrill, was the Director and Coordinator of Intelligence in Northern Ireland's MI5 branch at the time of the accident.

MI5 Branch. John Hayes. Aged 58. Was a Counter Intelligence agent for the Government Office in Northern Ireland.

Home Office CB-57. John Robert Deverell. CB. MBE. Aged 57 was Deputy Director General of MI5 in Northern Ireland who had formally worked for the agency in Counter Intelligence K Section.

Colonel Christopher John Biles. OBE. Born 3rd November 1952. Was an officer in the British Army Devon & Dorset Regiment. At the time of the accident he was Assistant Chief of Staff for the Northern Ireland branch of the regiment. He was cremated at Weymouth Crematorium. Dorset.

Lieutenant Colonel Richard Lawrence Gregory-Smith. Born 15th September 1951. Was an army officer in the Intelligence Corps at Army HQ Lisburn. He was cremated at Charing Crematorium, Ashford, Kent.

Lieutenant Colonel George Victor Alexander Williams. MBE. QGM. Born 5th March 1945. Was an officer in the Army Intelligence Corps. He was interred in Blaris New Cemetery, Lisburn, Near Belfast, Northern Ireland.

Major Christopher John Dockerty. Born 12th October 1960. Was an officer in the Army and served with the Prince of Wales Own Regiment. He was based at 8th Infantry Brigade HQ. Londonderry. He was interred in West Tanfield Parish Churchyard, Ripon, Yorkshire.

Lieutenant Colonel John William Tobias. MBE. Born 18th December 1952. Was an officer in the Army Intelligence Corps at the Army HQ Lisburn. He was cremated at West Herts Crematorium.

Major Gary Paul Sparks. Born 31st December 1960. Was a British Army officer with the Royal Artillery in Northern Ireland with 39 Infantry Brigade HQ. Lisburn. He was interred in the Royal Military Academy Cemetery at Sandhurst, Berkshire. Grave No.414.

Major Anthony Robert Hornby. MBE. QLR. Born 1st August 1955. Was an officer in the HQ No 3 Infantry Brigade, Portadown. Queens Lancashire Regiment. Anthony hailed from Bolton, Lancashire.

Major Richard Allen. Born 18th September 1959. Was a British Army officer with the Royal Gloucester, Berks and Wiltshire Regiment. He was interred in Tidworth Military Cemetery, Tidworth, Wiltshire. Sec. L. Grave.1.

Major Roy Pugh. MBE. Born 6th March 1957. Was a British Army officer in the Intelligence Corps based at the Army HQ in Lisburn. He was cremated at Roselawn Crematorium, Ballygowan Road, Belfast, Northern Ireland.

The Chinook memorial cairn near Beinn na Lice, Mull of Kintyre

Photo: Author's Collection

AIRCRAFT IN DATE ORDER

DATE:	TYPE:	SERIAL:	LOCATION:	LAND or SEA
03.03.1940	SWORDFISH	P4215	CAMPBELTOWN A/FLD	LAND
23.01.1941	WHITLEY	P5041	BALMAVICAR	LAND
26.02.1941	STRANRAER	K7299	NR CAMPBELTOWN	LAND
07.07.1941	FULMAR	N4038	KERRAN HILL	LAND
25.07.1941	HUDSON	AE640	FEORLAN	LAND
18.08.1941	MARTLET	AL259	LOW SMERBY	LAND
01.09.1941	LIBERATOR	AM915	ARINARACH HILL	LAND
12.12.1941	BLENHEIM	Z6350	NR KILLEAN	LAND
17.02.1942	SWORDFISH	W5982	OFF WESTPORT	SEA
15.03.1942	ANSON	R3344	NR CAMPBELTOWN	LAND
31.08.1942.	SWORDFISH	V4441	CAMPBELTOWN LOCH	SEA
31.08.1942	SWORDFISH	V4312	CAMPBELTOWN LOCH	SEA
31.08.1942	SWORDFISH	V4489	CAMPBELTOWN LOCH	SEA
02.09.1942	BEAUFORT	N1180	TOR MHOR	LAND
14.11.1942	ANSON	K6309	OFF MACHRIHANISH	SEA
06.02.1943	ALBACORE	N4330	OFF CROSSAIG	SEA
09.02.1943	SKUA	L2907	MACHRIHANISH A/FLD	LAND
09.02.1943	SWORDFISH	U/K	MACHRIHANISH A/FLD	LAND
17.02.1943	WELLINGTON	HX420	EASACH / SGREADAN HILL	LAND
27.02.1943	WELLINGTON	HX779	NR LOCH CIARAN	LAND
03.04.1943	ALBACORE	X9165	OFF ARDPATRICK POINT	SEA
01.05.1943	SWORDFISH	DK744	OFF SKIPNESS	SEA
28.05.1943	BARRACUDA	P9748	OFF CROSSAIG	SEA
10.06.1943	HUDSON	FK780	EAST OF PUTACHAN LODGE	LAND
28.08.1943	BEAUFIGHTER	LZ156	NE OF RUBHA CHLACHAN	LAND
01.09.1943	HURRICANE	NF867	OFF BELLOCHCHANTUY	SEA

Date	Aircraft	Serial	Location	Type
10.10.1943	ANSON	EF820	A`CRUACH, W OF STRONE	LAND
30.10.1943	BEAUFIGHTER	LZ455	BEINN BHREAC	LAND
09.11.1943	BARRACUDA	P9737	MACHRIHANISH BAY	SEA
18.11.1943	SWORDFISH	HS448	NR CROSSAIG	LAND
02.12.1943	WELLINGTON	LB137	BEINN NA LICE	LAND
06.12.1943	SWORDFISH	HS454	OFF BELLOCHCHANTUY	SEA
09.12.1943	ANSON	N4988	OFF WHITESTONE	SEA
07.01.1944	SWORDFISH	LS426	OFF MULL OF KINTYRE	SEA
29.01.1944	SEAFIRE	MB145	AROS FARM	LAND
30.01.1944	WILDCAT	JV494	MACHRIHANISH A/FLD	LAND
29.03.1944	BARRACUDA	LS582	NR GLENCRAIGS FARM	LAND
11.04.1944	AVENGER	FN878	NE OF CARRADALE POINT	LAND
11.04.1944	WHITLEY	BD393	E OF MACHRIHANISH A/FLD	LAND
27.04.1944	FULMAR	X8751	NR BLACK LOCH	LAND
28.05.1944	AVENGER	FN867	TORR MOR	LAND
24.06.1944	FIREFLY	Z1891	OFF SOUTHEND	SEA
04.07.1944	AVENGER	FN772	NR CALLIBURN	LAND
22.12.1944	BEECH TRAVELLER	FT529	NE OF TANGY LODGE	LAND
05.02.1945	WELLINGTON	LP351	OFF KILBERRY HEAD	SEA
28.03.1945	BARRACUDA	ME121	OFF RHUNAHAORINE POINT	SEA
01.08.1945	SEAFIRE	`411`	MACHRIHANISH BAY	SEA
14.12.1945	SEAFIRE	SW857	KILKENZIE	LAND
08.05.1952	FIREFLY	VT490	GOLF LINKS, MACHRIHANISH	LAND
10.10.1956	NEPTUNE	WX545	BALMAVICAR	LAND
19.04.1968	SHACKLETON	WB833	GLENMANUILT HILL	LAND
12.08.1970	WASP	XT879	NE OF RUBHA CHLACHAN	LAND
15.05.1973	F-111E	68-008	GLENREASDALE	LAND
22.07.1974	SEA KING	XV706	N OF CARSKEY BAY	LAND
02.06.1994	CHINOOK	ZD576	BEINN NA LICE	LAND

ROYAL NAVAL AIR STATIONS

FLEET AIR ARM STATION	LOC	HM SHIP NAME FOR STATION
ABBOTSINCH	SCOT	SANDERLING
AYR	SCOT	WAGTAIL
BURSCOUGH	ENG	RINGTAIL
CAMPBELTOWN	SCOT	LANDRAIL II
CRAIL	SCOT	JACKDAW
DONIBRISTLE	SCOT	MERLIN
EASTLEIGH /SOUTHAMPTON	ENG	RAVEN
EGLINTON	IRE	GANNET / SEA EAGLE
FORD	ENG	PEREGINE
GOSPORT	ENG	ST.VINCENT
GRIMSETTER	SCOT	ROBIN
HATSTON	SCOT	SPARROWHAWK
HENSTRIDGE	ENG	DIPPER
INSKIP	ENG	NIGHTJAR
LEE-ON-SOLENT	ENG	DAEDALUS
MACHRIHANISH	SCOT	LANDRAIL
MAYDOWN	IRE	SHRIKE
NEW SOUTH WALES	AUS	ALBATROSS
PUCKPOOL CAMP	IOW	MEDINA
SIMONS TOWN.	S.AFR	AFRIKANDER
ST.MERRYN	ENG	CURLEW
TANGA	TANZ	KILELE
TOWN HILL CAMP	SCOT	WAXWING
TRINIDAD	CARIB	GOSHAWK / PIARCO
TWATT	SCOT	TERN
WASHINGTON	USA	SAKER
WORTHY DOWN	ENG	KESTREL
YEOVILTON	ENG	HERON

BIBLIOGRAPHY

A Scientists War - The War Diary of Sir Clifford Paterson 1939-1945. *Edited by Robert C. Clayton & Joan Algar. Institution of Engineering and Technology. 1991.*

Action Stations 6. Military airfields of the Cotswolds and Central Midlands - *Michael J.F. Bowyer, Patrick Stephens Ltd. 1990.*

Action Stations 7. Military airfields of Scotland the North East and Northern Ireland. *- David Smith Patrick Stephens Ltd. 1989.*

Action Stations 9. Military Airfields of the Central South and South East.— *Chris Ashworth Patrick Stephens Ltd, 1984.*

Aircraft Wrecks—A Walkers Guide. - *Nick Wotherspoon, Alan Clark and Mark Sheldon Pen & Sword Books Ltd. 2009.*

Aircraft of World War II - *Chris Chant, Amber Books Ltd, 1999.*

Alone on a Wide, Wide Sea. - *E.E. Berringer. Leo Cooper books. 1995.*

Biplanes, Triplanes and Seaplanes - *Michael Sharpe, Amber Books Ltd, 2000.*

Blue for a Girl -The Story of the W.R.N.S. - *John D. Drummond, W.H.Allen & Co.Ltd. 1960.*

British Military Aircraft Serials 1911-1971 - *Bruce Robertson, Ian Allan publishing. 1971.*

Clipped Wings RAF Training Aircraft Losses 1939-42. - *Colin Cummings .Nimbus 2015.*

Chinook Crash - *Steuart Campbell. Pen & sword Books Ltd. 2004*

Chronicles of a Nervous Navigator - *John A. Iverach, published by Iverach, 1995.*

F-111 General Dynamics—Modern Combat Aircraft 2. - *Bill Gunston, Ian Allan Ltd. 1978.*

F-111 Success in Action - *Anthony M. Thornborough & Peter Davies. Arms & Armour. 1989*

Fairey Firefly - The Operational Record - *W. Harrison, Airlife Publishing Ltd. 1992.*

Fleet Air Arm Aircraft 1939-1945 - *Ray Sturtivant and Mick Burrow. Air-Brit 1995*

Fleet Air Arm Handbook 1939-1945 - *David Wragg, Sutton Publishing Ltd. 2001.*

For Your Tomorrow - RNZAF Losses since 1915 - *Errol Martyn, Volplane Press 1998.*

Growling Over The Oceans - *Deborah Lake. Souvenir Press Ltd. 2010.*

Hell on High Ground - Volume 2 - *David W. Earl, Airlife Publishing Ltd, 1999.*

Kintyre Aircraft Crashes - Duncan McArthur, Alisdair McKinley, Bobby Duncan and Chris Blair. Private Publication. 2003 & 2005.

Lockheed Hudson in World War II - *Andrew Hendrie, Airlife Publishing Ltd. 1999.*

Lost to the Isles 1914-1941 - *David W. Earl & Peter Dobson. Hanover Publications 2013.*

Lost to the Isles 1942-1943 - *David W. Earl & Peter Dobson. Hanover Publications. 2014.*

Lost to the Isles 1944 - *David W. Earl & Peter Dobson. Hanover Publications. 2015.*

Lost to the Isles 1945 - 1990 - *David W. Earl & Peter Dobson. Hanover Publications. 2017.*

Night Strike From Malta - 830 Squadron RN and Rommel's Convoys. - *Kenneth Poolman. Janes Information Group. 1980.*

Ocean Bridge - The History of RAF Ferry Command - *Carl A. Christie, Midland Publishing. 1995.*

Phoenix –Policing the Shadows - *Jack Holland & Susan Phoenix, Hodder & Stoughton.1996.*

RAF Bomber Command Losses Volume 7 Operational Training Units 1940-1947. - *W.R. Chorley. Midland Publishing 2002.*

RAF Coastal Command Losses 1939-1941 - *Ross McNeill. Midland Publishing. 2003.*

Royal Air Force Retired List 1986 - *H.M.S.O Publications, 1986.*

Royal Air Force Flying Training and Support Units - *Ray Sturtivant, John Hamlin and James J. Halley, Air-Britain Publications, 1997.*

Short Sunderland in World War II, *Andrew Hendrie, Airlife Publishing Ltd, 1994.*

Squadron Codes 1937-1956 - *M.J.F Bowyer & J.D.R. Rawlings. Patrick Stephens. 1979.*

Squadrons of the Fleet Air Arm - *Ray Sturtivant. Air-Britain. 1984.*

Squadrons of the Royal Air Force - *James J. Halley. Air-Britain. 1980.*

Telegraphist Air Gunner - Ken Sims. DSM. - *J&KH Publishing. 1999.*

The Hidden Truth - Maurice R. Hamlin, FeedARead.com Publishing. 2014.

The Lighthouse Stevensons - Bella Bathurst, Harper Collins Publishing, 1999.

War in a Stringbag - Cdr. Charles Lamb. DSO.DSC. Cassell & Co. Ltd. 1977.

Wings Over The Glens - *Peter V. Clegg, GMS Enterprises, 1995.*

Women of Glory - *L.C. Bagley. - Longacre Press Ltd. 1960.*

World War II Sea War, Vol 4: Germany Sends Russia to the Allies - *Donald A. Bertke, Bertke Publications 2012.*

OFFICIAL & OTHER SOURCES

Form 540 RAF & RCAF Squadron Operational Record Books for squadrons:

90, 95, 118, 204, 217, 221,232, 240, 281, 285, 333, 404, 502 and 7 (C) OTU.

RAF Forms 78, 412, 765c and 1180 For aircraft belonging to:

3 RS, 4 AOS, 1 (O) AFU, 6 (P) AFU, 9 (O) AFU, TTU, 304 FTU, 2 OAPU, 45 GP, 36 SQN, 204 SQN, 240 SQN, 6 OTU, 7 (C) OTU, 105 OTU, 502 SQN.

RN Casualty files Form D51:

ADM-358-2240, ADM-358-1449, ADM-358-2606, ADM-358-2166, ADM-358-1938, ADM-358-2318, ADM-358-30, ADM-358-2902. ADM 358/1914. AIR 81.

USAAF Aircraft Accident Reports / MACR:

General Dynamics F-111E 68-008 77th TFS, 20th TFW.

Public Libraries :

Campbeltown Heritage Centre, Kintyre, Library & Archives of Canada. Ottawa. Orkney Library & Archive, Kirkwall, Orkney. Southport Library.

Newspapers & Magazines

Aberdeen Press and Journal, Campbeltown Courier, Daily Star, Derbyshire Times, Irish Times, The Times, Liverpool Echo, The London Gazette, The Scotsman, Flight, Toronto Glasgow Herald, Daily Telegraph, Daily Mirror, The New Zealand Weekly News, The New York Times, Yorkshire Post.

Other Sources:

Ancestry.com. Archives of Australia, Australian War Memorial, Auckland War Memorial Museum, New Zealand, Canadian Virtual War Memorial, Commonwealth War Graves Commission. Department of Births, Deaths & Marriages registers, Find-a-Grave, Fleet Air Arm 836 Squadron Line Book compiled by the late John K.G.Taylor and transcribed by Mike Aggleton as a online history source. Pembroke Dock Sunderland Trust, Ipswich War Memorial, RAF Museum, Hendon. RAF Commands Forum, The Aviation Photo Company, Telegraphist Air Gunner Assn, The National Archives, London, The Institute of Royal Naval Architects, The Royal British Legion, The Scottish War Graves Project, Wikipedia.

ABBREVIATIONS

AA:	Anti Aircraft	EWO:	Electronic Weapons Officer
A&AEE:	Aircraft & Armament Experimental Establishment	FAA:	Fleet Air Arm
		F/E:	Flight Engineer
AC1:	Aircraftman 1st Class	F/Sgt :	Flight Sergeant
AC2:	Aircraftman 2nd Class	F/Lt:	Flight Lieutenant
AEO:	Aircraft Engineer Officer	F/O:	Flying Officer
AFC:	Air Force Cross	FRU:	Fleet Requirements Unit
A/F:	Air Fitter	FTS:	Flying Training School
AIR SIG:	Air Signaller	FTU:	Ferry Training Unit
A/G:	Air Gunner	Fw:	Feldwebel (F/Sgt Luftwaffe)
A.O.C:	Air Officer Commanding	Gefr:	Gefreiter (LAC Luftwaffe)
ARGOS:	Aviation Research Group Orkney & Shetland	GHQ:	General Head Quarters
		Gp/Capt:	Group Captain
A/S:	Anti-Submarine	GMT:	Greenwich Mean Time
ASR:	Air Sea Rescue	HAA:	Heavy Anti-Aircraft Fire
ASV:	Air to Surface Vessel (radar)	HCU:	Heavy Conversion Unit
ATA:	Air Transport Auxiliary	Hptn:	Hauptman (F/Lt Luftwaffe)
B/A:	Bomb Aimer	HQ:	Headquarters
BEM:	British Empire Medal	HSL:	High Speed Launch
Bty:	Battery	ITS:	Initial Training School
Capt:	Captain	I.O:	Intelligence Officer
CLT:	Central Local Time	KG:	Kampfgruppe. (Bomber Group)
Cdr:	Commander	Kplt:	Kapitänleutnant (Captain)
CFSO:	Critical Flight Safety Officer	L/A:	Leading Airman
C.O:	Commanding Officer	LAC:	Leading Aircraftman
Col:	Colonel	LARA:	Low Altitude Radar Altimeter
Cpl:	Corporal	Leut:	Leutnant (P/O Luftwaffe)
C of I:	Court of Inquiry	Lt/Cdr:	Lieutenant Commander
D/C:	Depth Charge	Lt:	Lieutenant
DFM:	Distinguished Flying Medal	Maj:	Major
DFC:	Distinguished Flying Cross	Met:	Meteorological
DLT:	Deck Landing Trials/Training	Mid:	Midshipman
DSC:	Distinguished Service Cross	MID:	Mentioned in Dispatches
DSM:	Distinguished Service Medal	M.O.:	Medical Officer
DSO:	Distinguished Service Order	MTB:	Motor Torpedo Boat
Eng:	Engineer	MV:	Merchant Vessel
EFTS:	Elementary Flying Training School	MU:	Maintenance Unit
ETA:	Estimated Time of Arrival	NA1:	Naval Airman 1st Class

NA2:	Naval Airman 2nd Class	R.O:	Radar Operator
Nav:	Navigator	ROC:	Royal Ordinance Corps
Obs:	Observer	R/S:	Radio School
O.C:	Officer Commanding	R/T:	Radio Transmitter
Oblt:	Oberleutnant (F/O Luftwaffe)	RU:	Repair Unit
ORB:	Operational Record Book	2/Lt:	Second Lieutenant (US & Nor)
OTU:	Operational Training Unit	SAAF:	South African Air Force
OAPU:	Overseas Aircraft Prep Unit	SFTS:	Service Flying Training School
P/O:	Pilot Officer	SGR:	School of General Recon.
P.O:	Petty Officer	Sgt :	Sergeant
POW:	Prisoner of War	S/Ldr :	Squadron Leader
Pte:	Private	SOC:	Struck Off Charge
PRU:	Photo Reconnaissance Unit	SOS:	Save Our Souls (Distress call)
Qm:	Quartermaster (Norwegian)	Sqn:	Squadron
RAE:	Royal Aircraft Establishment	SSQ:	Station Sick Quarters
RAF:	Royal Air Force	S/Sgt:	Staff Sergeant
RAAF:	Royal Australian Air Force	Sub/Lt:	Sub Lieutenant
RAFFC:	Royal Air Force Ferry Command	Sub/Lt (A)	Sub-Lieutenant (Air)
RAFVR:	Royal Air Force Volunteer	TAG:	Telegraphist Air Gunner
RC:	Recruitment Centre	TFR:	Terrain Following Radar
RCAF:	Royal Canadian Air Force	TRS:	Tactical Recon Squadron
RCN:	Royal Canadian Navy	T/Sgt:	Technical Sergeant
RCNVR:	Royal Canadian Navy Volunteer Reserve.	TT:	Target Towing
		TTU:	Torpedo Training Unit
RD:	Repair Depot	USAF:	United States Air Force
RDF:	Radio Direction Finding	u/s:	Unserviceable
Recce:	Reconnaissance	U/T:	Under Training
Regt:	Regiment	VC:	Victoria Cross
RFC:	Royal Flying Corps	VFR:	Visual Flight Rules
R/G:	Rear Gunner	VHF:	Very High Frequency
RN:	Royal Navy	W/AG:	Wireless Op & Air Gunner
RNAF:	Royal Norwegian Air Force	WAAF:	Women`s Aux Air Force
RNAS:	Royal Naval Air Service	W/Cdr:	Wing Commander
RNR:	Royal Naval Reserve	W/E/M:	Wireless Electrical Mechanic
RNVR:	Royal Navy Volunteer Reserve		
RNZAF:	Royal New Zealand Air Force	WET:	Western European Time
RNZN:	Royal New Zealand Navy	W.O:	Warrant Officer
RNZNVR:	Royal New Zealand Navy Volunteer Reserve.	W/Op:	Wireless Operator
		WRNS:	Women`s Royal Naval Service
R/Op:	Radio Operator	WSO:	Weapons Systems Officer

ALSO AVAILABLE FROM HANOVER PUBLICATIONS

ALMOST HOME

The Story of the B-24 Crash at Walliwall, Orkney - 31 March 1945.

This book is the result of over 14 years research and tells the story behind the worst aviation accident in Orkney history, that of a USAAF B-24 Liberator bomber returning from a perilous mission over Norway to drop a Special Operations Group over hostile territory, along with a store of arms and equipment during Operation RYPE. However, fate intervened and the crew had no choice but to abort the mission and return to their secondary base in Scotland, but sadly were destined to crash in a field on Orkney with the loss of thirteen men and only one survivor. Paperback. 76 pages. Fully illustrated with Colour & B/W photos throughout, the majority having never been published before. ISBN: 978-0-9523928-1-1 £9.99 + £1.60 P&P.

LOST TO THE ISLES

Accounts of military aircraft accidents around the Scottish Isles 1941-1990

Four volumes covering accounts on 164 accidents along with biographies of crews.

Volume 1 - 1914-1941

The result of research spanning well over a decade, this book gives detailed accounts of forty three aircraft accidents, on and around the Scottish Islands from 1914 to 1941, with a great emphasis on the crews involved. This first volume in a series of four, deals in the main with the pioneer aviators of military aircraft, from basic single engine wooden biplanes, seaplanes and airships held together with wires, fabric and glue, with top speeds boasting between 50 and 90 mph, to the big four engine monoplane bombers and flying boats, built of robust aluminium and steel reaching top speeds of over 300mph. Published in paperback 244 pages with 246 B/W photos, Profile drawings, maps and diagrams throughout. ISBN: 978-0-9523928-4-2   £14.99 + £2.95 P&P.

Volume 2 - 1942–1943

Having reached the seventieth anniversary since the end of the Second World War, it seems almost appropriate that we are able to shed light on the many aircraft losses that occurred around the isles, on events that had hitherto long since been forgotten, save of course for those directly involved. In this second volume, using archived documents, letters, and many previously unpublished photographs, you will find accounts of fifty six aircraft accidents and incidents. Some on land, others at sea, but all we feel being worthy of recognition in the annals of aviation history. Whilst book one mainly dealt with biplanes, seaplanes and airships, book two sees the Americans enter the war with their large four engine bombers B-17s and B-24s. As with volume one, this book includes biographies on all the airmen involved. Published in paperback 386 pages with 406 B/W photos, profile drawings, maps and diagrams throughout. ISBN : 978-0-9523928-7-3 £17.99 + £2.95 P&P.

Volume 3 - 1944

In this third volume we cover stories on a further 34 military aircraft accidents and incidents around the Scottish Islands. 1944 was a very busy year and aside from British aircrews, there were notably many lost from Commonwealth and European forces and several accounts of these are included in this book. Once again, as well as the many single engine types, the twin and four engine heavies were a prominent feature, both in a training and an operational role, and great tales of bravery among crews are recalled. Like previous volumes this book contains biographical details on all the airmen involved. Published in paperback 312 pages with B/W photos and aircraft profiles throughout. ISBN : 978-0-9523928-6-6 £15.99 + £2.95 P&P.

Volume 4 - 1945-1990

This final book in the series begins as the Second World War enters its final stages in 1945. Though sadly, not before further losses are incurred around the Scottish Islands. In this fourth volume there are thirty five accounts of accidents and incidents, seventeen occurring prior to VJ day, with a further eighteen post-war, taking us from the WW2 turboprops to the Cold War gas turbine supersonic jet age. Published in paperback. 360 pages with B/W photos and aircraft profiles throughout. ISBN: 978-0-9523928-8-0. £16.99 + £2.95.

All volumes are available on Amazon or by cheque or P.O. made payable to: Hanover Publications, 25 Hanover Street, Stalybridge, Cheshire. SK15 1LR, England.